D0635275

Understanding
Identity &
Organizations

SAGE has been part of the global academic community since 1965, supporting high quality research and learning that transforms society and our understanding of individuals, groups, and cultures. SAGE is the independent, innovative, natural home for authors, editors and societies who share our commitment and passion for the social sciences.

Find out more at: **www.sagepublications.com**

Understanding Identity & Organizations

Kate Kenny, Andrea Whittle & Hugh Willmott

Los Angeles | London | New Delhi
Singapore | Washington DC

© Kate Kenny, Andrea Whittle and Hugh Willmott 2011

First published 2011

Apart from any fair dealing for the purposes of research or private study, or criticism or review, as permitted under the Copyright, Designs and Patents Act, 1988, this publication may be reproduced, stored or transmitted in any form, or by any means, only with the prior permission in writing of the publishers, or in the case of reprographic reproduction, in accordance with the terms of licences issued by the Copyright Licensing Agency. Enquiries concerning reproduction outside those terms should be sent to the publishers.

SAGE Publications Ltd
1 Oliver's Yard
55 City Road
London EC1Y 1SP

SAGE Publications Inc.
2455 Teller Road
Thousand Oaks, California 91320

SAGE Publications India Pvt Ltd
B 1/I 1 Mohan Cooperative Industrial Area
Mathura Road
New Delhi 110 044

SAGE Publications Asia-Pacific Pte Ltd
33 Pekin Street #02-01
Far East Square
Singapore 048763

Library of Congress Control Number: 2011927202

British Library Cataloguing in Publication data

A catalogue record for this book is available from the British Library

ISBN 978-1-84860-679-1
ISBN 978-1-84860-680-7 (pbk)

Typeset by C&M Digitals (P) Ltd, Chennai, India
Printed in India at Replika Press Pvt Ltd
Printed on paper from sustainable resources

Summary of Contents

Contents

About the Authors

Kate Kenny is a Lecturer in Political Science and Sociology at NUI Galway. She is a Fellow at Cambridge University's Judge Business School in Cambridge. Her research interests centre on issues of subjectivity and identity in relation to work organizations. Projects include a year-long ethnographic study at a non-profit aid organization (funded by ESRC among others), and upcoming research into the concept of identity among organizational whistleblowers. Her work has been published in *Human Relations, Health and Place* and *Gender Work and Organization*. She is an editorial board member of the *Journal of Organizational Ethnography and Ephemera: Theory and Politics in Organizations*.

Andrea Whittle is a Professor of Organization Studies at Cardiff Business School. She joined Cardiff from the Saïd Business School, Oxford University, where she worked as an Economic and Social Research Council (ESRC) Post-Doctoral Fellow. She studied identity among management consultants for her PhD. More recently, Dr Whittle has conducted research on technological change in organizations, the branding of higher education and public testimonies in the banking and accountancy professions. Her recent research has been inspired by the fields of discursive psychology, discourse analysis and narrative and has been published in a range of journals, including *Organization Studies, Human Relations, Journal of Applied Behavioural Science* and *Organization*.

Hugh Willmott is Research Professor in Organization Studies, Cardiff Business School, having previously held professorial positions at the Universities of Cambridge and Manchester. He has a strong interest in the application of social theory, especially poststructuralist thinking, to the field of management and business. His other books include *Making Sense of Management* (with Mats Alvesson, Sage), *The Body and Organization* (with John Hassard and Ruth Holliday, Sage), *Management Lives: Power and Identity in Contemporary Organizations* (with David Knights, Sage) and *Organization Theory and Design* (with Richard Daft and Jonathan Murphy, Cengage Learning).

This publication was granted-aided by the Publications Fund of **National University of Ireland, Galway**.

Introduction to Understanding Identity 1

1.1 Introduction

Identity is a topic that is relevant to everyone. Identity relates to the timeless question: 'who am I?' and the related questions: 'who and what do I appear to be: to myself, to my friends, my boss, my bank, my neighbours, my lecturers?'. A person can appear to be many things at once, even where these different 'identities' appear inconsistent or even contradictory. Someone could be, for example, a politically conservative, religiously atheist, homosexual female surgeon. All these words act as categories that describe us in different contexts. Such identifiers are vital to our experience of life, both at work and outside of it. In effect, they act as landmarks as we navigate or negotiate our way through social landscapes.

Some aspects of our identity are hard, but not necessarily impossible, to control. Sex, height and colour of skin are all difficult to alter, but they can in some cases be changed – in the case of transsexuals, for example. Other aspects, such as religion, hobbies and occupation, are more open to being changed, managed and controlled (Muir and Wetherell, 2010).

We sometimes hear about identities being 'strong' or 'weak'. Fanatical sport team supporters, such as so-called 'football hooligans', who have fights with other people simply because they are supporters of rival teams, could be said to have too 'strong' a sense of identification (see Glossary) – a strong sense of belonging and attachment with their team and fellow supporters. In extreme cases, people are murdered simply because they are members of a rival street gang, to protect the 'honour' and 'reputation' of the gang. In contrast, other identities are thought to be too 'weak' nowadays. Attachment to the local community, for example, is often said to be weaker now, and this is associated with a breakdown in social cohesion and community spirit.

We see the importance of identity in work organizations too. Sherron Watkins' role at Enron illustrates this point. Watkins was a Vice President for Corporate Development. In August 2001, she tried to alert the CEO at the time, Kenneth Lay, to the presence of accounting irregularities within the company, which she felt were dubious and possibly illegal. As the corporation began to collapse, she advised her CEO to come clean and report its massive financial losses to investors, but the result was a sidelining of her role in the organization. When Enron was eventually brought down, with catastrophic effects, Watkins testified before US Congressional Committees that investigated Enron's business practices.

In subsequent interviews, traces of Watkins' sense of identity, and her multiple identifications, emerge. She describes herself as a professional accountant, a moral person and an Enron employee, citing all three as contributing to her sense of self – who she is (and was). In particular, she points to the importance (or 'strength') of her sense of professional values that were embedded during her training as an accountant which, she says, equipped her with an ethical sensibility and a moral perspective on the world:

> I started my career in the early 1980s at Arthur Andersen & Co. as an auditor. I have to say that it bothered me that we were told it was not a public accountant's job to detect fraud. We were told to maintain a healthy degree of skepticism, but our audits were not specifically designed to find fraud. The trouble is that most shareholders believe the opposite: that an audit does in fact mean auditors looked for signs of fraud. … Being an ethical person is more than knowing right from wrong. It is having the fortitude to do right even when there is much at stake. (Carozza, 2007)

Watkins recalls how, early on in her career, she experienced some conflict between two key elements of her identity: an accountant and a Christian (she discusses God and Enron in 'The Enron Blog' by Cara Ellison (2010), 17 November 2010). As time passed during her period at Enron, she became aware of the dubious 'creative accounting' taking place at her firm. Her identification with Christian values and professional ethics came into conflict with her identification as an Enron employee. She grew uncomfortable with wrongdoing that appeared to be at odds with the values that were central to her sense of identity. This conflict led her to 'blow the whistle' (see Figure 1.1) on her close colleagues by drawing her concerns to the attention of her boss, Ken Lay. In an interview that took place after she had publicly spoken out, Watkins said:

> The real lesson for me is that I should have left Enron in 1996 when I first saw behavior that I thought was over the line. If your own personal value system is not validated or if you are uncomfortable when your value system gets violated, leave that organization. Trouble will hit at some point. (Lucas and Koerwer, 2004)

Watkins' self-identity – how she saw herself – played an important role in her decision to expose one of the largest and most significant corporate scandals of the last century.

Figure 1.1   Corporate whistleblowers

What the Sherron Watkins example shows us is that workplace identity is a vital part of working life and has significant implications for ourselves and for those around us. This book focuses on the relationship between identity and workplace life. Our particular focus is upon how identities are shaped in and through organizations, such as accounting firms, Enron and religious institutions. By 'organizations' we mean anything from a large corporation, to a small family business, a single subcontractor, a public sector organization, a charity or voluntary organization – anywhere where people work that is formally organized and structured, whether paid or unpaid.

1.2 Identity vs Personality

Often the terms identity and personality (see Glossary) are used interchangeably, or are assumed to have rather similar meanings. Words can, of course, acquire all kinds of meanings, so we are not suggesting that 'identity' has any essential meaning. Here we are simply concerned to communicate how we intend to define and use the term 'identity' and, to do this, we distinguish it from 'personality'.

At first sight, the terms personality and identity seem very similar. They both seem to be about what makes us 'who we are'. For us, however, the terms signify quite different things. The term personality tends to be associated with a person's unique and distinctive 'inner world' and is widely used in the discipline of psychology. It refers to the idea that we have a distinct set of inner cognitive (i.e. mental) structures and processes (such as attitudes, dispositions, temperaments and stereotypes) that influence how we behave. For example, some people are considered to have a 'shy and introverted' personality while others are 'outgoing and extrovert'. These inner cognitive structures are understood to be either genetically predetermined (i.e. we are born with them), or formed primarily during the early stages of childhood – making them 'hard-wired' into the brain and therefore difficult to change. Social scientists study personality differences by using scientific methods such as tests, questionnaires and experiments. They attempt to categorize the different types of personality and study how personality types influence behaviour. They rely on the assumption that human beings are discrete, independent entities with unique characteristics.

The term identity, on the other hand, can be attributed to groups as well as individuals. Indeed, membership of a wider group is key to specifying and understanding identity. So, for example, Sherron Watkins understood herself in terms of being an accountant and a 'Christian', both of which indicate membership of a wider group (of accountants and Christians). In contrast to the term personality, reference to the term identity signals an approach to understanding 'who we are' that is found in the fields of sociology, politics, cultural studies and discourse studies. Identity, even self-identity, does not refer to a distinct set of inner cognitive (i.e. mental) structures, processes or dispositions. Rather, it refers to how a person makes sense of themselves in relation to others, and how others conceive of that person. Identity can refer to individual characteristics (such as being an 'outgoing person'), which may of course include ideas about the kind of 'personality' we have, as well as to social categories (such as 'being a gay person').

So, identity can include identification with elements that we call 'our personality'. But this approach does not treat such elements as 'hard-wired', genetically predetermined features of the brain. In general, identity refers to socially available categories, which can of course include how we think about our 'personality'. These categories provide ways of making sense of 'who I am' in relation to 'who you are'. Whereas the psychological use of the term personality assumes and refers to the existence of a comparatively rigid and unchanging set of cognitive structures or mental processes, the sociological term identity is conceived to be contingent upon the particular – local, cultural and historical – conditions of its production. In other words, identity varies according to:

- Local context (e.g. my identity at home vs my identity at work).
- Culture (e.g. what it means to be a man in Chinese society vs American society).
- History (e.g. what it meant to be a man in the twelfth century vs today).

The concept of identity helps us to appreciate how our ways of making sense of ourselves and others are influenced by social processes. Such processes include the local, day-to-day interactions we have with friends, family and colleagues as well as the broader context of the society and period of history in which we live. Consider the type of person who respects tradition and authority figures, who has a strong sense of 'duty' to others – which can be regarded as a 'personality trait'. Those interested in 'personality' might attempt to use personality tests to measure the differences between people in respect of their sense of duty and respect for authority. When engaging a sociological focus on 'identity', the emphasis shifts from individual differences to the social conditions that produced this type of 'personality trait'. For example, think about the differences between those born into so-called 'honour-bound' cultures, such as parts of India or China, where a strong sense of duty to the family and to (male) elders is upheld, with those born into the more 'individualistic' culture of North America. Table 1.1 outlines the main differences between the two concepts.

Table 1.1 Personality and identity compared

	Personality	Identity
Core tenet	Who we are is based on relatively stable *individual* traits, attitudes and beliefs	Who we are is based on our experiences of the society and *social* groups in which we live
Central academic discipline	Psychology	Sociology (and social psychology)
Main source of self-formation	Biology or early socialization – something we are born with, or formed at an early stage of childhood	Society – something we learn to be from our interaction with others and wider society
Approach to stability	Personality remains relatively stable for life	Identity can change as a result of interactions with others
Approach to difference	Personality differentiates us from others	Identity attends to similarities to others
Research methods	Use of quantitative instruments (e.g. personality tests) to measure individual characteristics	Use of qualitative instruments (e.g. interviews) to explore processes of identity (trans) formation
Level of analysis	Individual cognition	Individual-group-society interactions

An attentiveness to 'identity', we believe, helps to compensate for some limitations of studies that place 'personality' at their centre. Among these limitations are:

1 A view of people as atomistic, sovereign agents: that is, as isolated individuals who either have complete control over who they are, or are the prisoners of their 'personalities'.
2 A reliance on the idea that our sense of self resides 'within us', as an essential feature of our cognitive make-up.
3 A use of a power-free analysis: that is, the focus on personality ignores the role of power in shaping and directing processes of self-formation.

The value of a focus upon identity can be summarized as follows:

- It appreciates how people's sense of 'who I am' is embedded in social relationships.
- It views identity as a social phenomenon, based on (more or less dominant) collective understandings of what it means to be a person, rather than existing only 'inside our heads' as mental processes.
- It emphasizes the role of power in shaping our sense of self, including the reproduction of diverse forms of inequality (e.g. gender, ethnicity, class structure, etc.).

We will not be discussing 'personality' per se in this book. But we will be exploring many themes and issues that are highly relevant to anyone who is interested in 'personality'. That is because students interested in 'personality' are usually inquisitive about how they, and other human beings, behave: what makes them 'tick'. Studying identity, we will show, can provide penetrating insights into 'human behaviour' that are different to, and so can complement and perhaps surpass, those generated by studies of 'personality'. So, for example, applying a personality test (e.g. Myers–Briggs) to Sherron Watkins might help us to understand why she, rather than some other Enron employee, sent the 'whistleblowing' internal memo to her boss, Ken Lay. But, to understand the way she alerted her superiors in Enron, how and why she eventually decided to 'go public', might be better understood by considering her diverse and perhaps conflicting identities and institutional affiliations, as a loyal employee, as a Christian, as an ambitious accountant, and so on.

1.3 Identity on the Management Agenda: A Brief History

When did the notion of identity first get onto the management agenda? Early approaches to management, such as F. W. Taylor's *Principles of Scientific Management* (1911), viewed a person's identity – our affiliations with others and the thoughts, feelings and values which make up our sense of who we are – as an obstacle to effective management (Rose, 1988). Taylor thought that management should be a rational, scientific endeavour that is not 'messed' and 'muddled' by having to manage such subjective and emotional issues. In effect, Taylor believed that workers should leave their sense of identity at the factory gate, and so be prepared to fit whatever 'mould' had been prepared for them by management.

Taylor was influenced by his experience of working as a foreman at the Midvale Steel Corporation, in Philadelphia in the United States. Taylor thought that, when left to their own devices, workers had a highly 'irrational' and 'inefficient' way of organizing work. Workers developed informal status hierarchies in their work 'gangs'. The gang 'boss' decided who did what job, and how fast, based on their own informal 'pecking order', habits and customs. The 'leader' of the work gang was not appointed to that position by management based on their relevant skills or experience. Instead, the 'leader' emerged from an informal hierarchy based on principles that, in Taylor's estimation, had little or nothing to do with the workplace – such as who was the 'toughest', or the most 'senior', or the most 'respected'.

Taylor set out to reform, and perhaps revolutionize, such 'irrational', unproductive arrangements by developing an approach to management that he termed 'scientific'. Using stopwatches and other measurement instruments, he sought to root out needless inefficiencies by eliminating all trace of subjective and social factors – such as loyalties to each other that stood in the way of the scientific division and application of labour. Taylor regarded such factors as morally indefensible (unfair) as well as instrumentally flawed (inefficient). He objected to them morally because he saw them holding back the ability of workers to maximize their productive capacity and thereby increase their earnings which, in 'scientific management', were linked directly to output in a 'piece-rate' system. By abolishing the 'custom and practice' associated with established, traditional identification with the gang, workers would be efficiently organized like the very 'cogs' in Taylor's stopwatch.

Taylor was not so much uninterested in the 'identities' of workers, and whether these were being recognized or ignored at work, as he was morally and managerially hostile to them. He wanted employees to be fairly treated by adopting scientific methods of working devised by time-and-motion experts. Because he regarded established identifications as irrational and harmful to the interests of workers in maximizing their pay, Taylor was confident that employees would enthusiastically embrace this approach. That was because he believed human beings to be 'rational economic' creatures who were motivated to work by the prospect of economic gain (i.e. pay), and would therefore willingly accommodate new 'scientific' forms of job design that would enable them to maximize their earnings.

Taylor was surprised that workers (and foremen) resisted the application of 'scientific' principles of work organization. For him, resistance to the new 'rational' scheme was simply irrational. The remedy was to apply the principles even more stringently, insisting that management tolerated no deviation from the methods prescribed by scientific investigations. This approach proved counterproductive as it simply increased the resistance. Workers began to organize (e.g. in unions) in defence of the informal culture, hierarchies and controls. One way to understand such resistance is in terms of workers' attachments to identities and affiliations with each other that were disrupted by 'scientific' methods. In other words, workers resisted the changes, in spite of the fact that they might earn more money from complying, due to their identification with the norms and values of the work gang. Being 'part of the gang' was perhaps more important than earning more money. Money was perhaps not the only thing that motivated employees – see Figure 1.2. The question for management and their advisors was: if these 'irrational' identities and identifications could not be eliminated by 'scientific' management, could they be co-opted in some way?

Figure 1.2 Motivation at work

The 'human relations movement' (Rose, 1988) provided a way forward by showing the role played by 'social factors' in human motivation. Its advocates sought to incorporate, rather than exclude, the view that human beings have 'needs' that are 'social' (such as group affiliation) as well as 'material' (pay according to output). Such 'needs' were understood to include belonging, companionship, recognition, social status and esteem – and were most famously 'demonstrated' in the classic Hawthorne studies (Sykes, 1965). The irony was that Elton Mayo, the Harvard professor responsible for the experiments at the Hawthorne plant of the Western Electric Company (a telephone manufacturing subsidiary of AT&T), originally set out to apply scientific management principles in the factory. Instead, Mayo's experiments brought to his attention a completely unexpected and very puzzling finding. The experimental group produced higher levels of output regardless of whatever changes the experimenters made, such as altering lighting levels or rest breaks.

The Hawthorne researchers eventually came to believe that the positive results were attributable to an unintended effect of the experiments – namely, that employees felt more motivated because they felt 'special' somehow, because they had a sense of camaraderie as a group and because they felt people were taking an interest in them. For employees, the intervention of the researchers was a form of status, affiliation and recognition that led to higher productivity. More generally, the focus of the human relations movement which arose from the experiments at the Hawthorne plant, is, as the name suggests, upon relations between people, including relations between workers themselves and between workers and management. Its claim is that people are motivated by factors related to subjective things like identity – such as feeling recognized and feeling part of a group. This movement did not, however, celebrate or commend a restoration of the informal practices of work gangs abhorred by Taylor. On the contrary, it has sought to extend the control of management by constructing more 'human' kinds of workplaces as a means of overcoming the social obstacles encountered by Taylor. To this end, the human relations movement has favoured the adoption of an ostensibly more 'caring' and 'humanistic' posture in relation to workers. The intent has been to encourage employees to derive a stronger sense of affiliation, identification and esteem from the norms and values prescribed by the organization rather than by their work group, by unions or by affiliations outside of the workplace. The significance of identity was not simply recognized by management, it was identified as something that could be shaped and controlled by management.

In 'human relations' thinking, subjective elements such as identity were no longer to be eliminated by management. Instead, these elements were to be utilized (or, some critical thinkers would say, exploited) by management. The theories of motivation that emerged from the so-called 'human relations movement' (such as Maslow's 'hierarchy of needs', Alderfer's 'Existence, Relatedness, Growth' (ERG) and Herzberg's 'two-factor theory') all recognized that workers were motivated not only by money or the physical work environment, but also by social and emotional 'needs' like the need for a sense of belonging in a group, for example (Buchanan and Huczynski, 2004: Ch. 8). In Maslow's infamous 'hierarchy of needs', the top of the pyramid refers to needs for 'belonging', 'esteem' and 'self-actualization'. These can be read as addressing 'identity concerns' – the desire to feel like part of a group ('I am a team player'), the desire to be held in high regard by others ('I am respected by others') and the desire to reach our potential ('I am what I always dreamed of being').

Whereas Taylor's *Principles of Scientific Management* is almost exclusively concerned with organizing work in ways that are restricted to lower levels of the hierarchy (needs for survival and security), human relations techniques and more recent variations on this theme (such as 'corporate culture', see Chapter 5) can be seen to connect to ideas about 'esteem' and 'self-actualization'. From a management perspective, employees become more pliable and productive when they identify strongly with the organization. Strong identification is thought to lead employees to 'go the extra mile' (be more productive or flexible) for their organization – such as working late to complete a project. It is this so-called 'discretionary effort' (i.e. effort that is not formally required and that employees have discretion about whether to 'give') that makes the idea of exercising control through 'identity' so appealing to managers (Alvesson and Willmott, 2002). We will discuss the issue of identity and organizational control in more detail in Chapter 5.

1.4 How Do Individual and Organizational Identities Interact?

In this book, we are interested in any form of organization, any group of people who work in some way towards a common goal. That includes not just paid employment in companies, but also charities, community organizations, public sector or not-for-profit organizations.

How, then, does our individual identity relate to 'organizations'? At a basic level, being a member of an organization – an employee or an unpaid volunteer for a charity, for example – may itself provide us with a sense of identity. When people ask us about ourselves, we can say 'I work for Apple' or 'I help to run a local homeless shelter'. Beyond this simple aspect of 'membership', the way we relate as individuals to organizations can be much more complex and multi-faceted.

Parker (2007) notes that our sense of identification with (and within) an organization can be complex, multiple and contextual. By this he means that we can identify with different parts of the organization, or the organization as a whole, or indeed groups outside the organization (such as a geographical region, or a trade union, or a profession), at different times depending on the context. Figure 1.3 shows

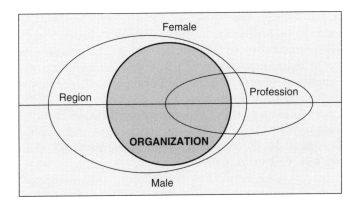

Figure 1.3   An organization with some 'externally' derived identity divisions

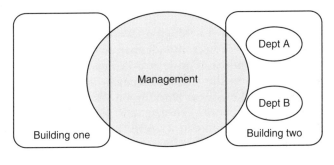

ORGANIZATION

Figure 1.4   An organization with some 'internally' derived identity divisions

what sorts of identifications outside an organization could be important to different workers. Figure 1.4 shows what sorts of identifications within an organization could be important to different workers. The box at the end of this chapter sets out some 'thinking tasks' that you can undertake to assess your own identity and identifications, or those within the organization you are currently studying.

Parker (2007) argues that identifications are contextual because the identity that is most important to a person depends on what is relevant to a particular situation. Let's imagine there is a Senior Marketing Manager for a factory called Mary. On Monday, Mary joins a staff protest to save the staff canteen in her building, 'Building One'. She is prepared to stand up and fight for everyone who works in Building One, even if this means going against the views of other members of senior management and other marketing colleagues. On Tuesday, Mary identifies more strongly with being a 'marketing' person when arguing at a board meeting for more resources for a new advertising campaign which is opposed by the Engineering Director, who is actually based in Building One. On Wednesday, the identity of 'manager' becomes more important when she is conducting an annual appraisal with a subordinate and has to enforce a disciplinary warning, in spite of being close friends with the person in question. On Thursday, the difference between her and her subordinates, and the differences between departments and buildings, is less important when they are discussing their shared concerns about a possible merger with another company. On Friday, she feels a sense of identity as a 'Northern' employee when she participates in a squash tournament against the 'Southern' branches of the company.

This book aims to explore these processes through which people come to see themselves as identified with (or within) the organization as a whole, or other possible identifications, such as hierarchical level (e.g. manager), occupation (e.g. engineer) or region (e.g. the Northern branch).

1.5 Introducing the Book

About Us: We are three people who have been working in the area of identity and organizations for a number of years.

Kate Kenny, a lecturer in the Sociology of Work at NUI Galway, Ireland, carried out a four-year research project into identity among people working for not-for-profit organizations. Andrea Whittle is a Professor of Organization Studies at Cardiff Business School in the UK, and studied identity among management consultants for her PhD. She is now working on research exploring the role of discourse and narrative in identity construction. Hugh Willmott is a Research Professor in Organization Studies at Cardiff Business School. Hugh became interested in identity in the 1980s. At the time, the study of such 'subjective' concerns were considered to be incompatible with the identity of sociologically minded researchers who were content to leave its examination to psychology. His PhD research was on the identity of single homeless people as seen by themselves and the agencies responsible for their 'management'. Since then his work has revolved around an exploration of the relevance of identity in relation to power, insecurity and inequality for the study of organizational work (see e.g. Knights and Willmott, 1999). For further details, see https://sites.google.com/site/hughwillmottshomepage.

The three of us share the idea that identity is a vital part of work and its organization. We noticed that there were few books around that dealt adequately with this important topic and so we decided to write one.

Of course, we cannot cover all the different contributions and perspectives on identity and its significance within workplaces. Our choices no doubt reflect our own interests and assumptions, even and perhaps especially where we remain ignorant of them. We acknowledge that this book, in common with all academic work, is not 'neutral'. It too is a form of 'identity work' rooted in a specific culture and written at a particular time. Our aim, nonetheless, has been to draw together our specific concerns and viewpoints to provide a good introductory coverage of the field.

About the Book: We want this book to provide teachers and students with a useful, relevant and engaging overview of the field of identity studies, especially in relation to business and management, and applied social sciences.

Theory: The book introduces a variety of different approaches to understanding identity. There is no one 'correct' way to study identity. What is the 'right' method or theory to use depends on the perspective adopted. Broadly speaking, this book adopts a predominantly social constructionist perspective on identity, which means that identity is viewed as an outcome of social processes through which people construct a sense of 'who they are'. This differs from a realist or positivist perspective which views identity as an entity or object that is 'real' and exists out there in the world, amenable to scientific methods of discovery (such as experiments, questionnaire surveys, etc.). We are particularly interested in, and therefore have included, some of the latest emerging theories – including poststructural perspectives and psychoanalysis. We also anticipate that these are likely to become increasingly influential.

Real-Life Examples: Colleagues around the world, who have similar interests in studying identity and organizations, have for years been carrying out fascinating research into real-life working situations. In addition to using cartoons and our own examples from everyday life and the media, we draw extensively upon their scholarship. We present mini-case studies which we call 'Case Points'. When selecting the studies to include, we endeavoured to choose examples from a range of countries and diverse work settings, although our choices are undoubtedly limited by the number of studies published in English-language books and journals.

1.5.1 Using the book

Students: We have organized the chapters around key areas of the study of identity and organizations. In Chapter 2, we present an overview of major theoretical approaches to the study of identity. In Chapters 3–7, we detail and explore key areas of study. In the final chapter, we consider what the future might hold for the study of identity.

Each chapter begins with the rationale for why we include certain issues and leave others out. Since the issues we explore remain open to debate, we encourage a questioning approach by including Thinkpoints in each chapter: inviting the reader to think about a certain topic. In addition, we provide Case Points where we draw on previous studies to illustrate the concepts or issues discussed in the text. To signal connections between different chapters and different sections within chapters, we use Links to other sections of the book. The Glossary at the end can be used for reference, along with the Index.

Course Instructors: This book can be used either as supplementary reading for a lecture on identity and organizations, or to structure an entire course (in combination with additional material – see Suggested Reading at the end of each chapter). Chapters 3–7 would work well as individual lecture topics, while Chapter 2 would perhaps require more than one lecture, depending on the number of theoretical perspectives you would like to cover in the class. We would recommend using the Case Points as a basis for class discussion or to design tutorial exercises. You might also want to select certain cases for further reading and discussion by giving the students the original book or article to read in private study time. We have provided sample questions at the end of each chapter that could be used to set an assignment or exam.

Suggested Reading

Jenkins, R. (1996) *Social Identity*. London: Routledge. Ch. 1.

Pullen, A., Beech, N. and Sims, D. (eds) (2007) *Exploring Identity: Concepts and Methods*. Basingstoke: Palgrave Macmillan. Introduction ch.

Webb, J. (2006) *Organisations, Identities and the Self*. New York: Palgrave Macmillan. Ch. 1.

Wetherell, M. and Mohanty, C.T. (eds) (2010) *The Sage Handbook of Identities*. London: Sage. Ch. 1.

Task 1: Think about the kinds of identifications that you think you have, at the moment, on this course you are currently studying. Think about whether your identification is (a) strong and positive, (b) neutral, (c) weak, or (d) negative, regarding the following groups:

- Your fellow students on this module.
- Your fellow students on the same course as you.
- Your fellow students at this institution (i.e. university, college).
- Your fellow students who are part of your friendship group that you socialize with outside of lessons.
- Your fellow students who live in the same student house or university accommodation (if applicable).
- Your fellow students who are from the same social category as you (e.g. gender, age, race/ethnicity, nationality, etc.).

Task 2: To 'test' the extent to which you identify with each of these social groups, think about the following scenario:

> A fellow student has asked you for help with their coursework assignment. You are already pushed for time, busy working on your own assignment and your various hobbies and social activities. You would have to give up your time to help them.

Depending on which group listed above the student belongs to, how willing would you be to help them?

For example, would you be more likely to help someone who was the same gender as you? Or someone who was part of your friendship group? Or part of the same 'cohort' of students studying the same course?

Your answer to this question will tell you how much you think you identify with the group, making you see yourself as 'just like them', with associated feelings of solidarity and duty.

Task 3: Use your answers to the questions in Tasks 1 and 2 above to develop your own organizational 'identification diagram', which plots which groups you identify with and which you do not, just like Figure 1.4.

Theoretical Perspectives on Identity 2

2.1 Introduction

Theories are an essential resource for making sense of identity. In this chapter, we map out a range of theoretical approaches that have been developed and applied by students of identity. We lack space to cover the full range, so we focus on theories that have been particularly influential in the field of organization studies. We acknowledge that it is not possible, or perhaps even desirable, to 'pigeon-hole' every study within one of these 'camps'. Most authors do not start their book or article with a full declaration of which 'camp' they belong to, or have drawn inspiration from. When studying identity, many scholars, ourselves included, depend upon numerous sources of theoretical inspiration. Many also attempt to synthesize insights from different perspectives.

It is useful to think of theory as a perspective, or perhaps as a 'lens' that leads us to see something in a particular way. But a lens is also a way of not seeing. Each theory foregrounds different aspects of identity. Some highlight dynamics of power, like the Foucauldian perspective outlined below. Others focus on relationships between individuals and the social groups they belong to, like the social identity theory approach.

While each of the six different theories presented here have their own strengths and weaknesses, we do not seek to evaluate different theories against each other, as if there were an authoritative benchmark (or omniscient way of seeing) for doing so. Instead, we tease out and examine the basic assumptions that underlie each one. But, of course, in doing so, we adopt a particular standpoint which will become clearer as we review the theories. For each theory, we will address the following questions:

- How does this theory understand the notion of 'identity' and what theoretical assumptions does it make?
- What are the most common methodological approaches adopted by scholars who favour this perspective?
- Who are the 'founding thinkers' that are most commonly associated with the theoretical perspective?
- What are some major studies that have drawn upon the perspective?
- What are the most frequent criticisms of the perspective?

In Table 2.1, we present the six perspectives alongside each other as a way of appreciating their key similarities and differences. At the end of the chapter, we introduce a fictional employee called Frances, who works for Apple. Her diary entries are used to

Table 2.1 Six theoretical perspectives compared

	Theoretical assumptions	Methodological approach	Founding thinkers	Example from org. studies
Social identity theory	People identify with certain social groups (the in-group) and dis-identify with other social groups (the out-group) People have a natural tendency to: • generalize from their experiences • underestimate differences within the in-group • overemphasize differences with the out-group	Identification with particular in-groups and out-groups can be understood and analyzed, from what people say or do, through interviews, observations or controlled scientific experiments (e.g. group role-play experiments)	Henri Tajfel, John Turner	O'Connor and Annison (2002)
Psychoanalysis	The psyche shapes our responses to everyday events • People form their identifications with particular social forces at the level of the psyche • A person's psyche is formed through life experiences that are internalized. These emerge in the form of repressed feelings, fantasies or desires. • Such elements can help us to understand the power of particular norms, in a given social context	The influence of the psyche can be studied through analysis of what people say or do, such as through interviews or observations. Gaps in people's speech, jokes and slippages can also point to unconscious, 'hidden' aspects of people's experiences, which in turn can help us understand the wider social context	Sigmund Freud Jacques Lacan	Schwartz (1990) Gabriel (1999) Driver (2005)
Foucauldian	People are formed within, and come to identify with, dominant discourses or systems of thought, which make available certain subject positions and self-understandings These comprise modes of liberation as well as modes of subjection. In each case, Foucauldian thinking questions the autonomy that is attributed to subjects while resisting any suggestion that human behaviour is determined by dominant discourses, power/knowledge regimes, subject positions, etc.	Identities are studied by looking at the dominant discourses through which people make sense of themselves and the world around them, drawn from interviews, observations or discourse analysis of various types of texts (e.g. documents, statements, technologies, etc.) Some scholars express a preference for historical data, based on the study of multiple texts that reflect a particular dominant discourse at a particular point in time	Michel Foucault	Brewis (2004) Knights and Willmott (1989) Zuboff (1988)

(Continued)

Table 2.1 (Continued)

	Theoretical assumptions	Methodological approach	Founding thinkers	Example from org. studies
Symbolic interactionism	People construct their sense of self through interaction with others: • Mead views the self as composed of the 'Me' (how we think others view us) and the 'I' (how we respond to the attitudes and behaviour of others) • Goffman views identity as a continuing process of managing how we present ourselves to others. He uses the metaphor of the theatre: we take on certain roles, scripts and costumes that suit the social setting, in order to manage these impressions	Preference for observation of naturally occurring social interaction, through participant or non-participant observation Preference for micro-level, in-depth studies of particular situations, rather than large-scale analysis of the surrounding context Identity can be understood as a way of presenting oneself to others, and to oneself, in social situations	George Herbert Mead, Erving Goffman	Gardner and Avolio (1998) Mangham (1986)
Narrative	People's identities are shaped by the narratives and stories they tell about themselves and their lives, and by narratives drawn from the wider social environment that surrounds them People search for a sense of meaning and coherence about themselves by telling stories with particular characters and plots	Preference for in-depth and loosely structured interviews, biographies or diaries which capture rich self-reflection Self-identity can be interpreted from the stories that people tell about themselves and their lives	Paul Ricoeur, Kenneth Burke	Czarniawska (1998)
Micro-interactionist	People make use of identity categories as part of their methods for accomplishing particular tasks Identity is not something that people 'have' but is something that people can make relevant in certain situations in order to achieve a particular social action, such as declining an invitation, making a compliment, reporting concerns and so on	Preference for tape-recording or video-recording naturally occurring conversation. Methods therefore adopt an in-depth, micro-level perspective, closely analyzing even small segments of communication Identity cannot be 'read off' from people but must be shown to be relevant to the participants themselves in their interaction	Harold Garfinkel, Harvey Sacks	Llewellyn and Burrow (2007)

illustrate how we might apply the six theoretical perspectives outlined in this chapter to analyze her 'identity'.

2.2 Social Identity Theory (SIT)

SIT is an approach developed in the field of social psychology in the 1980s by Henri Tajfel and John Turner (Matthewman et al., 2009: 147–8). SIT proposes that people have a natural tendency to identify with others whom they see as similar to themselves (known as the 'homophily' principle). Individuals are thought to form a strong psychological identification (see Glossary) or feeling of attachment with a particular social group known as the 'in-group' (for instance, as a woman, or a black person, or a working-class person). This bonding with the 'in-group' is further strengthened by processes of dis-identification (see Glossary) with the 'out-group' – regarding the out-group as somehow different or inferior to the in-group. This creates an 'us and them' divide.

The famous Stanford Prison Experiment (see http://www.prisonexp.org/) is a good example of how human behaviour is influenced by a sense of group membership, however arbitrary and artificial. An experiment was devised whereby undergraduate students were randomly divided into prisoners and prison guards. The students rapidly identified with the roles and group that they had been allocated. Whereas previously they had been part of the same social group (undergraduate class-mates), they suddenly saw themselves as members of rival groups (prisoners versus prison guards).

Violent clashes between fans of rival sports teams are seen by SIT to be rooted in the same socio-psychological processes of identification (with the in-group) and dis-identification (with the out-group). Some fans might even seek visual displays of their group membership: wearing the team shirt or perhaps even getting the team logo tattooed onto their body. The important point is that such processes of group formation and inter-group comparison can occur even in the absence of material conflicts of interests – such as a fight for resources in an organization, for example.

SIT assumes that individuals engage in forms of cognitive distortion in the identification process. First, people are thought to make cognitive generalizations (i.e. stereotypes – see Glossary) from limited experiences. For example, Figure 2.1 shows what the stereotype of a female employee might be. A cognitive distortion could emerge from a person seeing a woman crying and assuming, therefore building a stereotyped bias, that all women are 'over-emotional' and 'irrational'. Second, because of the complexity and variety of perceptual stimuli – we come into contact with so many different people with different behavioural patterns – we deal with this 'informational overload' by using convenient categories. For instance, despite the number of very different women we meet, we may remain wedded to the idea that (all) 'women are too emotional' simply because of a memorable experience of seeing a woman crying. Third, people are thought to underemphasize the differences within the in-group ('they are just like me') while exaggerating the differences between the in-group and out-group ('they are nothing like me'). This leads to problems in relating to and understanding members of the out-group as well as recognizing differences in the 'in-group'. An example would be a man who assumes that 'I couldn't be friends with the women I work with; they are too emotional and so we have nothing in common'. Finally, and related to the third point, people are understood to

Figure 2.1 Stereotypes

be motivated by a desire to maintain self-esteem derived from a sense of belonging. Esteem is boosted from seeing oneself as part of a group, and from attributing negative values to the out-group: 'we are better than them'. A man might gain self-esteem by, for example, thinking 'women are emotional, hence feeble and submissive' and thinking that men are 'strong and authoritative'.

O'Connor and Annison's (2002) study of a community hospital in the Midwestern United States provides an instructive example of how SIT has been applied to the understanding of organizations (cited in Fiol et al., 2009: 32). At the hospital, the medical staff saw themselves as part of a different group to the senior management and administration, leading to an 'us' and 'them' atmosphere. Administrators were seen as a direct threat to the medics' sense of 'who we are' and 'what we believe in'. Changes to services, for example, were understood to threaten their right to control decisions about patients. This led to the medical staff resisting the changes, and attempting to remove the CEO. Administrators, in return, started to withdraw their support for initiatives designed by the medical staff, further entrenching the 'us' versus 'them' divide. The processes of 'in-group' versus 'out-group' conflict led to a series of costly and unproductive battles that eventually spiralled out of control and damaged the running of the hospital.

What are the strengths and weaknesses of SIT? In its favour, we see it illuminating how people can become so over-identified with a particular group (such as a sports team) that other groups (e.g. fans of other teams) are regarded as inherently inferior. Taken to the extreme, it can lead people to view the out-group as evil, or even as less than human. In turn, this can justify their denigration, punishment, exclusion or even death (in cases of 'ethnic cleansing'). Given this strong connection with everyday experience and ugly world events, it is not difficult to grasp the basis of the plausibility of SIT. However, the theory is not without its critics and has been criticized as an approach for studying identity on the following grounds (Wetherell and Potter, 1992):

- It reduces identity to a cognitive phenomenon (what people think of themselves and others), rather than seeing it as a social process in which dominant discourses (systems of thought) influence who we identify with.
- It does not examine how or why cognitive processes of identification vary across different cultures and throughout different historical periods. For example, it does not help us to see why understandings of the categories 'men' and 'women' (and how they are related to each other) have changed so much since

the nineteenth century, or why they are so different today in China compared with the Western world.

- It fails to appreciate the ideological (see Glossary) conditions and consequences of identity processes: the forms of inequality and oppression that are generated, maintained or challenged. For example, who gains from the idea that 'all women are emotional and irrational'? How does that affect women's experiences in the workplace?
- It ignores the complex, shifting and sometimes multiple forms of identification people form or lay claim to – for instance, someone could identify themselves as a woman in one context but as a manager in another (see Chapter 1, Section 1.4).
- It fails to provide the basis for positive change or social transformation: cognitive processes are seen as simply part of human nature, 'hard-wired' into the brain, and therefore difficult to change.

2.3 Psychoanalysis

A psychoanalytic (or psychodynamic) approach to studying identity draws upon ideas that come from clinical practice. Psychoanalysis developed through the twentieth century as a procedure for treating perceived mental and emotional disorders in patients, and it is typically linked with the pioneering work of Sigmund Freud. A central assumption is that people identify strongly with particular things that they come in contact with, at different times in their lives, including aspects of working life. These identifications are emotional and relate to certain drives that emerge from the unconscious part of the psyche (see Glossary). Unconsciously, we are understood to act in ways that preserve our strongest identifications. In turn, we feel threatened (e.g. become anxious and even hysterical) when these identifications, or even our associations with them, are endangered. These identifications are not something that we are necessarily conscious of. Indeed, we may lack any conscious understanding of what triggers positive as well as negative reactions. Psychoanalysis is relevant for understanding identity precisely because it attends to the role of unconscious forces – feelings, desires and fantasies – in processes of identification.

People are understood to be driven by a desire to establish and maintain a stable, recognizable sense of themselves. To fulfil this desire, we identify and continuously re-identify with things as well as people. We may remember, for example, how we had a favourite soft toy or other object that enabled us to feel secure as we associated it with a sense of belonging (and proved a nightmare for our carers as well as ourselves if it became mislaid or even if it was accidentally washed). Psychoanalysis also teaches us that this stable sense of self is elusive, and so our identifications continually shift onto new things as we tirelessly seek out that something (a new car?) or someone (a new lover?) to make us feel both distinctive and secure. Figure 2.2 shows how fantasies may emerge to provide a sense of security and meaning.

Psychoanalysis rejects the idea that people possess a single, unchanging 'identity'. Instead, attention is given to processes of identification that are directed at different phenomena, at different times in a person's life. Rather than holding a stable and coherent identity, people are continually (re)constructing their sense of self (Driver, 2005). Roberts (2005) shows how managers strive for a sense of control and security in an increasingly chaotic world. Contemporary ideas of what a manager 'is' are

Figure 2.2 Fantasy at work

often intended to provide this security, partly because they tell today's managers how they are able to control the world around themselves by using different techniques and strategies (Mintzberg, 2011). The idea of control is a 'foundational fantasy for management'; the manager is encouraged to assume that the world 'moves as I will it to move' (Roberts, 2005: 630). This helps us to understand why some people identify so strongly with the concept of being a manager.

Jones and Spicer (2005) use psychoanalytical theory to understand why the idea of the 'entrepreneur' is so powerful. They argue that entrepreneurship is something of an empty idea because it is impossible to pin down what an entrepreneur actually is. Far from rendering it useless, the notion of entrepreneurship, assumes the status of a 'sublime' object as it allows people to project their fantasies onto it, thereby temporarily fulfilling a need for a stable and positive identification. A similar analysis could be applied to 'leadership', 'strategy' and other beguiling buzzwords in management discourse that exert a comparably irresistible allure. These ideas exert power and control over people, as they seek to become the elusive 'entrepreneurial' person or employee by striving to work harder and become more 'innovative'. We discuss this further in relation to du Gay's (1996a) analysis of 'enterprise culture' in Section 5.3.2.

Some scholars have used psychoanalytic ideas to understand how group identities come to be defended. For example, Brown (1997) draws on the concept of narcissism (egotistical self-love) to consider how, in organizations, people actively defend a collective identity – the 'self-esteem' of the group itself – through processes including denial, rationalization and aggrandisement. According to Schwartz (1990), employees can come to idealize their organization and identify with it obsessively, and this identification is manifest in strong forms of commitment and loyalty. In other work, Schwartz (1987a) applies these insights to understand the organizational processes for example – the denial of problems that surrounded the *Challenger* shuttle disaster.

Psychoanalysis, and more specifically its application in studying workplace identity, has been critiqued on a number of counts that include:

- Concerns about whether it is appropriate to apply concepts and ideas that were originally developed for clinical analysis of psychological problems to social settings like organizations.
- Criticism for not being 'scientific' because its claims can be neither experimentally tested nor refuted. For example, if a psychoanalyst claims that a person is driven by a desire to have sex with one of their parents and the person denied it,

the analyst simply replies 'you cannot see it because it is subconscious, repressed or latent'. Hence, the analyst is 'always right' and cannot be proved wrong.

- Criticism from a Foucauldian perspective (see Glossary and Section 2.4 below) about the claims to have uncovered universal psychological processes: viewing psychological processes such as internalization, fantasy, desire and repression as in-built, hard-wired aspects of human nature, rather than historically and culturally specific ideas or discourses (see Glossary) resulting from Western humanistic thinking (Parker, 1997: 484–5).
- Failure to recognize cultural differences in the subject positions (i.e. ways of thinking about being a person) (see Glossary) formulated by psychoanalysis. Many non-Western societies have different understandings of what a 'person' is, far removed from the kind of psychoanalysis popularized in aspects of contemporary Western culture (such as daytime TV talk shows and magazine problem pages).
- Tendency to legitimize (i.e. make socially acceptable) and reproduce a version of the self that is drawn from, and serves to reinforce, the narcissism associated most strongly with much North American ideology (Cushman, 1991).
- Criticisms of its misogynistic (i.e. women-hating) and patriarchal (i.e. assuming male superiority and authority) legacy, such as the Lacanian idea of the 'phallus' (a symbol related to the penis); it therefore has no place in contemporary organizational analysis (Butler, 1993; Kenny, 2009b).
- Inhibition of collective, political struggle by focusing on the 'inner world' of the individual: for instance, problems are addressed by going for therapy, rather than organizing collective action. For some, this represents a huge loss for political movements, which, under this lens, are denied a collective identity around which people can organize and struggle against oppression (e.g. discrimination) – we discuss this idea further in Chapter 3 in relation to the feminist movement, for example.

2.4 Foucauldian Perspective

The writings of Michel Foucault (1926–84) on power and subjectivity (see Glossary) have had a huge influence on the study of identity in organization studies. Foucault uses the term subjectivity rather than identity because it emphasizes the way in which our sense of who we are is shaped by the power relationships we are subject to and subjects of. So, for example, the very idea of being an 'individual' is understood to be the product of particular powerful, modern discourses (see Glossary) or systems of thought (Willmott, 2011a). The Foucauldian (see Glossary) approach focuses on how identity, such as our (common) sense of ourselves as 'individuals', is inscribed into dominant discourses – systems of thought – that structure how people think of themselves (self-image: 'I am an individual') and enable power to operate through, rather than against, subjects. For example, participation in a dominant discourse of 'human rights' can lead people to think: 'I will assert my rights as an individual'. In contrast, a dominant discourse of duty and honour can lead people to think: 'I have a duty to honour my family'. A Foucauldian perspective on identity conceives of subjects coming to occupy certain subject positions (ways of understanding themselves, see Glossary) within, and/or becoming positioned by, discourses that enable and constrain us by structuring our sense of self and our relationship to the world.

Brewis (2004) uses many of Foucault's ideas to analyze her own experience of nervous exhaustion and mental breakdown. 'Mental illness' is widespread, according to the Royal College of Psychiatrists, as mental health problems affect every family in the UK. However, these problems are generally stigmatized, hidden and taboo. To speak openly about mental illness is courageous (and potentially therapeutic). Speaking out is also politically emancipatory (i.e. enables people to be free) insofar as it 'outs' a condition that is hidden away and widely regarded and felt as an individual problem or stigma. Mental illness tends to be equated with some 'weakness' of character or personality disorder, and it is rarely linked, as Brewis does, to making excessive efforts to be strong or to trying too hard.

Brewis was diagnosed by the medical profession as suffering from 'nervous debility', or what she characterizes as chronic anxiety and depression following a highly stressful sequence of events. A change of job and a move to a different part of the country presented a significant challenge, particularly her ideas (ideals) of professionalism, high standards and self-control. It was, needless to say, that very sense of imperfect attainment which drove her on. When starting her new job, the 'violence' (e.g. high expectations) that she inflicted upon herself in order to maintain her self-image as a professional and model of self-control was even more severe than usual. Expressed in Foucauldian terms, she became very intensely 'preoccupied with satisfying a particular "truth" of "self"' (ibid.: 24) – that is, with living up to or maintaining (or performing) a 'perfectionist' sense of identity or self-image (e.g. of not letting yourself or others down – see ibid.: 30–1) irrespective of circumstances.

From a Foucauldian perspective, the key to understanding such processes is the particular discourses (such as that of 'professionalism') that produce such 'truths' about the 'self'. It is through 'techniques of the self', which include our internal, often punishing, conversations about 'who we are' and 'how we are doing', that we come to understand but also to discipline ourselves. In the premodern era, the 'truth' was conveyed in divine teachings. In the contemporary (largely) secular period, such truth is increasingly communicated through the authority of 'humanistic' sciences – in the form of psychology and psychoanalysis, for example, which establish what is 'normal' and, by implication, what is aberrant or perverse. For example, psychiatrists built asylums to treat people who were considered 'abnormal'. Patients were treated by 'experts' who were trained and certified to apply a variety of remedies to treat nervous conditions – including, for example, freezing showers, electric shocks and cocktails of chemicals – to make patients 'normal' again. From a Foucauldian perspective, we are seen to become 'normalized' (i.e. judged against a version of what is 'normal') by these 'regimes of truth' (i.e. disciplines that create bodies of knowledge).

As Brewis emphasizes, this does not mean that any discourse – of science, religion or anything else – enables us to get closer, or to become more like, what we 'really' are. Why not? Because we cannot escape a reliance upon some, particular, set of ideas about how to define and acquire the 'truth' of the 'self' (see also Prasad, 2009). Foucault analyzed historical changes in the understanding of the person, particularly the emergence of new forms of disciplinary power associated with the human science disciplines (Foucault, 1977) – power that operates by disciplining the mind as well as the body. Disciplinary power is contrasted with more traditional ideas of 'sovereign' power, where power was exercised in a very public and external way – such as when criminals were punished publicly through hanging or the guillotine. Order was maintained by command of the agents of the sovereign (e.g. king or queen) by making physical examples of those who deviated from their rule.

Under disciplinary power, in contrast, power operates internally through the mind rather than the body. Surveillance of behaviour using methods such as the examination, hierarchical observation (e.g. supervision within a bureaucracy) and normalizing judgement (deciding what is 'normal' and what is not) is widely deployed in modern societies – for example, in schools that could be a combination of codes of conduct, punishments from teachers and examinations. These disciplinary methods encourage subjects (school pupils) to internalize codes of behaviour in a manner which gradually leads them to discipline themselves (self-discipline). It is not simply the threat of punishment that channels our behaviour but, rather, the (positive) development of a self-identity that provides us with a pleasant sense of esteem, earned from 'being normal' and 'doing the right thing'. In the case of Joanna Brewis, and many other high achievers, the internalized desire to 'do the right thing' became (unrealistically) excessive and obsessive, with an eventual loss of self-control in the form of a nervous breakdown.

Foucault saw 'knowledge' not as a neutral thing, or as a positive thing – with its ideas of 'advancement' and 'enlightenment' – but as tied up with the exercise of power. The concepts and techniques of psychiatry, for example, are inescapably bound up with the exercise of power over subjects as the discourse of psychiatry tells people what is normal and what is neurotic or psychotic. The Foucauldian term power/knowledge is often used to describe the way in which power and knowledge are closely intertwined – in this case, the knowledge of psychiatry and psychoanalysis and their powerful capacity to define and treat what they deem to be abnormal. When this knowledge is popularized and disseminated, then everyone, not just patients, may come to position and discipline themselves and others through the discourse. The key point is that power does not operate simply as an external force that is imposed upon us but also acts to constitute us as subjects and to discipline us, for better or worse, in so many everyday, barely noticeable ways.

Foucault's analysis of the 'panopticon', a prison layout designed by Jeremy Bentham in the late sixteenth century where inmates' cells are organized around a central watchtower from which they can be continually observed, has become a popular image of disciplinary power. Its key feature, for Foucault, is not the efficiency of using a single watchtower to survey a large number of prisoners. Rather, it is how prisoners could never see or know whether they were being observed or not – which led them to act as if they were being observed (potentially) all the time. As a result, they became self-disciplined: watching their own behaviour to ensure it complied with the rules. The open-plan office, the town centre surveyed by CCTV cameras, or the 'wire tap' recording of call centre employees, are modern-day equivalents. Figure 2.3 shows the kinds of surveillance designed to ensure self-discipline that might be found in modern workplaces.

Zuboff (1988) uses Foucault's panopticon idea to study a pulp mill in which a computer system took a 'snapshot' of key instrument readings every five seconds. This prompted workers to self-discipline their behaviour out of fear that the Overview System would reveal any mistakes they tried to cover up. Printouts from the Overview System were placed into employees' record files and used for training, promotion and disciplinary procedures. In another telephone-switching circuit operation, computer terminals monitored the speed of each completed 'job', and workers had to speed up to meet the predetermined 'efficiency target' set by the machine. Again, the machine ensured that workers actively self-disciplined their behaviour and internalized the expectations made of them – changing their own internal thought patterns and feelings to comply with the system.

Figure 2.3 Disciplinary surveillance at work

Du Gay (1996a; 1996b) also draws on the work of Foucault to examine the effects of 'enterprise discourse' on workers' identities. This discourse is seen to promote ideas of market competition and entrepreneurship, which encourage employees to regard themselves in new, 'enterprising', ways. Rather than just being employees who do as they are told by managers, they are invited to conceive of themselves as self-managing, autonomous, responsible individuals who act like they are in business for themselves (du Gay, 1996a). When organizational change occurs, such as 'downsizing' that leads to some employees being made redundant, these employees are not expected to be resistant or aggrieved. Rather, when engaging in 'enterprise discourse', their apparent misfortune is presented as an 'opportunity' to take control of their careers, perhaps by pursuing a different career or setting up their own business. In other words, in this discourse, responsibility for coping with redundancy lies with the workers themselves, rather than the organization. Of course, as we stressed earlier, we are routinely subjected to diverse cross-cutting discourses, and so employee identification with the entrepreneurial discourse is by no means guaranteed (see Section 5.3.2, Chapter 5).

The Foucauldian perspective has been criticized for:

- Overemphasizing the 'fragility' of the self and its vulnerability to the power of discourse (Newton, 1998; Speer, 1999).
- Neglecting the importance of the structural forces (such as the drive for profit) that are thought to shape ideas; and, relatedly, failing to analyze the role played by material struggles over wages and control of the production process under capitalism (Thompson, 1990).
- A lack of attention to the degree of room for manoeuvre and resistance within, around and between discourses, including the variability and flexibility with which people relate to discourses (Fournier and Grey, 1999; Alvesson and Karreman, 2000).
- A tendency to 'reify' (treat as real) discourse: when the analyst assumes that discourse has a constraining influence by exerting influence on people in 'unseen' ways, without showing how this occurs through empirical analysis of data (Speer, 1999; Thomas and Davies, 2005a).

2.5 Symbolic Interactionism

Symbolic interactionism focuses on how people generate and modify meaning through social interaction with others. It has been used to study a wide variety of topics such as emotions, deviance and institutions. We concentrate here on two key thinkers that have influenced the study of identity specifically: George Herbert Mead and Erving Goffman.

Mead (1863–1931) argued that human beings construct their sense of self through their interaction with others. According to Mead, infants acquire an identity (a sense of 'who I am') through a process of socialization whereby they come to internalize understandings and expectations of 'the generalized other' – that is, from parents and guardians but also from the wider community. So, for example, the male infant will learn that everyone identifies him not just as a human child (with the expectations that brings compared with, say, a dog) but also as a 'boy' – with a baggage of expectations and associations that accompany this identity. Depending upon the culture in which the child grows up, a 'boy' might be expected to do certain things (like play with cars rather than dolls), and act in certain ways (like not cry when he hurts himself).

Understanding 'the generalized other' enables us to establish what kind of behaviour is deemed appropriate (e.g. 'boys don't cry') in different social situations. Mead also distinguishes between the 'I' and the 'me'. The 'I' refers to the active, responsive quality of individuals in interactions with others. It is the 'I' that undertakes the process of internalizing elements of the 'generalized other' by forging a sense of what the world is like, including how other people are interacting with us. So, for example, it is the 'I' that senses the world, or particular elements of it, to be friendly or hostile. The 'me', in contrast, refers to the sense that we build up of how others perceive us. The 'me', then, is what the 'I' identifies itself to be. It is an outcome of processes of identification based primarily upon how the 'I' thinks others view the 'I' – for example, as a sexed (male or female), rather than androgenous, human being. As the male infant is talked about, and treated as, a boy, he is urged to identify himself with the meanings associated with 'boy'. In effect, 'significant others' provide the 'I' with a kind of looking glass or mirror (Cooley, 1902: 183–4) in which the 'me' is seen. Taken together, the 'I' and the 'me' form a person's self. Of course, as we know from cases of 'gender reassignment' (sex change), the 'me' conferred by the 'generalized other' may be rejected by the 'I'.

Weierter (2001) uses Mead's concept of 'me' (among other things) in his study of a network direct-selling organization he calls 'Netto' (a pseudonym, which is unrelated to the supermarket store). Netto uses a kind of 'pyramid structure' to recruit distributors and relies on face-to-face methods (such as family and friendship networks) to sell a range of products from computers and clothes to furniture. Distributors are paid to recruit new distributors as well as being paid a percentage for each product sold. Netto spreads its vision and values among distributors by using a series of audio and visual tapes, books, seminars and group 'rallies'. Weierter (2001) applies Mead's concept of 'me' to understand how these artefacts and events motivate distributors to attain the 'ideal' image of themselves, as presented to them by Netto. The 'I' is exposed to these values and ideals through Netto books, tapes and group events. Through the various media, Netto presents a model of the effective distributor that provides a basis, or mirror, for self-examination ('who am I; am I as good as that model?') and self-production ('who can I make myself into; can I become as good as the model salesperson promoted by Netto?'). If these values and ideals are identified with and internalized by the 'I' of trainees, they come to form part of their 'me'. This 'me' is then actively mobilized and enacted by the 'I' in the everyday activities of selling. Some distributors are seen to have identified so strongly with the 'me' commended by Netto that they displayed a commitment to the company that approached religious fervour.

Erving Goffman (1922–83) was a chief exponent of a dramaturgical perspective which views social life as comparable with a theatrical performance. People are seen to play particular roles (like actors in a play) or, in Mead's terminology, they perform a variety of 'me's'. The main difference between Goffman and Mead is that Goffman emphasizes the more self-conscious, strategic presentation of 'me's'. Whereas Mead conceives of the 'me' as received and then routinely reproduced by the 'I', Goffman, in contrast, is attentive to the ambivalent and manipulative relationship between the 'I' and the 'me'. People are seen wilfully to adopt and play (at) roles rather than be defined by them. People prepare for interaction with others when they are in private, or just around close family and friends (known as the back-stage region), and they actively cultivate and control the impression others have of them when performing for the audience (known as the front-stage region). For example, when a person is preparing at home for a job interview (back-stage), they might carefully select the outfit to be worn and practise their interview responses in front of a mirror, in an attempt to present a favourable image of themselves at the interview (front-stage).

For Goffman, making a favourable impression is very much part of everyday life. It is going on whenever we are in the company of other people (either face to face or 'virtually', such as on the telephone). The term face is important here. 'Face' refers to the desired (positive) sense of self we want to portray to others. For example, if we accidentally trip up in public, accidentally say something embarrassing (such as a Freudian slip), or reveal our incompetence, we are said to have 'lost face'. Goffman contends that 'face' is not inherent to a person – it does not 'belong' to the individual as such. Nor is face an enduring or permanent feature because its preservation relies continually upon the actions and reactions of others. At any moment, we can be 'tripped up' and embarrassed or discredited by the unpredictable interventions, intended or random, of other people. So, if we are concerned to preserve 'face', which Goffman argues we are, then we are obliged continuously to manage the impressions that we 'give off' about ourselves in our social interactions (known as impression management). In order to minimize the risk of 'goofing up' or being 'tripped up', we manage and monitor what we say as well as our body language. Failure to do so effectively discredits or even destroys our identity, thereby undermining this valued source of security.

A classic example of dramaturgical analysis within organization studies is Mangham's (1986) study of the face-to-face performances of eight senior male executives during company boardroom meetings. Mangham shows how small details, such as facial expressions and bodily movements, are important in the 'performances' of managers. Gardner and Avolio (1998) also use Goffman's dramaturgical perspective when analyzing how so-called 'charismatic leadership' is performed by managers. Leaders who are identified as 'charismatic', they contend, are more likely to have a sophisticated 'self-monitoring' ability. Like successful salespeople, magicians and con-artists, they are especially skilled at monitoring and controlling the impression others form about them, and they are quick to adjust their behaviour to different or changing situations. Managers who are deemed more 'charismatic' are seen to present themselves (their self-identity) as trustworthy, credible, morally worthy, innovative, esteemed and powerful in order to inspire confidence in their abilities and influence others. In other words, they are skilled at a particular type of impression management and presentation of self.

Just like a chameleon changes the colour of its skin to match its environment, Goffman highlights how people artfully adapt and change their identity performances to blend in with, or gain control of, the social situation. This might not necessarily be a fully conscious thing, as the process can become habitual or 'second nature' with practice. A manager might (play) act aggressively and authoritatively at work in the expectation that subordinates will be compliant, but then behave in a more caring and loving way outside of the workplace. From a symbolic interactionist perspective, it is difficult to view identity as an essential, invariant inner 'core' that we carry around with us. Instead, it is conceived as context specific, and therefore fragmented.

The main criticisms typically directed at symbolic interactionist approaches are as follows:

- Symbolic interactionism leads to a focus upon micro-interactions that are abstracted from the wider social context and structure (e.g. class, gender or racial hierarchies).
- Symbolic interactionist approaches overly emphasize meaning-making, to the detriment of material constraints (e.g. wealth, poverty). Mead's splitting of the self into the 'I' and 'me' has been criticized for making speculative assumptions about the nature of the human mind by presuming the existence of distinct and concrete cognitive entities (mental objects) (Potter et al., 1984: 159).
- Goffman has been criticized for implying that the front-stage is somehow more 'real' or 'authentic' than the back-stage and also for failing to develop his penetrating insights into everyday interactions into a coherent theory.

2.6 Narrative Approaches

The narrative approach to identity is based on the idea that human beings are both tellers of stories and subjects of the stories told by themselves and others. The terms narrative and story are often used interchangeably. Both terms refer to the process of arranging events and characters in a meaningful way (Czarniawska, 1998). They can refer to writing (such as a book or diary entry), speech (such as an interview with a researcher) or another type of creative performance (such as a ballet that tells a story through music and dance). The term narrative is a more general concept, compared with the relatively structured idea of a story with a well-defined beginning, middle and end. As Watson (2009: 427) puts it: 'human beings both make narratives and engage with those which are discursively available to/imposed upon them'. A narrative approach to studying identity has been used in many disciplines, including psychology, sociology, communications, literary theory, philosophy and psychiatry (Brockmeier and Carbaugh, 2001).

The work of Paul Ricœur (1913–2005) has been particularly influential in narrative research. Ricœur distinguishes between how we conceive of time as a linear experience and how we experience it in practice, phenomenologically (i.e. as it is perceived and given meaning by human beings). Linear time refers to the experience of time mechanically moving forward in hours, days and years. Phenomenological time refers to the way in which we weave meaning around our past, present and future. We are always in the present and so we render the past and future meaningful through our immersion in the present. Ricœur uses the term human time to refer to the combination of linear and phenomenological time. For example, thinking 'tomorrow is my birthday' is both a linear time (e.g. a date in a calendar) and a phenomenological time concept (e.g. all the meanings surrounding the expectations and rituals of a birthday). Time is particularly important in the building of a narrative, and the telling of a person's life history, because it gives sequence and structure to the events and experiences that shape our sense of who we are (and what we may become). For example, an interviewee could explain their choice of career through a life story narrative that arranges past, present and future in the following way:

> I was brought up in a poor family [past] and never thought I would go to university [future], so the idea of entering a profession like accountancy never crossed my mind. My family is so proud of me for getting such a good job and I love the money [present], but I'm not sure I want to be in the corporate 'rat race' anymore. I think I want to do something more meaningful and work for a charity in the future, to give something back to society [future].

The particular plots we choose to narrate our experiences (known as 'emplotment') enable certain connections to be made between elements (e.g. wanting to escape a poor family background motivated me to go to university, which in turn led me to secure a well-paid professional job) and enables self-understanding – which is central to the formation of self-identity. As time goes by, new experiences enable us to reflect upon and renarrate our past and bring new meaning, whether of coherence or uncertainty, to our future.

The narrative approach is important in identity research because stories not only describe events, but also describe the identities of those involved. Stockoe and Edwards (2006: 56) argue that 'it is through storytelling that people's lives are experienced and made meaningful, and their identities constructed'. When we tell a narrative about our personal experiences, we also weave, mould and fashion our sense of self in the process (Vásquez, 2007). For example, in a study of a new information system being implemented, Whittle et al. (2009) found that different people told different stories about the new system, positioning themselves as the hero or victim of the story, but never, unsurprisingly, as the villain.

Stories often draw on certain literary and poetic genres (Gabriel, 2000), such as the tragedy or the comedy. In fact, the 'genres' that are available in our culture have a profound impact on how we make sense of our identity. Think about how young children can easily become immersed in the romantic and heroic storylines of Disney movies, such as *Beauty and the Beast*. If children begin to internalize the meanings and identities embedded in these storylines, they can begin to shape their identities as they grow up. A boy might start to think about how he can become a 'brave hero' when he grows up. A girl might start to dream of being rescued by a 'handsome prince' when she grows up. Research by feminist scholars has revealed the confused and sometimes hostile reactions by children and adults alike to stories that do not adhere to the traditional (hetero-normative) plots and roles: for example, where the princess slays the dragon with her sword and rescues the prince (Potter et al., 1984). This suggests that stories play a central role in forming our expectations of gender roles: what is 'appropriate' for a man or woman to do. Hence, narrative approaches can help us to understand both the freedom we have to make up stories and the constraints that dominant stories place upon us.

Recent work has emphasized that stories can be distributed and fragmented (Boje, 1991). Stories are not always told by one person from beginning to end, with their recipients just passively accepting them. They can also be told in many small fragments by many different people, who might alter or refine the story-in-the-making during this process. As a result, the identities of the characters involved can be contested and perhaps even 'recast' in the process (Whittle et al., 2009). Not surprisingly, people often attempt to portray themselves in a positive light in the stories that they tell, 'for instance as virtuous, honourable, courageous, caring, committed, competent, and so on' (ibid.: 438).

There have been surprisingly few critics of the narrative approach, at least in organization theory. However, some of the same kinds of criticisms that are often directed at other approaches also apply here:

- It is difficult to build theory from diverse narratives (i.e. how stories can be connected together to build an overall theory).
- The process of selecting between diverse narratives that offer conflicting interpretations of the same actions or events can be difficult and sometimes opaque (i.e. how do you decide who is 'right' and 'wrong'?). This is, of course, only an issue if you believe that research can uncover the 'truth'.
- Narrative approaches place an individualistic emphasis on the person-as-storyteller, ignoring the wider social context and structure (e.g. class, gender or racial hierarchies).
- There is a tendency to isolate work-based identity narratives from the overall life history in the way that narrative perspectives have been used in organization studies (Watson, 2009).
- This approach overemphasizes meaning-making, to the neglect of material constraints (e.g. wealth, poverty). Some would argue that these things affect us regardless of how we 'narrate' ourselves and our lives.

2.7 Micro-interactional Approaches

We use the term micro-interactional approaches to group together three distinct but related research traditions – ethnomethodology, conversational analysis and discursive psychology – because they all focus on detailed analyses of naturally occurring talk and text. However, there are some differences between these three perspectives, which we will discuss below.

Ethnomethodology emerged as a distinct research programme in the 1960s, particularly associated with the writings of Harold Garfinkel. Ethnomethodologists focus on the methods people use to produce a sense of meaning and social order. They question whether grand categories – such as race, gender or class – should be used by social scientists to explain social behaviour. Rather, they argue, the analyst should focus on the categories that are demonstrably (i.e. visible in their interaction) part of the methods of ordering accomplished by members of social groups. Instead of imposing social scientists' categories, such as class or race, to analyze people's actions and forms of social order, ethnomethodologists study how everyday categories (such as 'being a woman' or 'being a man') are used by members of social groups to (re) produce their particular sense of order. Ethnomethodologists are interested in questions such as: how is order accomplished by the use of a category, such as identifying oneself as a woman?

Conversational analysis (CA) developed as a branch of ethnomethodology. CA attempts to develop a 'science of interaction'. It seeks to map the order, structure and sequential patterns of ordinary conversation and is associated particularly with the work of Harvey Sacks, Gail Jefferson and Emanuel Schegloff. CA takes a very different approach to studying identity than the other perspectives we have detailed already in this chapter. It does not ask about how people develop cognitive categories of in-groups and out-groups, how unconscious processes drive our behaviour, how we are socialized into viewing ourselves, or how we are made into subjects in dominant discourses. Instead, CA examines how identities are relevant and consequential for members themselves, in the 'real-time', moment-by-moment unfolding of social interaction (Llewellyn and Hindmarsh, 2010). This means that the analyst does not bring in certain categories (e.g. gender) to explain conduct, because 'questions of identity are confronted and resolved by members and their solutions, rather than by analysts and theirs' (ibid.: 22). Hence, CA looks at 'how people orient to various categories of personhood as they go about their business'.

Widdicombe and Wooffitt's (1995) study of subcultural identities is an example of how CA approaches the study of identity (see Hutchby and Wooffit, 1998). They wanted to investigate whether processes of group identification – as understood by SIT (see Section 2.2 above) – could help to explain why young people joined subcultural groups such as 'punks', 'skinheads', 'goths' and 'rockers'. Semi-structured interview schedules were designed for researching the respondents, who were typically approached either on the street or after music concerts. These young people were asked to identify which subgroup they belonged to by answering the question 'How would you describe yourself?' (or something similar).

In some cases, the respondent stated their group identity immediately (e.g. 'I am a punk'), but in other cases the respondent reacted with a question (such as, 'do you mean describe my style?') or even with a lengthy description of their appearance (e.g. 'I have long hair', and so on), or by reference to some wider affiliation (e.g. 'I am a student'). In the last case, the respondent displays their identity as a widespread type of person, a student, rather than as a member of some subculture like 'punk'. Perhaps they are resistant to being 'pigeon-holed' into a particular identity category favoured by social scientists and media pundits. Whether they are a 'punk' or an 'ordinary person' is not, it would seem, a continuous or core part of their self-concept, nor an outcome of their cognitive processing (as in SIT, in Section 2.2 above). Instead, how they identify themselves is the outcome of an interactional method for presenting identity to others – in ways that are relevant to the interaction in hand.

Many of the classic studies conducted by Harvey Sacks concerned what he called 'institutional' settings – settings where the participants have particular kinds of institutional tasks and roles to fulfil, such as doctors or managers. Doctors, teachers and police officers have all been observed to initiate question–answer sequences, in which they ask the questions. CA focuses on these implicit organizational 'rules' or methods that people use when they are enacting certain institutional roles. Ethnomethodology and CA view institutional identities, such as 'doctor' and 'patient', as 'emergent properties of talk-in-interaction' (Benwell and Stockoe, 2006: 87). This stance differs from the structural view in which identity is more 'fixed' or even a 'position' (ibid.: 87) that reflects pre-existing and enduring power structures (e.g. power asymmetries between doctors and patients). It also differs from psychodynamic approaches that emphasize the deeply embedded nature of personal biographies and psyches (Llewellyn and Burrow, 2007: 302). CA does not ask whether someone really has or is a particular type of person, such as a 'lady', a 'teenager' or a 'regular customer'. Nor does CA ask what difference identities make to the individual person at a cognitive level (such as sense of self-esteem) or to society at a social–structural level (such as class inequalities). Instead, CA attends to 'how people accomplish, do, or otherwise draw upon' various identities in the process of interacting with others (ibid.: 302). In this respect, there is some affinity with Goffman's dramaturgical perspective where people are seen to take on roles that they present to others. However, CA does not assume that the accomplishment or 'doing' of identities can be readily placed or squeezed into Goffman's dramaturgical framing of interaction, nor does it assume a conscious manipulation of impressions.

Llewellyn and Burrow (2007) use CA to study how homeless people try to sell the *Big Issue* magazine to make some money. The *Big Issue* is a magazine published in eight countries, written by professional journalists and sold on the street by homeless people. Llewellyn and Burrow found that sellers routinely use gender identity categories, such as 'guy' and 'lady', to identify particular passers-by as potential customers. So, for example, they step towards the prospective purchaser and ask: 'Big Issue, guy?' (Llewellyn and Burrow, 2007: 306). This shows that gender identity categories, rather than say categories based on height, race or weight, are deemed in such situations to be most relevant by *Big Issue* sellers. Other categories, such as 'mate', could well be used in cases where the seller orients to the customer as a 'regular' rather than a 'stranger', to invoke the notion of 'friend'. The sellers also use flexible identity categories to describe themselves – such as 'homeless', 'poor' or 'ordinary bloke just like you', depending on the particular conversation that is unfolding. The key point is that CA is interested in the categories that 'members' (e.g. *Big Issue* sellers) use themselves, rather than the categories that social scientists might use to categorize people.

In one instance observed by Llewellyn and Burrow (2007: 312), a buyer of a *Big Issue* identifies herself as 'Catholic' in order to explain why she wants to donate some money without purchasing the magazine. Her identity as a 'Catholic' is invoked to produce an account of why she wants to make a donation to the *Big Issue* seller instead of purchasing a copy. CA does not ask whether or not she actually is a Catholic or not, or how often she attends church, or whether she has internalized the values of the religion regarding charitable giving. Identity is not used by CA to explain behaviour. Rather, the analyst focuses on how identity is 'relevant and consequential for the daily activities of people', including 'the concerted activities of the workplace' (Llewellyn and Burrow, 2007: 313).

Discursive psychology (DP) is an approach to discourse analysis (i.e. the analysis of talk and text). It is strongly associated with the work of Jonathan Potter, Margaret Wetherell and colleagues. DP focuses on how 'psychological' aspects – such as memory, emotion, attitudes and also identities – are constructed (i.e. assembled using words) and constructive (i.e. shape how we see things) through language. DP deploys many of the methods (such as the detailed transcription of naturally occurring talk) of CA but it foregrounds the process of social construction through language use (Potter and Hepburn, 2008). Some DP scholars, such as Margaret Wetherell, have sought to develop insights from combining the micro-interactional perspective of CA with poststructuralist (see Glossary) thought, such as Foucauldian theory. For example, Wetherell (1998) draws on both CA and the poststructuralist thinking of Laclau and Mouffe (1985) in an attempt to connect instances of talk with patterns of 'discourse, power and subjectification' (Wetherell, 1998: 388).

DP rejects the traditional view, which is dominant in psychology (see also the discussion of 'personality' in Chapter 1, Section 1.2), that language is a neutral medium for the expression of mental states and cognitive processes. For example, describing a person who collects unemployment benefits as a 'scrounger' or a 'victim of the recession' constructs two very different versions of who the person is. The former constructs an image of a claimant as lazy, and perhaps also unethical: a 'cheat' who is deliberately claiming benefit even though they are able to work. Describing the claimant as a 'victim of the recession', in contrast, constructs an image of a hard-working person who has been laid off work through no fault of their own. Instead of being condemned as a possible cheat, they are to be pitied and helped by society. Crucially, through its attention to the social construction of reality – that is, the performative effects (i.e. what social actions are performed) of identifying the claimant as a 'scrounger' or as a 'victim' – DP has the potential to incorporate analysis of the wider social consequences of discourse (Phillips and Jørgensen, 2002: 105–6), such as issues of power and inequality (see e.g. Wetherell and Potter, 1992). Media use of the term scrounger could, for example, be used ideologically by a political party to shift responsibility for unpopular policies, to justify cuts to benefit payments, and thereby further inequality and poverty in society.

Micro-interactionist approaches have been criticized in several ways, but such criticisms have to be tempered in relation to the particular variants of these approaches:

- They place a 'one-sided individualistic emphasis upon the rhetorical strategies of speakers' (Fairclough, 1992: 25).
- They lose analytical power by refusing to treat what people say as a source of information about themselves and the world (e.g. attitudes, events, etc.) (Hammersley, 2003).
- They fail to take account of wider contextual elements, including non-discursive and material elements, such as the 'social relations of power in a given social economic and political/historical context' (Sims-Schouten et al., 2007: 137).

2.8 Application Exercise – The Case of Frances

Approaching the study of identity for the first time can be a daunting prospect. To help with this, we now provide an exercise that involves analyzing a short piece of text from the standpoint of the different theoretical perspectives outlined above. We invite you to read the following excerpt from the (fictional) diary of 'Frances' (see the box below), and to think about how the different theories might make sense of her identity. To assist, we have outlined some possible insights, in Table 2.2. There are no definitive 'right and wrong' answers to this exercise (see Conclusion below), but working through it will help you appreciate how different theories provide different understandings of, and insights into, the diary entries.

The (Fictional) Diary of Frances

This is a fictional excerpt from the diary of Frances, a Marketing Director at Apple Inc. in Dublin, Ireland.

Thursday

I haven't written in a while because work has been so hectic. Since the i-book device was launched, it really hasn't stopped. I felt so stressed today – I woke up actually thinking about the 'to-do' list in my head! Lunch was at my desk again, oh well. Somewhat depressing but at least I got the report on our advertising in to James. I got annoyed with him today. He's my boss, fair enough, but he should be doing more to protect me from getting stressed out – I mean, from taking on too much work. This is not why I joined Apple – I did not think that the company would treat employees like this – like factory workers!

Back to James, today he told me he'd signed me up for lunchtime volleyball … of course, Apple has its own volleyball court (as well as pin-ball, a gym, a crèche and as many bean bags as you could possibly want to sit on). It would be easier to take part in these great 'we-are-all-Apple-employees-together' types of events, and even stay for the barbeques afterwards, if there was less pressure to meet the deadlines!! I'm also annoyed with James because of the way he told me – he just forwarded an email from someone else with all the details. I mean – what is that?? If you are signing someone up, do it face-to-face or at least make it a bit personal! You can be sure that I will let him know where he can stick the volleyball, face to face.

Friday

So, today someone came in with a flyer for the Apple Women's Executive Meeting next month. James of course turned to me straight away. … 'I suppose you'll be first to put your name down etc. etc.?' I hate that. Just because I'm female why do I have to hold the fort for women everywhere? I don't even have that many female friends … James is always teasing me about this. If it's not that, it's being Croatian. Normally that's when he is praising me for my work ethic, as an excuse for loading more work onto me. I suppose he means well but sometimes his teasing can hurt. And most importantly: he's my boss. I want him to see me and my work, not the female Croat in the office. … It's frustrating.

Saturday

I hadn't cleaned the apartment in ages so today I started on the rubbish tip that has gathered under my bed. I found some old diaries from when I finished university and went travelling! I cannot believe what a hippy I sounded then: all I wanted to do was to change the world, save the planet and live on an organic farm somewhere in Australia. So idealistic! I did come across one bit that made me think – when I was deciding to

(Continued)

(Continued)

come home and study for a Masters in Marketing. I was afraid that I would turn into a 'corporate lackey' and so put down these rules for myself: I would only do things that go along with my own personal ethics, and I would use my salary for good. … God, I wonder how the last few years at Apple would stack up against these 'to dos'! I think things might have started to change for me when I did that Marketing Masters degree in CDU. There were so many modules in finance and accounting – we were taught to look at everything through a money lens. Suddenly everything seemed like Marketing, and everything else was just about the bottom line. I suppose it is, but I know that I got into this game hoping that there was something more …

Anyway my little clean-out also reminded me that I have really lost touch with some of the gang from the Masters. Marketing's not really like other 'professions': law, or medicine or whatever: people don't really hang out together after college, either through professional networks, or socially. Not really sure if it is a profession, despite all the many times we were told at college that it is. I suspect it's just selling. Whatever. I still want to do it well, and do it on my terms. Nice to know that not much has changed in that respect, then! …

At least I'm not with IBM or another of the really big corporates. We ended up in a bar in town tonight for one of those IT industry networking events, and a bunch of those IBM guys walked in together. You could spot them a mile away – blue shirts, cream trousers, the stripey ties still on. And mostly men … I would say it's such a boring place to work. It's a bit incestuous, but we Applers tend to hang out together at these things. I always feel a bit out of place though. My clothes are not all 'designer' like the other girls. I made sure I wore my smartest outfit, feminine but not too sexy – I don't want to get a reputation as a tart. I never say that I am 'Croatian', just 'European', it sounds more 'cultured' and less 'backward'. I never get too drunk either, try to stay professional. You never know whether a future employer could be at such events. Besides, I've heard of people being put on 'gardening leave' and asked to leave the company if they act like an idiot.

I found out that Steve Jobs is going to be in the Times at the weekend. He's quite strange but it's always fascinating to see what he will do next. He's one of the reasons that I joined Apple. I heard him talk in Australia and started to read up on him – his goals just really seemed to reflect my own views on life! James has a picture of him in a heart-shaped frame on his desk. It's pretty funny. We do talk about Steve a lot though …

Monday

We got an email from James about our annual evaluations next month. I'm not too worried because I think that I've been doing well, but I know Margaret is nervous. She was off on maternity leave right up until Christmas – away for our busiest period! She cannot help it of course and she has the right to take time off – of course! – but I know that there were some comments made in the coffee room about how she hadn't been around to help out. I heard from one of the girls that Margaret might be pregnant again, poor thing, just six months after her first. I wonder what James will do? There's no way that she will be able to handle the meetings with Google – it will be an intense few months of late nights and travelling to New York. Hmm, maybe I will be in line? Still, I hate all the comments about maternity: it brings up the difference between men and women workers

(Continued)

(Continued)

yet again. I mean, I'm in my late twenties. I'm not planning to have kids any time soon. But are Head Office looking at me and assuming that I'm about to start breeding and therefore shouldn't be given anything important to do? I'm sure that no one really thinks like that, and I am also very sure that, legally, they cannot talk that way, but still …

Tuesday

Yuk – we have to do one of those psychological tests before our annual evaluations. Hate them. The questions are so stupid … e.g. And for what? Just to find out whether you are an introvert or an extrovert? For me, it depends on how many espressos I've had, or glasses of wine for that matter. And who you are with, and all that … who is just one or the other? I guess it just helps the bosses to justify their decisions about who would be good in different roles, but I hope that they don't rely on them – yuk!

2.9 Conclusion

In this chapter, we have mapped out some of the main theoretical perspectives on identity and illustrated them by reference to studies of workplace identity. Our review of different perspectives has by no means been exhaustive. Our selection and discussion of them are inevitably coloured by our own preferences which have led us to exclude many – such as the work of theorists such as William James, Carl Rogers, Georg Simmel, Anthony Giddens, Kenneth Gergen and Jonathan Shotter.

Our intention has been to illustrate and underscore our earlier point that ways of seeing are also ways of not seeing. By this, we do not imply that different ways of seeing mirror different aspects of social reality. Rather, each perspective presents a different understanding of the 'reality' of identity. Social identity theory (SIT), for example, views identity as a largely cognitive phenomenon, something that goes on 'in our heads' as we try to process social information. Foucauldian approaches, in contrast, conceive of identity as a thoroughly social process, linked with the historical emergence of certain discourses, and imbued with power.

It would make no sense to 'combine' all the approaches in the vain hope of producing a more 'complete' picture. Instead, as a student, you are being invited to get to grips with these different ways of understanding identity in order to make an informed decision about which theory (or combination thereof) you consider as most plausible, most illuminating and/or most useful for your own study. Especially when considering the possibility of combining perspectives, it is relevant to pay attention to the assumptions that inform the theories. While some theories share some assumptions (e.g. some discursive psychologists and Foucauldian scholars have compatible understandings of power and discourse), others are much less compatible (e.g. the cognitivism of SIT and Foucauldian analysis).

Finally, it is worth acknowledging how academia is subject to waves of fashion. Identity theory is no different. In recent decades, Foucauldian approaches have had a considerable impact on European scholarship, including organization studies, but its influence has been comparatively weak in the United States, especially in business schools. SIT and

Table 2.2 Illustrative analysis of Frances from different theoretical perspectives

Perspective	Approach to studying identity	Example from Frances' diary	Analysis of example using theoretical approach
Social identity theory	People identify with certain social groups (the in-group) and dis-identify with other social groups (the out-group)	Frances' boss, James, seems to hold many assumptions about which groups she belongs to. For example, he automatically assumes that she would join the Apple Women's Executive Meeting, simply because she is a woman (see Friday entry) James also refers to Frances as 'Croatian', placing her in a different social category than him and the rest of the company, based on nationality Frances also worries that Head Office may think that all women want to have children, making generalized assumptions about members of the whole category, leading to women of a child-bearing age being given less responsibility (see Monday entry)	A social identity theory approach would explain Frances' experiences in the following way: • Frances' colleagues and superiors placed her into a certain social identity category (i.e. women, Croatian) • They emphasized the differences between this group and others (e.g. men versus women, Croats vs non-Croats) • They also made generalizations about the similarities within the social group (e.g. women all want to have children, Croats are all hard working)
Psychoanalysis	Unconscious forces within the psyche shape our responses to everyday events. The effects of these forces are felt in the form of feelings, fantasies or desires of which we are barely conscious	Frances feels angry and stressed because James is placing more work on her desk, even though he should know that she is overloaded. Nonetheless, she finds herself agreeing to do the work but also continues to feel frustrated (see Friday entry)	A psychoanalytic approach to analyzing this text might read it in the following way: • Frances joined Apple because she believed that the goals and mission of the organization reflected her own values (see Saturday entry). Her perception of who she came to be tied up with her perception of the company, in an 'imaginary' identification

(Continued)

Table 2.2 (Continued)

Perspective	Approach to studying identity	Example from Frances' diary	Analysis of example using theoretical approach
	Attending to these elements can help us to understand how our identifications and associated actions are conditioned by powerful unconscious forces		• When day-to-day life at this company appears to cause her stress and frustration, this conflicts with her image of the organization and with her reflected self-image. This conflict emerges in emotional ways: through feelings of stress and frustration • Frances does the work anyway, because of her psychic attachment to Apple. In this way, Apple has power over her
Foucauldian	People form their identity through dominant discourses or systems of thought, which make available certain subject positions and self-images	Frances mentions the many social activities employees are encouraged to attend, including lunchtime volleyball (see Friday entry). Later, she reflects on the annual performance evaluation (see Monday entry) and being asked to do a personality test by the company (see Tuesday entry). She mentions that employees are sacked if they behave inappropriately at social events (see Saturday entry). She also comments on the way in which the owner of the company, Steve Jobs, is idolized by most of the staff, including her boss. At one point, Frances even talks about 'we Applers'	A Foucauldian approach would analyze these experiences in the following way: • The company uses disciplinary *technologies of the self*, such as appraisals and personality tests, to try to get employees to *internalize* the values and ideals of the company ('corporate discourse') • The company encouraged a strong sense of *identification* with the company through 'bonding' activities such as sporting and social events, so that employees come to see themselves in corporate terms – as 'Applers' • Certain leaders – such as Steve Jobs – are held up as 'role models' for employees to strive to emulate, changing themselves to fit with the corporate ideal • These mechanisms exerted power over employees by creating high levels of identification that reduced resistance to the 'colonization' of the self, e.g. long working hours, work intensification
Symbolic interactionism	People construct their sense of self through interaction with others, in an ongoing process of interpreting and shaping how others see us	Frances talks about how she thinks others might see her (and judge her) at social events where other business people go (see Saturday entry). She mentions being very	A symbolic interactionist perspective might interpret these experiences as follows: • Frances makes sense of who she is, and who she would like others to think she is, in her social interactions with others

Table 2.2 (Continued)

Perspective	Approach to studying identity	Example from Frances' diary	Analysis of example using theoretical approach
		careful about how she dresses and how she behaves, trying not to drink too much	• Frances engages in impression management to try to shape how others see her (e.g. feminine but not too sexy) • Frances forms an impression of others based on the verbal and non-verbal signals they give off (e.g. blue shirts, boring people) • Frances changes her understanding of who she is, or should be, based on her interactions with others (e.g. trying to look 'professional' to 'fit in' with others)
Narrative	People's identities are shaped by the narratives and stories they tell about themselves and their lives, and narratives that surround them	Frances mentioned her dreams when she finished university of 'changing the world' and how studying for a Masters changed her ideas about what she wanted in life (see Saturday entry)	A narrative perspective would make sense of these experiences as follows: • Frances narrates her life story by drawing together events and characters in a meaningful way through a plot, e.g. a story of disillusionment and lost dreams • Frances draws on certain plot-lines to make sense of her experiences, such as the Quest (following her dreams to 'save the world') and the Tragedy (how she got 'lost' and 'corrupted' in the corporate world of money)
Micro-interactionist	People make use of identity categories as part of their methods for accomplishing particular social actions	Frances' boss, James, always seemed to refer to her identity as a 'Croatian' before he gave her more work (see Friday entry) Frances talks about herself in terms of being a more ethical person, not only caring about 'money' and the 'bottom line'. She also mentions describing herself as 'European' rather than 'Croatian' at networking events (see Saturday entry)	A micro-interactionist approach would analyze these experiences as follows: • Reference to the identity category 'Croatian' performed certain social actions, such as justifying and excusing James' actions – overloading her with work • Talking about oneself as an 'ethical person' helps to accomplish the action of presenting oneself as more compassionate and moral than others • Describing herself as 'European' rather than 'Croatian' can accomplish actions such as appearing more 'cultured', or perhaps more similar to others

symbolic interactionism have appealed more strongly to US-based researchers (with some exceptions, of course). We recognize that we too, as authors, have been 'swept along' in a strong Foucauldian current, and that some have actively contributed to its flow.

Suggested Reading

The table at the start of this chapter (see Table 2.1) gives additional reading for each of the six theoretical perspectives, giving at least one source that applies the perspective to the topic of work, management and/or organizations.

Additional suggested reading for each of the theories is suggested below:

Social identity theory

Benwell, B. and Stockoe, L. (2006) *Discourse and Identity*. Edinburgh: Edinburgh University Press. Ch. 1.

Haslam, S.A. (2004) *Psychology in Organizations: The Social Identity Approach* (2nd edn). Thousand Oaks, CA: Sage.

Wetherell, M. and Mohanty, C.T. (eds) (2010) *The Sage Handbook of Identities*. London: Sage. Ch. 2.

Psychoanalysis

Benwell, B. and Stockoe, L. (2006) *Discourse and Identity*. Edinburgh: Edinburgh University Press. Ch. 1.

Lawler, S. (2008) *Identity: Sociological Perspectives*. Cambridge: Polity Press. Ch. 5.

Wetherell, M. and Mohanty, C.T. (eds) (2010) *The Sage Handbook of Identities*. London: Sage. Ch. 1.

Foucauldian

Benwell, B. and Stockoe, L. (2006) *Discourse and Identity*. Edinburgh: Edinburgh University Press. Ch. 1.

Lawler, S. (2008) *Identity: Sociological Perspectives*. Cambridge: Polity Press. Ch. 4.

Wetherell, M. and Mohanty, C.T. (eds) (2010) *The Sage Handbook of Identities*. London: Sage. Ch. 4.

Symbolic interactionism

Benwell, B. and Stockoe, L. (2006) *Discourse and Identity*. Edinburgh: Edinburgh University Press. Ch. 1.

Jenkins, R. (1996) *Social Identity*. London: Routledge. Ch. 1.

Lawler, S. (2008) *Identity: Sociological Perspectives*. Cambridge: Polity Press. Ch. 6.

Narrative

Benwell, B. and Stockoe, L. (2006) *Discourse and Identity*. Edinburgh: Edinburgh University Press. Ch. 4.

Lawler, S. (2008) *Identity: Sociological Perspectives*. Cambridge: Polity Press. Ch. 2.

Wetherell, M. and Mohanty, C.T. (eds) (2010) *The Sage Handbook of Identities*. London: Sage. Ch. 4.

Micro-interactionist

Antaki, C. and Widdicombe, S. (eds) (1998) *Identities in Talk*. London: Sage.

Benwell, B. and Stockoe, L. (2006) *Discourse and Identity*. Edinburgh: Edinburgh University Press. Chs 1 and 2.

Wetherell, M. and Mohanty, C.T. (eds) (2010) *The Sage Handbook of Identities*. London: Sage. Ch. 4.

Sample Exam/Assignment Questions

- Compare and contrast the social identity theory and Foucauldian perspectives on identity.
- Drawing on a range of theories, discuss the role of the social environment in the formation of identity.
- Critically assess the psychoanalytical perspective on identity.

Diversity and Identity 3

3.1 Introduction

When we think of identities, we often think of the different 'categories' that people ascribe to themselves and to others. If you were asked to describe all the lecturers that teach you on the course you are currently studying, how would you do this? Perhaps you would mention each person's gender, their age and physical characteristics such as race or ethnicity, weight and so forth. All these categories would help to differentiate one lecturer from the others. We frequently use categories like this in day-to-day life, and at work. The categories that other people use about (or for) us are not necessarily the categories we would choose for ourselves. For example, in the diary entry of an Apple employee in Chapter 2, Frances describes her dislike at being referred to as 'Croatian' by her boss.

These categories, or 'labels', of identity are central to the study of diversity at work. They affect how we think about others, and how we think about ourselves. Words such as 'black' or 'white', 'man' or 'woman', often carry particular connotations and value judgements (e.g. which is 'better' at certain things or in certain respects) when used in different contexts. So, the identity categories that we attribute to people come with a certain amount of 'baggage'. In the context of workplace diversity, it is important to study these categories: how they impact upon people, where they come from, whether they can be changed and, if so, to what extent.

In what follows, we develop ideas around diversity and identity. In the first part of the chapter we discuss different aspects of this perspective, including the idea of homosociability (the presumed tendency to associate ourselves with other people who are like us), the experience of being outside of the dominant identity (the 'norm'), critiques of workplace diversity and the idea of using identity categories as resources in social struggles. The second part of the chapter addresses the question of whether the identity categories already presented can be considered an essential feature of people and organizations, or whether there are other ways of understanding them. We present two important perspectives: first, the idea of identity as embedded in particular cultural, historical, economic and political contexts; and, second, the notion that workplace identities are multiple and revisable. Throughout this chapter we provide illustrations drawing on studies of identity at work, and outline common critiques of the various perspectives presented.

3.2 Identity as a Social Category

As noted above, people at work can be seen to belong to certain social categories, such as 'man' or 'woman', 'black' or 'white'. We know that in different workplace contexts, people are treated differently based on how they are perceived. For example, statistics suggest that being female can hamper the career prospects of women; in the UK, even after 30 years of legislation against sex discrimination began in the 1970s, the distribution of women in the higher echelons of organizations had changed only marginally by 2007 (McKinsey, 2007). The category of 'older worker' is also associated with a number of negative stereotypes (Posthuma and Campion, 2009; Fineman, 2011). Older workers are often seen as less able to cope with change, less able to learn new things, and more expensive to employ – even though such views (or stereotypes) often lack any credible basis. Given such prevailing assumptions, in particular industries like retail and catering, managers are often reluctant to employ workers that bear some kind of social stigma (Posthuma and Campion, 2009). Age, in particular, leaves people vulnerable to being laid off in certain conditions, as De Bruin and Firkin (2001) show in their study of enterprise-led reforms and the resulting impact on ageing employees. Similarly, Ainsworth and Hardy (2007) discuss the impact of workplace reforms based on a drive for new 'enterprising approaches'. They discuss how older workers were constructed as unattractive 'products' and risky 'projects'.

Similar stereotypes affect workers of certain races or ethnicities. Jenkins' (1996) research into racism at work notes how the colour of one's skin affects how employees in the UK are assessed by their managers. Black workers were seen as potentially problematic for the organizations in question, and the problems associated with employing black workers were attributed by management to the black workers themselves, rather than to persistent racism within the organization. In Ogbonna and Harris's (2006) study of ethnic minority workers in Harmony Bakeries, a UK cake manufacturer, white managers justified their reluctance to promote non-white workers in terms of their purported difficulty with the English language, inability to handle the pressures of the job, and problems with complex decision-making. This in-depth study shows how, despite the presence of a wide range of nationalities and ethnicities at the bakery factory, non-white people tended to be perceived and spoken about as a somewhat homogeneous group: the 'ethnic minorities'. At times, these workers were simply referred to as 'coloured', a term experienced as ignorant and hurtful by non-white workers.

Over the past few years, organization researchers have been investigating how such categories play out at work. In particular, research has focused on how inequalities and disadvantages related to these categories persist over time. Some important ideas are presented here.

3.2.1 Networking and 'homosociability'

A key part of the way particular groups are disadvantaged in their workplace is through subtle ways in which people tend to prefer the company of their 'own kind'. The idea is that people are 'homosocial' – they prefer to associate with, and give preference to, people who are more like them (i.e. part of the same social category – whether this is 'class', 'age', 'ethnicity' or some other kind of identification, such as 'manager'). This relates to the social identity theory (SIT) perspective (see Chapter 2,

Section 2.2) which focuses upon how people tend to group others into particular categories. The idea of 'homosociability' points to how we tend to be drawn to those who we identify (or implicitly label) as similar to ourselves and view in a positive light. Groups of people who are different are perceived as being 'other' and are often attributed negative, stereotypical characteristics. However, it is important to remember criticisms of SIT which challenge the idea that homosociability is part of human nature and 'hard wired' into our brains. Critics of SIT instead point to the role of discourse (see Glossary) in shaping who we see as 'one of us' or 'one of them'. Hence, our sense of the 'in-group' may be flexible and contingent on the context we are in – as the discussion of organizational identification in Chapter 1, Section 1.4, illustrated.

Homosociability acts to maintain the status quo in a particular organization. It also serves to maintain our own 'comfort zone' of identity as we effectively exclude or at least distance ourselves – cognitively and emotionally and where possible physically – from experiences that might unsettle it. When certain groups informally 'hang out' with each other, in this informal socializing, common languages and meanings develop and are (comfortingly) reinforced. Such informal activities tend to lead to friendships and acquaintances between people whose values and interests are, in effect, broadly shared. An example is the 'old boys club', where typically white, middle-class men socialize together in particular types of interaction, such as on the golf course. Gaining membership of the 'club' often means having access to special favours such as being given important, prestigious projects that will help to secure promotions (Dalton, 1959). In this way, homosociability tends to reproduce the existing hierarchy; this is often how informal mentoring relationships begin, for example (Kanter, 1977).

For those in the minority, including women in junior management positions, such informal networks are difficult to foster. Ibarra (1993) shows the significance of being left outside such networks. Research supports these observations: Poggio (2000) observes that relationships at work tend to be more equal where women cease to be in the minority. For Simpson (1998), this mix of genders is the most significant factor in ensuring that women's career advancement is supported and enabled.

In some cases, the homosociability of those who remain outside the dominant order can contribute to maintaining existing divisions. Marginalized groups stay marginalized because they tend to associate mainly or even exclusively with others in the same group as them. Westwood and Leung (1994) highlight this in the case of female expatriate managers in Hong Kong. Chattopadhyay et al. (2004) show how people who identify as minorities are often themselves drawn to an out-group, contributing to their marginality. In Collinson's (1992) well-known *Managing the Shopfloor*, he reports how these kinds of strong homosocial ties, supported by in-jokes and humour, characterized the team of shop-floor workers he studied. However, it was this homosociability that contributed to the men being unable, or unwilling, to change and adapt to new structures and cultural practices within the organization, leading to their eventual redundancy. Cockburn's (1983) case of male print workers (see Case Point 3.1) also shows how identifying with particular categories can reproduce one's position in the social order, in a negative way.

🗁   **Case Point 3.1   Male Dominance in the Printing Industry**

Cockburn (1983) examined how technological change was implemented in the male-dominated printing industry. The men who were in the majority in this sector saw mechanization as a threat to their masculine identity. These print workers feared that mechanization would lead to the influx of women and 'unskilled' men into their profession – they interpreted both groups as threats to their sense of masculine identity. Masculinity was aligned with pride and self-respect in two ways: (1) in terms of their role as breadwinner for the family; and (2) emphasizing the heavy, dirty, physically strenuous nature of their work.

To resist the entry of women into this profession, women were ascribed varied and contradictory identities, such as:

- Too 'soft' to do the job.
- Too 'innocent' and liable to corruption by the sexual banter of the men.
- Too 'sexual' and likely to distract and corrupt the men at work with their sexuality.

Interestingly, there was another side to this attachment to a masculine, working-class identity: male print workers excluded themselves from engaging with out-groups such as managers and those above them in the organizational hierarchy. This meant that, in the end, it was more difficult to resist or even negotiate on the introduction of new machinery, due to the identity defence that was occurring.

3.2.2 Outside the 'norm'

In many social settings, particular 'norms' persist. Norms are taken-for-granted ways of perceiving the world. For example, among students in the UK, the 'norm' might be seen as being relatively young, able bodied and perhaps English speaking. Only 50 years ago, we might have added (predominantly) 'male' to this list. What this 'norm' means is that people tend to invoke these categories when hearing the word 'student'. What if a student is in their forties, or wheelchair bound? What happens to people who fall outside the dominant norm? The concept of accepted norms is central to the study of identity at work.

Cockburn's (1983) study (see Case Point 3.1) shows how particular occupations or industries become associated with a particular gender, or it could be a certain age group, race or ethnicity. As we saw above, in the printing industry studied by Cockburn, the norm was for workers to be men. This gendering of occupational identity is not exclusive to this study. In fact, it is a widespread phenomenon, as Figure 3.1 illustrates: occupations such as science and engineering are highly male dominated in many countries around the world. This can apply to other identity categories, such as race, ethnicity or religious belief. In many parts of India, for example, members of certain castes (social classes) are only allowed to do certain jobs, such as working in sewers or cleaning. In certain areas, each caste group has its own occupation: high-ranking castes have official administrative and management roles; middle-ranking castes are associated with crafts and trades such as pottery,

Figure 3.1   Gendered assumptions about occupations

hairdressing and carpentry; while very low-ranking 'untouchable' castes are butchers, launderers and cleaners.

Identity-based assumptions apply not only to occupations (known as horizontal segregation) but also to levels of the organizational hierarchy (known as vertical segregation) – see the box below for an explanation of these terms.

Gender Segregation Explained

- Vertical segregation refers to the clustering of certain groups (e.g. men, women) at different levels of the organizational hierarchy. The idea of the 'glass ceiling' refers to the invisible but real difficulties faced by women in getting promoted to senior management.
- Horizontal segregation refers to the clustering of certain groups (e.g. men, women) in different occupations or industries. The idea of nursing being a 'woman's job' and car mechanic being a 'man's job' are two examples.

For Kanter (1977), the cultural norm within many organizations is to assume that a manager is male. This is also an example of a norm that is in the process of change but which, nonetheless, retains a residue of meaning such that the role continues to be ascribed masculine qualities which makes it difficult (not impossible!) for women to occupy and retain a sense of femininity. To the extent that others (more senior managers as well as subordinates) have expectations about who is suitable for such roles and how they should be performed, there are consequences for those who do not 'fit' the norm, namely women managers. If it is assumed that managers are, or should be, male, this view is likely to affect recruitment practices, locking women into the lower reaches of the hierarchy and into particular sex-segregated jobs, such as secretarial roles.

Even if a woman moves up through the ranks of her organization, Kanter notes, she must often conform to rules that assume that a manager must be a man. These might include assumptions that childcare responsibilities are not going to fall on the manager, that an aggressive style of management is to be expected, or that typically male-oriented social events such as going to bars or playing golf are suitable forms of socializing. Despite being outside the norm, the woman manager must choose either to live with these, or to find herself excluded from institutions (e.g. socializing after work) that are central to the culture of her fellow managers (see also Wajcman, 1998, on this), and deal with the consequences. Examining these forms of disempowerment at work, Kanter finds that identity plays a key role in how women (and men) engage with dominant norms. Finding oneself outside a norm that subtly and implicitly privileges masculine norms, women may, for example, come to internalize relative notions of worth. They might experience a feeling of being lesser than the (male) norm, due to the category of 'female' that they are assigned, with all the negative connotations associated with it in the context of their workplace.

Traditional management theories are largely silent on such matters as they present the workplace as an asexual, unemotional place. Shows of sexuality, for example, are frowned upon and discouraged. Against this asexual backdrop, recent studies suggest that women and their bodies are, nonetheless, seen as somewhat sexualized. The idea is that because of their difference to the male norm, their presence commands notice and is seen not only as different but as problematic (MacKinnon, 1979). For Tretheway (1999), women's bodies, their breasts, long hair, pregnant bellies and monthly menstruation are all signals of how women are sexed, while the male body is not seen as standing out or causing problems, because it reflects the norm. (Imagine a situation where the position is reversed, when men are introduced into an all-female workplace. Would they be welcome to use the same toilets? See also Case Point 3.2.) To overcome such issues, women try to 'blend in' at work through bodily adjustments which include adopting business suits styled on the padded shoulders and sombre colours of the male version, ensuring that their hair is worn short (but not too short) and neat. In some (extreme) cases, strategies include using contraceptives like the pill to ensure that their periods occur only at the weekend (Kenny and Bell, 2011; Sheppard, 1989).

However, in some occupations, women are encouraged to play up their sexualized identities as part of the job. For example, Pringle (1989) shows how women secretaries can find themselves adopting the role of 'office wife' in order to construct an identity for themselves that works. For instance, they undertake duties more commonly associated with 'wives' than 'employees', such as buying presents for family members or collecting dry-cleaning. Interestingly, Pringle shows how the secretaries themselves 'played with' this adopted identity: far from acting as passive participants in male-dominated workplaces, they collectively imitated, exaggerated and ridiculed many of the stereotypes under which they laboured, making fun of this sexualized identity.

Hochschild (1983) describes how airline attendants are encouraged to play up to a variety of sexualized images. She talks about how airlines use photographs of beautiful, smiling flight attendants to sell their services, frequently accompanied by slogans replete with sexual innuendo, including 'we really move our tails for you to make your every wish come true' (Continental) or 'Fly me, you'll like it' (National) (ibid.: 93). She discusses how part of the work of the female airline attendant is to maintain this sexualized fantasy that anything might happen between the passenger and the worker. Her book *The Managed Heart* represents an in-depth exploration of just what the emotional cost might be for this kind of labour as workers internalize the demand for such displays of sexuality. The result can be confusion and stress between experiencing an 'authentic' emotion of this kind and when it has to be 'turned on' for one's employer. Hochschild (1983) uses the term emotional labour to describe the work that flight attendants have to put into displaying the 'correct' emotions to customers, such as smiling, being friendly and acting in a subservient way. Emotional labour is often associated with a particular gender and a particular type of sexual orientation, such as women and gay men. Whitty and Carr (2003) show how practices of flirting on the Internet involve playing with one's sexual and gendered identity; this can amount to the reconstruction of the body online. The authors draw on a psychoanalytic approach, namely Winnicott's object-relations theory, and suggest that this kind of play enables psychological growth, but can also result in destructive behaviour against others.

This internalization of norms can similarly relate to how people perceive their ethnicity or age. Chattopadhyay et al. (2004) find that people in work who occupy lower status roles, such as ethnic minorities, can internalize and act out some of the negative traits associated with particular categories. This can result in behaviour that is somewhat debilitating and self-deprecating. Posthuma and Campion (2009) argue that the negative stereotypes around older people that pervade society can be strongly held by older workers themselves. Just being part of this group does not mean that people disassociate themselves from those stereotypes.

Some of the identity categories that shape our experiences at work are not as visible as age, gender or race (Clair et al., 2005). Religion and sexual orientation, for example, are not always immediately 'obvious' when you look at someone. People face unique challenges when dealing with these aspects of their identities, when they are outside of the norm. Clair et al. (2005) discuss a scenario where a lesbian women has to decide whether to 'come out' to her boss as a lesbian because she wants to request time off for the arrival of her partner's baby. People with an 'invisible' illness, such as depression or MS, may have to try to hide their illness to avoid being stigmatized as 'strange' or 'lazy' (ibid.). Ogbonna and Harris (2006) found that discrimination could occur due to aspects of identity that were not as immediately visible as race and ethnicity. The ethnic minorities they studied experienced discrimination because of their perceived lack of English-language skills, not simply because of the colour of their skin.

3.2.3 When the 'other' becomes the norm

In some situations, what is traditionally an 'othered' (i.e. not the dominant norm) identity becomes a dominant norm. An example could be a gay bar that favours employing people who are openly gay, lesbian, bisexual or transgender. This can lead to accusations of 'reverse discrimination', as found in Creed et al.'s (2002) study of different forms of sexual discrimination policies in the workplace. The authors note that the civil rights discourse was used by both gay rights activists and its opponents. One group saw gays as 'simply immoral' in their behaviour: as such, they did not represent a distinct class of people deserving special treatment. This group argued that they were being discriminated against by gay-friendly policies in work organizations, and that this reverse discrimination represented an attack on their civil rights (Creed et al. 2002). Case Point 3.2 discusses the example of how men handle working in occupations dominated by women, such as nursing and primary school teaching.

☞ Case Point 3.2   Being a Man in a Feminized Occupation

Pullen and Simpson (2009) interviewed 25 men about how they dealt with working in traditionally 'feminine' occupations like nursing and primary school teaching. The men in their study often felt out of place and worried about being seen as a 'freak' or a 'wimp'. To make sense of being in the minority, the men drew on both discourses of masculinity and femininity, emphasizing both their 'sameness' and their 'difference' to the women who dominated the occupation. Many of the men in the study sought to resist the discursive subject positions that are institutionally expected of men (e.g. what is 'men's work'), for example by emphasizing the value of their non-traditional attributes like caring, or being good with children.

However, many of the respondents also sought to differentiate themselves from the women who dominated their profession by drawing on ideas of masculinity. Some of the male nurses, for example, claimed to be more 'detached' and 'rational' when dealing with patients, enabling them to present themselves as more competent than their more 'emotional' female counterparts. They also appealed to their sense of 'belonging' with senior male colleagues, particularly those in managerial positions. The stories they told emphasized their equal status with other (hierarchically senior) men, particularly the stories that involved displaying assertiveness in interactions with male doctors. Pullen and Simpson see these stories as attempts to show the aggression and dominance typical of masculine identities, a tactic that was perhaps used to differentiate them from the lower status women they worked with.

In Ogbonna and Harris's (2006) study of workers in a British bakery, the majority of workers were from ethnic groups that would be in the minority in the wider UK context. Workers were largely practising Muslims, displaying outward appearances like wearing headscarves. The white British men complained that they were discriminated against because they were given extra work to do for which the ethnic minority workers were considered by management to be poorly suited due to language problems. It might be assumed that because they were in the minority in this setting, the white workers would be relegated to a lower status position. Interestingly, the authors found that this was clearly not the case. Hence, it is possible to have a disadvantaged majority in an organization, at least with regard to particular issues, such as workload allocations. It is relevant to note that Ogbonna and Harris found that the minority white workers occupied more of the management and supervisory positions at the bakery than the majority non-white employees.

While older workers can be discriminated against in some sectors and indeed in Western society (Tretheway, 2001; Fineman, 2011), age can be also be seen as an asset, for example when applying for jobs that require maintaining an impression of being 'reliable' and 'trustworthy'. Ainsworth and Cutcher (2008) found that older female employees were favoured in this way in the banks that were studied. What these studies show is that power and position appear to be more than a 'numbers game': just being part of the majority is not always an advantage. Rather, power depends on the dominant discourses (see Glossary) that afford certain groups privilege and prestige.

Thinkpoint

What are the categories that you belong to? Can you think of any that might be seen as an advantage in one job or occupation, and a strong disadvantage in another?

In some cases, a norm which might be considered debilitating or negative can be turned around and actively appropriated. Some commentators think that this has happened in recent years around the notion of the 'feminine' in management. A trend has emerged whereby supposedly 'female' qualities – such as empathy, collaboration and emotional awareness – are celebrated and hailed as offering a new and potentially profitable way of managing. Articles and books have been written about how the old masculine ('command and control') way came to be seen as no longer appropriate when getting the best from others: an aggressive, individualistic style, it has been suggested, must be replaced by a more caring, participative and engaging approach (e.g. Rosener, 1990). Such 'feminine' qualities, it is argued, are particularly suitable to flatter, facilitate and empower forms of organization, which have fewer levels of hierarchy, fewer rules, and are based on trust relationships rather than traditional forms of discipline (ibid.).

This celebration of feminine attributes, it was anticipated, would lead to females gaining more power and status within organizations, which would help to overcome the barriers mentioned above. Empirical evidence does not suggest that this has occurred. Even as this 'celebration of the feminine' gained popularity in management rhetoric, studies showed that few organizations applied it in practice. Instead, successful managers were found to rely upon traditionally masculine styles, marked by competition and aggression, while frequently espousing more feminine ideals (Thompson and McHugh, 2009). Moreover, some authors claim that this approach merely served to reinforce the gulf between men and women by reinforcing the idea that they have radically different styles, when, in fact, men and women are more similar than such studies allow for (Izraeli and Adler, 1994). This also relates to the criticisms of the growing 'rhetoric of diversity' which commentators observe in today's workplace, as we describe next.

3.2.4 Diversity at work: a form of control?

Most researchers study the experiences of minority groups, such as ethnic minorities and gay and lesbian workers, to try to understand how and why their experiences are different to those who are part of the 'norm'. However, not all organizations marginalize and disadvantage minority identities. In fact, some organizations actively encourage and cultivate certain identity categories that they feel are 'good for business'. By encouraging employees to 'express' their identities in the workplace, managers hope that employees will be more likely to identify with their work, feel committed to the organization and invest passion into their jobs. As such, being given the 'freedom' to exhibit your 'abnormal' (e.g. gay) identity can be seen as a method of exerting power and control over an employee, 'funnelling' their sense of self into the job. Case Point 3.3 shows an example of how an employee's sexuality (e.g. as a gay or lesbian employee) was used by the call centre firm studied by Fleming (2007). This study shows how a person's sexuality not only is an important part of their identity, but can also be used by organizations to manage and control them in subtle ways.

📁 Case Point 3.3 Sexuality, Resistance and Control at 'Sunray'

Fleming (2007) studied an American-owned call centre called 'Sunray' (a pseudonym) based in a large Australian city. The company had a reputation as a high-performance organization with a workforce of highly committed and motivated staff.

The study involved loosely structured interviews, focus group interviews (with three human resource managers and 30 employees), workplace shadowing, non-participant observation and the collection of company documents (particularly around the 'culture programme' of the company). It was only after the data had been collected that the importance of sexuality was noticed by the researcher.

The company slogan of Sunray '3Fs: Focus, Fun, Fulfilment' indicated the company's emphasis on freedom of expression, good humour and playfulness. Employees were encouraged to just 'be themselves'. The dress code, for example, was very relaxed and workers could have any tattoos, piercings and style they wished. One human resource manager described the culture this way:

> It all comes down to our environment – the culture, the freedom to enjoy being themselves and to enjoy being at work.

Sex and sexuality were openly condoned and even encouraged. While sexuality was not explicitly mentioned in the interviews with senior managers, one team leader did state:

> We like to think of ourselves as fun, sexy and dedicated.

Flirting, dating, flings, gossip and affairs were commonplace. This acceptance of sexuality also applied to homosexual men and women. The CEO publicly stated in the local press:

> We've tried to create a workplace in which people of either sex, gay people and people from other places can come and really enjoy the time they spend with each other and their managers in the environment.

This environment meant that gay sexuality was openly discussed. During one of the 'fun' theme days the call centre held a 'fashion day' where employees came to work dressed as models. As one employee commented:

> It was amazing the different costumes people wore … they really got into it. Many of the gay guys dressed in drag, in tiny mini skirts … and one of them won.

Although many of the employees seemed to welcome Sunray's open and fun culture, others viewed it as 'false' and obscuring the exploitative side of working there. The open sexuality was viewed negatively, associated with 'sluts' and 'sleazy guys'. The firm was cynically renamed 'Gayray' and the 3Fs were rephrased as 'Fuckwits, Faggots and Freaks'. One employee, Kim (a pseudonym), disliked the favouritism at Sunray:

> Well, to 'succeed' at Sunray you are basically gay, have to be really 'alternative' and Sunray likes people who have different coloured hair and who are into [in a sarcastic tone] 'being themselves' or you're just a complete loser. Now I'm not too sure which one we fitted into, but basically we are plebs. Just plebs.

Kim felt that you had to be 'cool' and 'sexy' to be respected by peers and promoted by management. Rather than expressing their 'real selves', these people were being duped into adopting a fake and shallow personality (bubbly, extrovert and fun) because it enabled management to create a culture of commitment.

🗯 Thinkpoint

Do you think the culture at Sunray is liberating? Or controlling? Or both?

Fleming (2007) views the Sunray culture as a way for managers to use the identity of employees for corporate purposes: 'the 3Fs philosophy enlists the private dimensions of the individual as a corporate resource' (ibid.: 251). For example, the feeling of being able to 'be myself' can encourage employees to be more creative and flexible in their jobs, such as wanting to work late to help to solve a difficult problem for a customer, making them 'go the extra mile' for the company (often referred to as discretionary effort). However, and more positively, Fleming notes that the Sunray culture also enabled people with marginalized gay identities to have a presence and 'voice' in the organization. Fleming concludes that Sunray is an example of the 'politics of recognition (redressing marginalized identities)' but not the '[politics of] redistribution (redressing economic inequalities)' (ibid.: 251). In other words, encouraging the expression of sexuality was positive in one way, because it opened up space for marginal identities to become expressed, but did not enable the employees to question or improve their labour process (via pay and working conditions). The resistance that was present in the study (such as with Kim above) was directed at exposing the politics of redistribution (issues of exploitation and control, for example) but it also partially repressed the politics of recognition (by using homophobic language, for example). It is alleged that a particular, narrow and stereotypical notion of 'gayness' (bubbly, extrovert, fun) was encouraged and rewarded discouraging and inhibiting other, broader forms of self-expression. Fleming concludes that 'sexuality is an aspect of managerial control, a site of empowerment and an object of resistance' (ibid.: 252). This case study by Fleming (2007) resonates with the growing scepticism around the rhetoric of diversity, as described in the box below.

The Business Case for Diversity

In some industries, managers have started to become interested in how to make their businesses more suited to people with diverse identities, such as women, ethnic minorities, gay and lesbian employees, etc., because they think there is a good business case for having a diverse workforce (Noon, 2007). A homogeneous workforce, composed of only white, heterosexual men, for example, means that the firm misses out on the talents of other workers and might not appeal to a broad range of customers. However, there is limited evidence that major changes are actually occurring to make workplaces more diverse (ibid.). Noon (2007) also argues that the very concept of 'diversity' actually makes equality harder to fight for (by ignoring the social justice argument) and downplays the significance of factors such as ethnicity. Diversity is seen as a 'personal trait' that can be utilized by the firm (but only when it is good for business), rather than a social group characteristic that demands certain universal rights. Fair treatment is therefore only offered when there is an economic rationale. For example, what happens when a particular business thinks it would benefit from only employing people of one particular ethnicity or race?

For some critics, the effect of the diversity rhetoric is to yield something of a smoke-screen: in playing up the differences between gender styles of management, for example, women continue to be portrayed as different, and continue to experience the kinds of material disadvantage outlined above.

3.2.5 Using social categories in struggles over equality

Some groups use particular labels to organize around, and this helps with struggles for greater recognition and equality. Traditionally, work organizations are technically supposed to be neutral. As Max Weber observed, bureaucratic structures claim to be run along roughly 'rational' lines, where promotion is based on merit alone (known as 'meritocracy'), and personal characteristics of employees and managers do not interfere with how people are treated. We can see the rhetoric of impersonality and fairness in the ways that many organizations account for themselves and their own practices. However, as we noted above, statistics imply that often this is not the case. For instance, women still lag behind men in promotion and pay, even in cases where their qualifications are superior (Kanter, 1977/1993). According to the UK Higher Education Statistics Agency (HESA), average salaries for full-time academic staff across universities in 2009 were £43,162 for women compared with £49,382 for men, despite decades of campaigning and policy initiatives on this issue (THE, 2011).

Some think that the solution to inequality lies in ensuring that organizations are truly 'category blind', so they do not 'see' racial differences, for example. Once this occurs, the idea is that stereotyping and mistreatment will disappear and fairness will emerge. Fairly recent equal opportunity movements in the UK, for example, take this perspective (Symons, 1992). However, other more 'radical' commentators argue for more progressive action, such as quotas for the number of women or ethnic minorities in senior management, as the only solution.

3.3 Identity as a Process of Social Construction

Do the identity categories that we belong to determine our experiences? Those scholars who would answer 'yes' come from what we call an 'essentialist' position. Such a perspective assumes that all who fall within a certain category share an 'essential', inherent or 'core' set of characteristics or experiences. For instance, the assumption could be that men are always more aggressive than women, and always have an advantage over women in organizations.

For some, an essentialist perspective is important because it enables social change and emancipation to happen. The idea is that the history of some categories makes them unique, and this means that the category can be used as something to struggle around. A particular radical feminist perspective, for example, may argue that women possess a unique and privileged way of viewing the world, partly due to a history of oppression and disadvantage (Thomas and Davies, 2005b). Thus women are seen to be closer to a 'truer consciousness'. This shared history of pain is thought to both unite women and be useful as a catalyst for collective action (Ferguson, 1984). Such a radical feminist approach advocates privileging and refocusing on the feminine, creating new organizations and alternative structures that avoid the embedded gender hierarchy of the existing ones (Thomas and Davies, 2005b).

There are some problems with the assumptions of essentialism. For example, we know that not all biologically 'male' people can be said to be overly masculine, just as not all females fit into the assumptions about what being 'feminine' means. In work-places dominated by a masculine norm, for example, not all men will find themselves part of the privileged group that embrace this norm. Some men may find themselves the 'other' to the dominant masculinity as they are not 'macho' enough, or not suffi-ciently interested in the 'right' sports. They might not act the 'right' way, or they might not take part in particular jokes and banter that others in the dominant group share.

Some commentators would therefore answer 'no' to the question above. They point out that it is not 'men' that are dominant, but rather particular forms of hetero-sexual white masculinity. Hence, a gay man, or a non-white man, would both be bio-logically male but not part of the dominant norm. In contrast, a woman could make herself part of the dominant norm by acting in a masculine way. This perspective views identity not as something you just 'are' (e.g. a man or woman), but something that is constructed through social processes (e.g. the dominant social norm). This is known as the social constructionist perspective.

The social constructionist perspective argues that the meaning of a particular iden-tity (such as 'woman') is not 'given', but rather is dependent on how people in a given social context (which could be an organization or a society) make sense of it. It is people themselves who continually construct and 'reproduce' the categories that exist, and are given weight, in a given social context. If the categories were used in different ways, the meanings that they hold for people could well change. If they stopped being used, they would disappear.

As Grint (2005) points out, gendered work identities change over time; the role of women at work, for example, has changed dramatically over the last 100 years. In Europe during the First and Second World Wars, the typical gender-based occupa-tional boundaries broke down for very practical reasons. While the men were away from home fighting the wars, women carried out jobs traditionally reserved for men. Even the heavy, dirty and dangerous work in factories that produced the equipment and supplies for the war effort was performed by women. With this change, women experienced a sudden rise in wages as a result of being paid the wages previously given to men. This helps us to understand why forms of gendered occupational seg-regation (see Figure 3.2) are not set in stone and can sometimes change. However, as Grint (2005) observes, when the wars ended, women swiftly left these occupations and the traditional gender boundaries and hierarchies were, in the main, reinstated. The rest of this chapter discusses the social constructionist perspective in more detail.

 **Thinkpoint**

Can you think of other aspects of social life that are 'socially constructed'? Which ones have changed over time, and have any disappeared? Can you think of aspects of social life that you feel have more 'essentialist' features?

We begin by discussing the historical changes in how identity – particularly gender identity – has been socially constructed.

3.3.1 Identity as embedded in historical context

In Section 3.2, we described how 'identity categories' can operate in different workplaces. Perhaps, however, the issue is larger; people can find themselves placed, or socially positioned, within particular racial, age-related and gendered hierarchies that reach beyond the workplace, spanning experiences of childhood, schooling, family life and other social settings.

An historical viewpoint, such as that taken by Grint (above) when considering how gendered identities change over time, reveals the problems of an essentialist approach to identity categories. In addition to the historical context, understandings of gendered workplace identities are influenced by social and cultural settings too. For example, huge changes have happened fairly recently to the understanding of women's work in post-reform China (Jacka, 1997). Yet, while some gendered work boundaries have been challenged, the traditional saying 'Men rule outside, women rule inside' still seems to hold influence over what Chinese women are expected to do. Nevertheless, what 'being a woman' means in post-reform China now includes working outside the home, with challenges for how women perform their traditional roles as wives and mothers. Some feminist writers point out that the category 'woman' is not useful as the experiences of white Western women are likely to be very different to non-white, non-Western women. They argue that there is no homogeneous 'woman', no homogeneous 'black employee' and that talking about 'minority' experience is always problematic.

 Thinkpoint

How do you think the dominant ideas about what is a 'man's job' have changed over history? What sorts of jobs are men allowed, expected or discouraged from doing nowadays that they were not permitted or not allowed to do, say, 50 years ago? A hundred years ago? A thousand years ago? An example to study in more detail might be that of male midwives (see box below).

Midwifery: A Man's Job?

Man-midwives were male doctors who attended at births instead of female midwives. They were also known as 'he-midwives' or (more fashionably) as accoucheurs. After thousands of years of women-only births, male midwifery started suddenly in the early 1700s. University medical graduates, trained in modern anatomy, had become more confident. They also used forceps for difficult births. The midwifery forceps were invented by the Chamberlen family in the 1600s, and remained a family secret until the 1730s. Midwives complained of hundreds of male competitors taking up this lucrative new trade.

In England the wealthiest and most influential man-midwife was the Scottish surgeon William Smellie. Smellie improved the forceps and wrote a bestselling practical midwifery

(Continued)

(Continued)

handbook. He taught many pupils, including the famous surgeon and obstetrician William Hunter. Hunter's pupil William Shippen successfully introduced male midwifery to America. But in Germany female midwives were protected by being given better training and a new licensing system. In France, Italy and Spain the Catholic church insisted on the use of female midwives, to protect female modesty.

Source: http://www.sciencemuseum.org.uk/broughttolife/people/manmidwives.aspx

As with women at work, ideas about what it means to be a 'man' at work are not uniform. Different cultures, regions, religions and countries have different ideas about what 'being a man' means. These ideas also change over time. For example, the idea that a man can (should?) take time off work to help look after children when they are born is a relatively recent idea, and is certainly not the same around the world (Meriläinen et al., 2004). Therefore, as Bishop et al. (2009: 9) argue, masculine identity is a 'varying product of cultural and historical forces'. Poggio (2000) shows this, describing the different types of masculinity that arise in a variety of organizational cultures: the 'locker room culture', an in-group of privileged men, the traditional 'gentleman's club', and the latest 'gender-blind' and feminist-pretender cultures, where 'new men' support equal opportunities, regardless of change.

The same also applies to other diverse identities, such as the identity of gay and lesbian workers. According to Rumens and Kerfoot, ideas about sexuality are 'historically specific and vary across cultures' (2009: 770). For example, homosexuality has in the past been understood as a sin, a disease or a psychological disorder (ibid.) – in some societies it is still understood this way. Similarly, we might argue that the category of the 'ageing worker' is in decline as we enter an era in which 'the cult of youth' pervades, to the detriment of older people (Fineman, 2011). Ways in which people experience their age as an important identity category change over time, as highlighted in Figure 3.2.

Figure 3.2   Age stereotyping at work

3.3.2 Identity embedded in the social context

In addition to a historical perspective, identity categories at work are shaped by particular expectations from the wider social environment. For example, researchers have shown that a person's ability to enter the labour market and rise up the career ladder is strongly affected by domestic responsibilities, and that these are in turn related to societal conceptions of what entails a 'woman's role' and a 'man's role' at home and at work (Wajcman, 1998).

When technologies such as mobile phones and the Internet were first being used on a large scale in the workplace, many commentators were initially very optimistic about their potential to be used to 'liberate' women, in particular by enabling them to work from home, combining work with domestic responsibilities. Case Point 3.4 explores how cultural assumptions about gender identity influence the experience of teleworkers.

> ### ⬚ Case Point 3.4 Teleworking: When Work Comes Home
>
> Teleworking involves using technology such as telephones, computers and Internet connections to enable employees to work from home or other locations outside the office. As a lifestyle choice, teleworking is often presented as something of a liberating, utopian dream, where workers can achieve a better balance between work and home life. On this view, teleworking offers the potential of harnessing technology to make workplaces more equal: those with onerous domestic responsibilities and a full-time job will find both more manageable.
>
> Bryant's (2000) study of 38 teleworkers in Canada shows that the situation might be slightly more complex. She argues that gender plays an important role in people's experiences of what it is to 'work from home'. Her study found that due to gendered assumptions around whether men or women should take care of housework and childcare, women frequently did not find teleworking particularly liberating. Bryant's respondents reported facing more interruptions during the day when teleworking, which often led to their having to finish off the formal, paid work at night.
>
> Bryant concludes that telework does not realize its promises of a balanced work and home life, nor a liberating lifestyle choice: the superwoman complex, with women doing the majority of home work, in addition to their 'day job', appeared to persist. Interestingly, the gender bias when it comes to unpaid work in the home crosses national boundaries; a 2007 report on 'Working conditions in the European Union' reflected Bryant's observations from Canada, finding that across Europe, 'women do most of the childcare and eldercare, as well as housework' (Burchell et al., 2007: 15).

It is not only women that are socialized from an early age into what is 'right and proper' for a woman to do. The same also applies to how men learn the dominant form of masculinity – that is, how to be a 'proper' man. This dominant (or hegemonic) masculinity can have many consequences for how men behave in the workplace, as well as what job they decide to do. Hegemonic masculinity can explain why men might be reluctant to report instances of abusive behaviour in the workplace, as the example of male bus drivers studied by Bishop et al. (2009) shows (see Case Point 3.5).

📁 Case Point 3.5   Masculinity and Bus Drivers

Why do bus drivers fail to report incidents of anti-social behaviour, where they are threatened, abused or attacked by passengers? This question is important for organizations that are attempting to collect accurate data about anti-social behaviour. Bishop et al. (2009) used semi-structured interviews, observation and documentary analysis in their study of (exclusively male) UK bus drivers to attempt to answer the question of why bus drivers systematically under-report anti-social behaviour. They found that it was their identities as men that proved significant. The authors identified four main themes relating to masculine identity in the reasons why the bus drivers under-reported anti-social behaviour, summarized in Table 3.1.

Table 3.1   Role of masculinity in the under-reporting of anti-social behaviour among UK bus drivers

Theme	Rationale	Image of masculinity
'I am too big'	Bus drivers claimed they did not experience anti-social behaviour because the customers were too intimidated by their physical strength and size	Being a man involves being big and strong
'I can sort it out myself'	Bus drivers claimed that they did not need to report anti-social behaviour because they could deal with it themselves, either physically or verbally	Being a man involves being able to handle situations yourself without complaining or needing support
'Management inaction'	Bus drivers claimed that there was no point in reporting anti-social behaviour because management were bureaucratic 'pen pushers' who failed to do anything proper about it	Being a man involves doing a 'real' job rather than pushing paper behind a desk
'Paperwork'	Bus drivers claimed that reporting incidents took too much time, was a 'tick box exercise' and gave managers control over the handling of future incidents	Being a man involves sticking up for yourself, taking control of situations and dealing with them your own way

Source: Adapted from Bishop et al. (2009: 13–19)

When men enter traditionally feminine occupations, their sense of masculinity is often threatened (although see the box on p. 53 where their use of new technology (the forceps) enabled them to leverage their masculinity). In such cases, a typical strategy for preserving the sense of self is to distance a privileged sense of self (e.g. 'manliness') from their work. For example, male employees could state that their job is 'not important to

them', preferring instead to invest their time and energy into other more masculine pur-
suits such as sport. Another strategy is to de-emphasize the feminine elements of their
job, to avoid the idea that they are not 'real men'. Pullen and Simpson's (2009) study
of male nurses certainly supports this idea, as we discussed above (see Case Point 3.2).

Research has found that working-class men often refuse to work in menial service
occupations, such as being a cleaner or receptionist, because the idea of being deferent,
subordinate and servile clashes with their sense of masculinity (Nixon, 2009). The idea
of 'emotional labour' (Hochschild, 1983) discussed earlier is important here. Nixon
(2009) found that the working-class British men were reluctant to engage in the kind
of 'emotional displays', such as smiling to customers, that they associated with 'feminine' service jobs. Batnitzky et al. (2009) show how the gendered categories of what
is 'men's work' and 'women's work' are affected by the country of origin of migrant
workers. They conducted an in-depth study of migrant workers in a hospital and hotel
in London. Those who migrated to the UK for financial gain – to support their families –
were more flexible in their gender assumptions about work. They were prepared to
undertake what was traditionally seen as lower status 'women's work', such as cleaning, in order to fulfil their duties to provide for their families. Ethnicity and migration
combined to break down the traditional gender segregation of occupations in this case.

Similarly, Chattopadhyay et al. (2004) explore how negative racial stereotypes per-
sisting in US society inscribe employees' identities at work. Interestingly, they observe
how, in the United States, 'white values and stereotypes' come to inform black employees' aspirational identities (ibid.: 186). Regarding issues of age, Tretheway's (1999)
interviews with female members of a US Chamber of Commerce association showed
how women perceive their professional identities as necessarily incorporating a 'fit
body'. In this way, cultural discourses of health and vigour come to determine how
managers 'ought' to look. Tretheway notes how this disadvantages the ageing woman
manager – who finds that the greying hair, lined skin and thickening waist can signify
wisdom and experience for older male professionals but tends to signify 'decline and
asexuality' in women at a similar career juncture (ibid.: 447). More generally, as we
noted earlier, a cultural bias towards youthful appearances, according to the 'master
narrative' of ageing-as-decline (Gullette, 1997) impacts upon how older workers are
perceived and treated (Tretheway, 2001).

The box below explores the issue of age in more detail. Many authors argue that a
shift towards valuing youth is symptomatic of the precarious nature of selfhood in late
modernity. Collinson's *Managing the Shopfloor*, described above, shows how masculine
identity at work was inscribed by wider societal discourses of class and status. What
such studies show is that workplace identity is inextricably interlinked with wider discourses in society, and must therefore be explored with this complexity in mind.

Age and the Workplace

Fineman (2011) argues that age is not just something that we have, like a 'fact' that we
carry around with ourselves. Our chronological age (our age in 'number of years') might
be very different to our subjective age (the age we feel like) and also our performance

(Continued)

(Continued)

age (the age we like to present to others) (Fineman, 2011). For example, a manager could be in her forties (chronological age), but feel very 'young at heart' (subjective age) and do many of the things normally associated with younger people – such as going to pop concerts and doing extreme sport activities. She could also try to deliberately dress in a 'young' fashionable style, and might even have cosmetic surgery such as a facelift to make herself look younger (performance age).

Fineman (2011) puts forward the concept of 'age work' to describe the things that people do to work upon and manage their perceived age. Age work is particularly relevant for work organizations because they often have implicit, unspoken assumptions about what is the 'right' age for certain jobs or occupations. For example, an organization might expect managers to be experienced, and equate that to age by only employing people who fit the 'look' of an 'older' person. Alternatively, another organization might believe that people who have not shown themselves as a 'star' by rising up the hierarchy by their early thirties are not 'star material', leading to a preference to 'younger' (or younger-looking) managers.

As Fineman (2011) points out, some occupations and professions are more strongly associated with, and troubled by, age-related identity than others. Sports stars, dancers and models often know that their career is age limited. It is a huge trauma to have your occupational identity stripped from you simply because of your age. People feel like they have lost a part of themselves when they can no longer say 'I am a dancer' or 'I am a model', for instance.

The discourses of age have changed a lot over time (Fineman, 2011). For example, 50 years ago the category 'teenager' did not even exist. Back then, the idea of an executive in their twenties was seen as 'laughable'. Nowadays, with the rise of young millionaires, such as the founders of 'dot com' companies like Facebook, the meaning around age has changed. Some people say that you have to have 'made it' in your career by the time you reach your twenties, otherwise you are left behind in the race.

Building on the idea that workplace identity categories are historically and socially contingent, for some, these categories may nonetheless be deeply embedded in the very structure of workplace organizations themselves (Thomas and Davies, 2005a: 716). For example, many of the communication strategies embedded within workplace structures and practices act to marginalize or even exclude women. This is because they frequently contradict styles of communicating that are 'learned' by girls growing up in Western societies. Tannen's work (1994) shows how, from an early age, boys and girls are taught different ways of expressing themselves. Communication styles are thus socially embedded, reproduced in family life and education structures. If this is the case, we can see how organizations in which more 'masculine' communication styles – such as those associated with power and authority – act to exclude women.

Hakim (1995) argues that women's position in lower paid, lower status jobs is often the result of their choosing such alternative career paths over other, higher status ones. Hakim suggests that women have different motivations to men: preferring flexible hours, friendly workmates and good relations with their boss, and eschewing the kind of self-driven ambition required for career progression. However, upon deeper examination, critics have pointed out that these decisions are inscribed by experiences in society, family and other contexts, all of which shape and constrain the ostensibly 'free choices' that people make during the course of their careers. Acker's (1990) work shows us that organizations are frequently built on implicitly gendered substructures. The rules and arrangements that guide practices at work, many of which often remain unsaid, can present obstacles to women's advancement. Even so, these practices are frequently presented as rational and therefore neutral. For example, promotion decisions might be affected by having a 'gap' on your CV from a break in your career, which is more likely to affect women because of the gendered expectations around child rearing.

 Thinkpoint

To what extent is the disparity in pay between male and female academics (see Section 3.2.5 above) explainable or excusable in terms of gendered expectations around child rearing?

Looking more broadly at differences in life-changes between men and women, the UK Women and Work Commission (2006) claims that women tend to be clustered into certain 'traditionally feminine' occupations. They call these the 5Cs: caring, cashiering, clerical, cleaning and catering. These types of occupations also tend to be among the lowest paid, which helps to account for why the gender pay gap remains persistent. Put simply, being a woman means that you are more likely to enter jobs that are low paid, insecure and have fewer opportunities for advancement. Without the expectations around looking after the home, men are often able to work longer hours, including evenings and weekends, to demonstrate their commitment to the organization, which is valued in organizations with a culture of 'presenteeism'. Women frequently cannot stay as late, due to commitments they have to children and other dependent family members, which arise from the cultural 'norm' that women are responsible for the domestic sphere (Simpson, 1998).

3.3.3 Questioning categories

From a social constructionist perspective, simply belonging to a certain 'social category' does not mean that any kind of collective identification must be involved. For example, simply being a woman does not make a person automatically identify with all other women and want to show her solidarity in the global fight against women's oppression. Hence, social constructionist perspectives expose the flaw in the assumption that identity is just about what social category a person belongs to. Foster and Fosh (2010) reveal the complexity lying beneath the apparently straightforward identity of the 'disabled worker'. They found that many people who fall within the technical remit of the category 'disabled', according to the UK's Disability Discrimination Act for example, did not identify with this term. Workers might prefer not be labelled as 'disabled' due to its negative connotations with regard to what they can, and especially cannot, do (e.g. you won't be capable of doing your job). Disability is also often understood using a medical model, which emphasizes the individual medical circumstances of each person. Disabled workers are therefore less likely to see themselves as part of a group with a common identity, making collective action ('we are the same and should fight for our interests') difficult to achieve. This lack of identification with the term disabled, and a related lack of group identity as 'disabled people', led to serious challenges for trade unions seeking to get disability onto the management agenda.

Ranciere (1991) is also critical of how academics, and other 'experts' like scientists and politicians, use particular categories. He argues that using categories, such as 'working class' or 'ethic minority', actively reinforces those categories or labels in ways that 'box', confine and restrict those people. So, for example, a commentator on gender who talks about the category of 'woman' as if it were a stable, reliable way of describing a person (unintentionally) reifies (treats as 'real') this idea, making it seem natural and normal. Paradoxically, this exertion of 'categorical power' occurs even as commentators are busy critiquing the categories, offering explanations as to why people are, for example, ignorant of their own domination. Analyzing and critiquing the category 'working class', for example, can have the effect of symbolically type-casting and trapping people in a particular social situation (Ranciere, 1991), even if its purpose is to engender solidarity and dignity. Accordingly, the interventions of well-known social scientists must be highlighted and critiqued. For example, Bourdieu's claim that people occupy a particular 'habitus' (ways of behaving) that reinforces their social status is itself seen to endorse a conservative view of social relations and inadvertently contribute to trapping people in this situation. Bourdieu indicates that working-class people are somewhat restricted in their ability to enjoy, say, classical music and fine wines. This may be empirically the case, but this claim also reinforces the status quo. The net effect of social theories, Ranciere argues, is often the reproduction of domination through reinforcing identities that are a product of politically charged processes of categorization. The question arises as to how we could start to talk about particular groups of people without using categories like gender, race and so on, to which we have become accustomed. The conundrum is as follows: how can we talk about people without 'identifying' them? Ranciere proposes that we think of people as different 'speaking beings' whose identifications are multiple, changing and cannot be categorized (Pelletier, 2009b).

3.3.4 Identity and discourse

A social constructionist perspective draws our attention to the ways in which dominant discourses (see Glossary) shape our understanding of diversity and identity. The work of Michel Foucault (see Chapter 2, Section 2.4) has been particularly influential in this area. For example, in Case Point 3.2 above, Pullen and Simpson (2009: 566) examine how the 'dominant discourses of heterosexual masculinity' affected the experience of men in traditionally 'feminine' jobs, such as teaching and nursing. Harding (2003) examines the content of leading management textbooks. Drawing on Foucault's work, but also on psychoanalytic ideas from Lacan and Butler, she highlights how assumptions about managers' identities that emerge in these texts are underscored by discourses of masculinity. Knights and Kerfoot (2004) offer a useful review of the debates between the Foucauldian perspective on gender identity and work organizations and more recent criticisms that have formed an 'anti-Foucauldian' perspective.

The field of discursive psychology (see Chapter 2, Section 2.7) also offers an approach to studying how diversity and identity are constructed in and through discourse. DP draws inspiration from poststructuralism (see Glossary), such as the work of Foucault, but also from micro-interactionist perspectives such as ethnomethodology and conversational analysis (see Chapter 2, Section 2.7). DP is critical of some approaches, such as SIT (see Chapter 2, Section 2.2), where identity is presumed to be formed through psychological processes that reside within individuals, as they cognitively process information about the world. Instead, DP views psychological processes and subjectivity as themselves 'constituted through the social domain of discourse'(Wetherell and Potter, 1992:75).

Wetherell and Potter's (1992) study of racist discourse in New Zealand illustrates how DP differs from other approaches. One of the interviewees in their study distinguished between 'average Māoris', 'Māoris who are friends', 'Māoris who can be invited into the house', 'Europeans', 'the Māoris people' and 'extremists' (ibid.: 77). These identity labels, Wetherell and Potter suggest, are not simply the outcome of cognitive patterns of in-group and out-group categorization, as SIT might characterize them. Rather, 'identity – who one is and what one is like – is established through discursive acts' (ibid.: 78) – such as acts of describing and categorizing ourselves and others. What people say is part of a broader discursive context (e.g. by drawing on what a person might have read in a newspaper, or heard a politician say) and social milieu (e.g. by using labels that reproduce racial inequality).

Wetherell and Potter (1992) adopt a performative or action-oriented perspective on discourse – which includes talk about 'who I am' and 'who they are'. This means that discursive acts are understood as forms of social action. They do certain things, such as defending a particular course of action. The interviewee who describes herself as having 'Māori friends', for example, conveys a sense of herself as someone who is not bigoted or racist (her self-identity), which in turns helps her to present and defend her arguments (such as being against the compulsory teaching of the Māori language) as more balanced, fair and rational. In turn, this discursive move serves to justify (or legitimate) certain practices – such as neutralizing Māori issues so that they are kept off the political agenda. Unlike other approaches (e.g. SIT, symbolic interactionism and other micro-interactional approaches), DP has a keen interest in the consequences, or performative effects, of presenting identity in a particular way. In work organizations, therefore, racism (for instance) is not an outcome of individual psychological attributes, as SIT would propose (e.g. bigoted attitudes and racist values). For DP, identity is not just a cognitive process, it is also a discursive process.

Wetherell and Potter's (1992) study also reveals the variability and flexibility of talk about identity. For example, in the case of the interviewee above, a range of flexible (and sometimes contradictory) identity categories and labels were invoked. This emphasis on variability and flexibility of language use can help us to understand how and why discrimination and inequality in work organizations are maintained and reproduced. For instance, Wetherell et al.'s (1987) study of workplace equal opportunities discourse shows that contradictory positions on gender inequality can be produced in interviews. When asked about issues such as the gender pay gap, interviewees simultaneously talked about their positive attitudes towards 'egalitarian' and 'fairness' ideals, while also justifying gender inequality by appealing to the 'biological inevitability' and 'practical necessities' of female child rearing. The field of DP (see Chapter 2, Section 2.7), in which scholars like Wetherell and Potter are located, questions the idea that people have a fixed set of attitudes, dispositions and values that make up their 'identity'. It shows that people can take up multiple, some-times conflicting, discursive positions in their talk. Inequality at work (e.g. racism, sexism, etc.), therefore, is not just an outcome of individual psychology (e.g. bias or prejudice), but part of the 'collective domain of negotiation, debate, argumentation and ideological struggle' (Wetherell and Potter, 1992: 77).

3.3.5 Workplace identities as multiple and revisable

If we reject the idea that identity is simply a social category to which we belong, something that we 'have', we can see that – at any one point in time – a person can 'occupy' a multiplicity of different identities, and that each of these is open to change. Hence, we can talk of identity as something of a subject position (see Glossary), with people coming to occupy different positions, at particular junctures in their lives. For example, to focus solely upon a person's gender is inadequate when that same person is also identified in terms of the colour of their skin, their religion and also their class. What is relevant in one situation, moreover, could be different in another situation. A woman might be subject to judgement based on gender when the organization turns her down for promotion on the belief that she might have children in the near future. Yet when she finds herself subject to some racist jokes, her identity as a Pakistani Muslim is the 'node' of her identity that matters most.

The 'intersectionality' approach to identity involves understanding how identity categories, or identifications, can be linked to, overlap with and operate through the other possible identifications available to a person in a given context. Identity is seen as multiple, and people tend to find themselves at the intersection of a number of different identity categories and cross-cutting identifications: one is not simply a 'student', or a 'worker', but occupies, or identifies with, many intersecting roles such as mother, sportswoman, activist and so on. Multiple 'nodes' of identity can there-fore intersect at any one point. Sometimes, we can find ourselves subject to gender, ethnic, age and religious 'identities' simultaneously. This approach tends to draw on a number of theoretical orientations, including queer theory (more about this below), postcolonial theories and gender studies. A key author is Anzaldúa (1987), who uses the term 'mestizaje' to express how people can exist beyond a binary, 'either–or', conception of identity (e.g. either male or female, heterosexual or homosexual). Instead, Anzaldúa argues for a 'new mestiza' way of thinking, which allows for the conflicting, overlapping identities that people experience. This awareness can help to challenge previous ways of thinking about identification. Anzaldúa draws particularly on her own experiences of complex and multiple racial and sexual identifications. In the case of gender identification, Judith Butler draws on Anzaldúa's work to point out that gender 'intersects with racial, class, ethnic, sexual and regional modalities of discursively constituted identities … it becomes impossible to separate out "gender" from the political and cultural intersections in which it is invariably produced and maintained' (Butler, 1990: 6).

What this perspective offers is an appreciation of how subject positions, and our sense of identity in relation to these, are open to change. This perspective is often associated with poststructural approaches, for example the so-called 'third-wave feminist' approach. Case Point 3.6 offers a brief case study of how these multiple nodes of identity are experienced by a group of female entrepreneurs of Turkish and Moroccan origin, based in the Netherlands.

> ### 🗁 Case Point 3.6   Gender, Ethnicity and Entrepreneurship: An Uneasy Combination?
>
> Essers and Benschop (2007) conducted a study of female entrepreneurs of Turkish and Moroccan origin based in the Netherlands. The women in the study struggled to reconcile their desires to run their own business with the traditional expectation of the Turkish and Moroccan communities that women should remain within the domestic sphere. The combination of their gender and ethnic identity meant that they faced many obstacles to establishing their own businesses. For example, some people assumed that the women were not sufficiently educated to run a business or unsuited as they wore a veil. Banks were reluctant to offer loans because of an assumption that their ethnic female identity meant they were not creditworthy.
>
> While some of the women sought to adhere to the dominant expectations of their ethnic communities, others rejected them: they resisted the notion that their identity as a female ethic minority was relevant in their business relationships. In contrast, some other women took the 'best parts' of Dutch and Moroccan/Turkish culture to make their business work for them. For example, they identified with being Dutch in the sense that it liberated them to run a business rather than stay at home. They also saw their entrepreneurship as contributing to the 'honour' of their family, as valued in their ethnic community. They were motivated to succeed in order to avoid bringing 'shame' on their family.

This viewpoint has a number of implications. For one, we cannot talk about a person's gender without seeing it as being simultaneously inscribed by class, race, age, nation and so forth. The way we experience gender identity depends on other (socially constructed) aspects of our identity, such as our age, disability, sexuality, ethnicity and religion. Women from a white, Western background, for example, are more readily able to have diverse experiences in the workplace compared with women from ethnic minority communities. Ainsworth and Hardy (2007) examine an Australian public parliamentary inquiry into the 'problem' of the older worker to show how age is discursively constructed alongside other aspects of identity, such as gender. Older men are constructed as somewhat helpless and vulnerable, requiring assistance, while older women are seen to be more self-sufficient and therefore less in need of government support. Here we can see how an 'aged identity' cannot be separated out from conceptions of gender. Leonard (2010) shows how ex-pat British managers in Hong Kong experienced a shift in their sense of self. Significant 'identity work' was required when these groups found themselves in a geographic and culturally strange place, in which formerly taken-for-granted ideas of race, gender and nationality no longer made sense, and needed to be renegotiated. Leonard discusses how powerful discourses of whiteness, Britishness and gender were reworked as aspects of people's identities in this new location. Jack and Lorbiecki (2007) also show how national identity, specifically Britishness, intersects with globalized identities in British organizations who are attempting to introduce diversity initiatives.

For intersectionality theorists, the idea of multiplicity is suggestive of a crossroads, where many different paths are in front of us, of different discourses that inform identification. This metaphor is useful because it implies the presence of many possible 'identification roads' that a person might take. However, it is this same analogy that draws criticism from commentators who read it as implying that at any given point in time, a person is free to choose between many possible 'roads' or identifications (McNay, 2003). Critics wonder whether such approaches adequately account for the material circumstances, particularly oppressive ones, in which people find themselves and which mitigate against free and open identification 'choices'.

3.3.6 Performing our identities

Building on the ideas put forward in the previous section, the performative perspective on identity offers an important way of understanding how people actively, but not necessarily consciously, work on displaying and managing their identity. Rather than viewing identity as something that is 'given' to us, as categories that we are 'trapped' into, the performative perspective views life as a series of 'identifications', whereby we identify with particular categories at different times, and work on displaying them to others. In doing so, we perform our identities and in this performance, these identities are subject to change (Butler, 1990). In the context of gender identity, for example, it is argued that while masculinity, as a discourse, is often problematic, we need to decouple this from the 'male sex'. The same is true of femininity: both are subject positions that are open to revision. This relates to the argument presented at the beginning of Section 3.3 around the problems of adopting an essentialist view of social categories. Studies taking this approach show how categories like gender, race and class can be seen merely as situated social scripts that guide identity performances, not some sort of concrete, fundamental division. Identity is what emerges when we examine the day-to-day negotiations of these scripts. Studies of performative identities in the workplace tend to draw on a psychoanalytic approach (Harding, 2003; Roberts, 2005).

The idea of identity as a 'performance' also relates to the work of Erving Goffman (see Chapter 2, Section 2.5). Social constructionists argue that our identity – as, say, a man or a woman – is not something that we have, but rather something that we have to continually construct, perform and achieve in social interaction. Harold Garfinkel, one of the founding thinkers in the field of ethnomethodology (see Chapter 2, Section 2.7), studied a person called 'Agnes' (Garfinkel, 1967: 167–72). Agnes was born with male genitalia and raised as a boy. However, she always felt herself to be female. At the age of 17, Agnes began living as a woman and started to take female hormone supplements. Garfinkel studied the 'methods' Agnes used to 'pass' as a woman. Agnes spoke in a soft and light tone, spoke often about her boyfriend and carefully dressed herself like other women in her age group – unlike the sometimes 'over-feminine' dress and make-up associated with some transvestites, from whom Agnes was at pains to distance herself. Garfinkel viewed gender identity not as something that people simply have, and bring to social situations, but as a 'situated accomplishment' (ibid.: 121).

It is in everyday negotiations that, for some authors, the potential for resistance resides. We have already mentioned how the secretaries in Pringle's (1989) study laughed at the 'office wife' image that they adopted, playing with and reinterpreting the identity. Figure 3.3 looks at the dominant expectations around the role of secretary.

Figure 3.3   Performing identities: boss and secretary

Similarly, in a study of Japanese women sweet factory workers, Kondo (1990) high-lights processes of playing with identities; women would draw on national, gendered and class identities at different times, often using these as forms of resistance through joking and parody. Interestingly, however, these apparent challenges to power did not result in a lessening of status difference between the workers in question and their employers.

The idea of the performative perspective is that identities can be performed on the local scale, meaning they are open to revision. We can also use these diverse and multiple positions to effect change. In the performance lies the potential to alter the discourse. For example, a woman could playfully comment on the length of her skirt or the amount of 'cleavage' she is displaying in order to subtly criticize current norms of female sexuality in the workplace. The potential for change arises in the space between competing discourses – such as woman as 'nurturing earth mother' and woman as 'sexual object' – and in the realization that there may in fact be no fixed or final gender identity.

The way that physical signs of identity are carried out/performed through bodily work is an important part of the way such identities, and the power structures that inform them, are reproduced. Research shows how women dress in particular ways or adopt other bodily styles of behaviour at work – referred to as 'embodiment' (Kenny and Bell, 2011). For some authors (Butler, 1990), bodily performances form an important way in which people can perform 'who they are' in different ways. Butler's 1990 book *Gender Trouble* discusses how this can work with 'drag artists' – men who dress up as women – and how traditional, taken-for-granted identities such as 'man' or 'woman' can be troubled, or put into jeopardy. Again, the idea is that bodily forms of identity are merely subject positions that are revisable and contingent (see Chapter 2, Section 2.4, on Foucault). If so, notions of bodily performativity might be drawn upon to trouble traditional identity characteristics (Harding, 2003). Drawing on queer theory, Parker (2001) explores ideas around how workplace roles such as 'manager' can be performed and subverted in a number of ways. It must be noted, however, following Tretheway's (2001) study of older women professionals, that the material body can be difficult to 'perform' differently. Yet, as Fineman (2011) points out, some ageing workers go to extreme lengths, such as having plastic sur-gery, to achieve the embodied image of the 'ideal' young-looking worker.

Critics of the idea that multiple and changeable identities provide us with resources for resistance argue that it plays down the material realities of situations in which some groups simply dominate over others. For example, if women are oppressed, not paid equally, and denied the opportunity to vote or gain paid employment, what difference does it make that they can 'play' with their gender identity beyond offering some distracting compensation for their oppression? A related question is: how far do people get towards altering power structures by their 'subversive' identity work (Wajcman, 1998)? Some commentators think that recognizing, or even celebrating, multiple identities actually limits the capacity for collective action. Some (so-called 'second-wave') feminists argue that the sense of identity invoked by the idea of multiple identities is so tenuous and shifting that it loses political weight. The material inequality (such as unequal pay) that oppresses women as a group may be lost by focusing on how gender is performed by individuals. Brubaker and Cooper (2000: 1), for example, ask:

> If [identity] is fluid, how can we understand the ways in which self-understandings may harden, congeal and crystallize? If it is constructed, how can we understand the sometimes coercive force of external identifications? If it is multiple, how can we understand?

In response, advocates of a more complex and plural understanding of identity formation and membership argue that identities can be, and are, invoked strategically, as a 'necessary but contingent' category (see Butler et al., 2000, for example). The context of each situation is vastly different, and so theorizing about gender, race or ageing identities in the abstract is of limited assistance. In this regard, it is relevant to recall how much of the literature on identity comes from the halls of 'Western' (US/European) academic institutions. We must be careful: the issues debated by these scholars may bear little relation to the experiences of people in developing countries. Postcolonial feminist critics argue that such perspectives are products of, and contribute to, continuing Western hegemony (Spivak, 1988). More studies are certainly needed from other cultural contexts and perspectives.

3.3.7 'Troubling' and 'queering' identities

Critical thinkers, who want to think about new ways of disrupting (and improving) social inequality, have begun to think about the potential of identity for changing society. Largely drawing from psychoanalytic perspectives, research has focused on how people seek to 'trouble' (question) or 'queer' (reverse or turn upside down) dominant assumptions about identity. The box below explains 'queer theory' in more detail.

Queer Theory

Queer theory tends to reject an essentialist way of viewing self and identity: for example, women are not necessarily 'caring', gay men are not necessarily 'effeminate'. Such understandings come to be constructed at particular periods of time, in particular ways. For queer theorists, categories, identities and norms that are often seen as unchangeable, particularly those involving sexuality and gender, should be continually problematized and challenged. For this reason, it is helpful to think of it as a practice of queering, rather than a theory about a particular group of people (i.e. non-heterosexuals).

Queer theory emerged from radical gay activism by groups such as ACT UP, who argued that traditional categories for understanding 'gay issues' were insufficient and

(Continued)

(Continued)

oppressive, and that a different way of thinking about politics was needed, away from the usual focus on gaining recognition for identity categories. Key authors in the area include Butler (1990), Sedgwick (1990), Fuss (1991), among others, and the influence of Foucault (see Chapter 2, Section 2.4) is strong.

Eve Kosofsky Sedgwick's book *Epistemology of the Closet* focuses on considerations of what can be known, and what remains unknown, in social life: how and why some things 'come out' and others remain 'in the closet'. What is 'out' in a text depends on something else that remains silenced. Moving on from this, Sedgwick explores the idea of pure difference: a way of thinking of something so that it is not necessarily related to, and therefore dependent upon, another thing, but simply different (for example, thinking about 'woman' without thinking of the difference to 'man'). It is about being open to difference without seeking to pin it down with a category. It is about renouncing such efforts to control the world by subjecting it to cultural specification.

Sedgwick wonders whether it would be possible simply to allow people and phenomena to exist in their own specificity, without any categories. This would require overcoming an aversion to such practice in which processes of identification and dis-identification are wholly playful, not representational. People tend to desire and defend relational links between concepts (e.g. man and woman), and so maintaining these connections often takes primacy, at the expense of paradox, inexplicability and disconnection.

Butler considers how categories of gender can be oppressive, and how we might move away from this by showing how they can be troubled. She is interested in how people upset gender norms and famously draws on the example of the drag performance. For her, drag practices act to temporarily upset our pre-existing assumptions about gender identity (Butler, 1990). When we see a person in drag, we momentarily draw on our assumptions about what a man 'is', and what a woman 'is', as we try to make sense of what we are seeing. The confusion that drag prompts at this moment hints at how there may be no reality behind the illusion: there may be no 'is' for a woman, or a man, but rather the 'isness' associated with, or bestowed by, categories is one that is constructed, contingent and therefore subject to transformation.

Ranciere argues that research should pay attention to the day-to-day lived reality in which people deal with identity categories. He shows that people regularly disrupt their 'allocated' identities, giving the example of working-class people who fantasize about, mock and imitate their social betters in ways that effectively upset existing hierarchical norms. Ranciere (1989) studies workers' movements from the 1830s in France, highlighting activities that workers carried out in their spare time, including writing poetry, creating art and crafting letters. For Ranciere, it would be a mistake to talk about such activities as some form of 'resistance' against an identity category, as other theorists might, but rather should be seen as the performative enacting of a lack of identity – a disentanglement and troubling of what we might have expected in the particular situation (Ranciere, 1989).

Although working within different theoretical traditions, what Ranciere's and Butler's approaches to identity have in common is a focus on how, why and when categories break down as they play out in day-to-day life. Instances where boundaries are transgressed present us with ideas of how categories might be played with, and how oppressive discourses and norms that regulate and restrict 'isness' might someday be changed.

Queer theory (see box above) is about acknowledging how social reality is politically constructed and reproduced, and then performing this politics through everyday work: things we do and things we say. As such, queering represents an active and embodied critique of conservative and ostensibly apolitical or 'scientific' conceptions of identity. Rather than a concern with 'gay' or 'lesbian' issues, it is about opening up and queering categories of knowledge through practice: for example, dressing in 'drag' disrupts categories of 'male' and 'female'. Herein lies the difference between queer theory, social constructivism and ethnomethodology: while each can be said to highlight the contingency of particular identity categories, to show that these are open to change, and to focus upon the performed and ongoing nature of identity as practice, queer is different in that it aims to problematize categories for explicitly political reasons – to denaturalize categories so that new forms of being and new ways of occupying a place in the world can emerge (Parker, 2001). The question therefore is not what 'is' queer theory, but what can it do?

Queer theory examines how identification of, and with, particular norms and categories limits and oppresses people. It explores the different forms of being that might disrupt or 'trouble' the authority of categories, even where these forms of being appear fantastic and unlikely, and where the end result is unknown and difficult to imagine (Butler, 1990). Queer theory has become increasingly influential across a wide range of scholarly areas including organization studies. In this area, Parker (2001) attempts the apparently outrageous (for the identity of the management scholar) to 'fuck management'. Drawing on queer theory, he proposes that academics would first of all see management as a 'doing' – a performance. That is to say, 'management' does not describe the world or even a slice of the world (i.e. a set of particular tasks done by certain people) but, rather, subjects the world to a particular description that is conveyed by the meaning(s) assigned to 'management'. Parker suggests that perhaps 'camp' management would be a way of performing this practice in ways that could highlight its contingency and fragility. For Parker, this might be a practice of continually showing up camp, as contrasted to macho, aspects of management practice and knowledge that, as Sedgwick argues, tend to be secret or taboo.

In *Leadership as Identity*, Ford et al. (2008) attempt to practise this kind of queering in relation to leadership and organization. They illustrate how leadership, as it is widely conceptualized, tends to create secrets and closeted features. The hidden, often embarrassing, and somewhat disconcerting aspects of leadership that are explored by Ford et al. include anxieties, stresses and difficulties faced by 'leaders' in coping with positions of authority. Gibson-Graham's (1996) study of a conference setting is another such engagement with queer theory in the context of workplace studies. In short, the point of queering in studies of management and organization is to disrupt and change the meaning and hegemonic force of categories and associated forms of identification. The idea is to open up ways of 'doing things differently'.

3.4 Conclusion

The perspective that a person takes to studying diverse identities depends a lot on how they view identity. Is it conceived as something that we 'have', as a result of membership of certain social categories, or something that we 'get' from the particular culture we are a member of (the social constructionist perspective), or something that we 'perform' to others (the performative perspective)? It also depends on the understanding that the person has of how social and political change occurs in organizations and the wider set of social relations in which organizations are embedded. Some commentators believe that tackling inequality is achieved by ensuring organizations are 'neutral' – where decision-making is 'blind' to a person's gender, race, age or sexuality. Reflecting this approach, contemporary employment legislation is generally based on the idea that certain social categories, such as gender, sexual orientation, race and ethnicity, should be protected from discrimination by law. People who view diverse identities as socially constructed would point to the limited effectiveness of such interventions in the absence of a change in wider cultural beliefs and assumptions about gender, race, age or sexuality. Such change extends beyond decisions about who to hire or who to promote to demand a transformation about how positive or negative values and life-chances are associated with diverse identities. They would argue that only by changing deeply ingrained assumptions about, for instance, can gender injustices be tackled. People who view diverse identities as multiple and revisable would point to the potential for the identity performances of individuals to challenge or subvert stereotypes (Hodgson, 2005; Thomas and Davies, 2005a), offering the potential for change at a more micro and local level.

Suggested Reading

Aaltio, I. and Mills, A.J. (2002) *Gender, Identity, and the Culture of Organizations*. London: Routledge.

Konrad, A.M., Prasad, P. and Pringle, J.K. (2005) *Handbook of Workplace Diversity*. London: Sage.

Liff, S. (1999) 'Diversity and equal opportunities: room for a constructive compromise?', *Human Resource Management Journal*, 9(1): 65–75.

Noon, M. and Ogbonna, E. (eds) (2001) *Equality, Diversity and Disadvantage in Employment*. Basingstoke: Palgrave.

Thomas, R., Mills, A. and Helms Mills, J. (eds) (2004) *Identity Politics at Work*. London: Routledge.

Sample Exam/Assignment Questions

- Using a range of case studies and evidence, discuss the ways in which racial/ethic identity and sexual identity affect experiences of work in modern society.
- How do dominant forms of masculinity and femininity shape the contemporary workplace?
- Critically assess the ways in which an individual's age might influence the experience of work in organizations.

Occupational Identities 4

4.1 Introduction

One of the first things that people in modern societies tend to ask strangers in a social situation, such as a party or a business function, is: 'What do you do?' The job that we do – or perhaps even the fact that we are not in paid employment – is one of the most defining aspects of our identities. In other words, what we do is intimately linked to who we think we are, or at least what we believe to be helpful in learning about strangers. In this chapter we will explore how occupations are related to our sense of identity, and what that means for how work is experienced, organized and managed.

In this chapter, we first explore how the meaning of work is tied up with our sense of identity. Meaning is of central importance to understanding the link between our job and our identities because it is how we make sense of the significance of 'what we do' for our sense of 'who we are'. For instance, as we note below, a person employed part-time to clean dishes in a café might view the work as unimportant and fairly meaningless: as just a job to pay the bills. The café owner, in contrast, might view the same task (cleaning dishes) as meaningful, because they are proud of owning their own café, and dirty dishes are not consistent with retaining this pride. The next section looks at how certain occupations develop their own distinct meanings, norms and values, which shape how members see themselves and their work.

Following our broad discussion of the importance of meaning in relation to identity, we look in some detail at one occupation in particular. Given that many of the readers may be studying business management, or related subjects, we have chosen to focus on how management has been understood and enacted in recent years. Next we turn our attention to professional identities. Who or what counts as a 'profession' is a contested subject – as this section explores. The final two sections attempt to explore our 'common-sense' ideas of occupational identity in two ways. First, we consider how people relate to occupations that have traditionally been shunned or dismissed as dirty, deviant or degrading. We ask: how do people build a sense of identity while doing these kinds of jobs? Second, we examine what happens to identity when people have no occupational identity because they are out of work. We ask: how do people build a sense of identity when they are unemployed?

4.2 The Meaning of Work

Work is not just a collection of tasks to be performed. How we view those tasks, and how they relate to our sense of self, are both crucial for influencing how we do the job. Take the task of cleaning, for example. If a person views cleaning as a chore that they do just to earn money to pay the bills, it is unlikely that they will be highly motivated when doing the job. On the other hand, work that has a positive sense of meaning that is related to our sense of who we are (or would like to be) is more likely to be personally fulfilling and motivating as well as satisfying and frustrating. For example, a person who has just become self-employed and opened their own café could take great pride in cleaning the café every morning before it opens, because they care a lot about their new venture. They are proud to say 'I own my own business, I am my own boss'. The job is the same – cleaning – but the meaning of the job has changed because it is related to the person's sense of 'who I am'. Whereas the person who is cleaning simply to pay the bills may be indifferent to whether the café is thoroughly cleaned, the owner may be mortified to receive a complaint about food being served on dirty dishes or tables being inadequately wiped down.

4.2.1 Occupations and class-based identities

Early studies of occupations examined the relationship between a person's occupation and their sense of class identity. Lockwood and Glass (1958) studied the emergence of a new type of worker: the office clerk. They argued that although clerical work is a typically 'working-class' job in terms of income, clerks often identified with the middle class. This middle-class identity led them to resist the idea of unionization, which was associated with a working-class identity.

Goldthorpe et al. (1968) studied manual workers in three factories who earned relatively high wages, so-called 'affluent workers'. They set out to test the idea that the diminishing power of the British labour movement (i.e. support for the Labour Party and union strength) was due to the rising 'embourgoisement' of the working classes: their movement into the ranks of the 'middle classes'. They found that despite having the income typical of middle-class occupations, the workers did not see themselves as middle class. In fact, the workers identified little with either their workplace or their colleagues. They did not 'climb the social ladder' or seek promotion to jobs higher up in the company hierarchy. They saw their job as simply a 'means to an end', a way of earning money to spend, typical of other working-class attitudes. They were interested only in money, not power and prestige. The researchers concluded that the rise of affluent workers did not indicate a shift in the class identity of these workers.

What these studies show is that a person's sense of class identity cannot simply be 'read off' from their occupation. The idea that class is something that can be interpreted and negotiated is a strong theme in Skeggs' (1997) longitudinal study of working-class women. Skeggs studied the life courses of 83 women over a 12-year period, starting from when they enrolled on a Social Care course at a local college in the north-west of England. She found that the women tried to gain 'respectability' and shake off the dirty, dangerous and value-less associations of being 'working class' through various occupational and social strategies. For example, the women saw that getting an education, getting married, staying slim and well presented (not 'letting themselves go') helped them to become respectable by addressing the concerns as a source of self-respect. This search for respectability also led them to value their jobs in the care industry – as hospital nurses, nursery assistants or workers in homes for the elderly. Some women even entered voluntary caring roles, working for charities or community organizations. Caring was viewed as a 'natural expression' of their personality and part of being a 'good' person.

Skeggs argues that being a 'caring person' was bound up with the women's strong identification with popular notions of femininity, but also their dis-identification with the negative stereotypes of being working class. Skeggs (1997: 63) also interprets her findings using the work of Rose (1990) (see box on p. 104 in Chapter 5). Rose notes a trend towards the creation of new types of subject positions for workers. In the 'old' subject positions, people sought emancipation from work because it was regarded as a chore that had no significance for identity and was viewed simply as a means of earning money. The new discourse of work presents people as seeking fulfillment through work, as a site where we can discover, improve and produce ourselves. The women in Skeggs' study could be seen to perform (see Chapter 3, Section 3.5) being a 'caring person' because it gave them a sense of 'self-actualization' (realizing your potential) and 'self-esteem' (as morally superior). Caring jobs were valued for enabling the women to affirm their sense of worth, femininity and morality at the same time.

4.2.2 What is 'good' work?

Ezzy (1997) argues that a job is not inherently fulfilling and worthwhile, nor alienating and degrading. The 'worth' of a job depends on how the person doing the job relates it to their sense of identity. Compare, for example, how a grandmother might describe the task of sewing an item of clothing for her new-born grandchild (i.e. an integral and worthwhile part of her self-identity as a grandmother) to how a sweatshop worker might describe the task of sewing items of clothing in oppressive factory conditions (i.e. unrelated to their self-identity, simply a means to earn money to survive). In both these cases, the task is the same (i.e. sewing), but the meaning changes because of how it relates to the person's identity.

Ezzy has been criticized for relying on a humanistic conception of subjectivity, where the 'self' is somehow free to construct the 'value' of a particular job (O'Doherty and Willmott, 2000). In other words, Ezzy is understood to assume an essential, sovereign human nature – in the form of a capacity to assign meaning to a job. For O'Doherty and Willmott, conceptions of 'who we are' are not simply invented by us as autonomous individuals, but rather are produced by particular historically specific modes of production (see Case Point 7.4 for an example of this, Chapter 7).

Those in capitalist and communist societies, for example, are likely to see themselves and their work in very different ways. Workers in communist societies might come to identify the value of their job as something which gives them pride in performing their duty to society and contributing towards the collective good. The Chinese slogan 'Serve the People', first employed in the 1940s, can still be found in use today. In certain capitalist societies, in contrast, a job might be valued because it gives a person the status that sets them apart from others, and enables them to consume goods (such as designer clothes and sports cars) that further separates them from those 'below' them. A psychoanalytic perspective can help us to understand how perceptions of 'good work' might come about. Contu and Willmott (2006) examine a well-known case study of photocopy technicians. The people in this study fantasized about being heroes as they successfully fixed machines in their care. These fantasies ultimately contributed to a relationship of workplace subordination, despite the technicians' valorization of their heroic positions.

4.2.3 Multiple identities in and of work

Fine's (1996) study of restaurant chefs provides an example of how the same task can have different meanings depending on the identities involved. Fine found that chefs do not all view cooking the same way. Four distinct identities emerged from his study:

1 Professionals – cooking as a respected, high-status occupation, with standards of training, skill and conduct.
2 Artists – cooking as an expression of creative instinct and flair.
3 Businessmen – cooking as a means for producing profit.
4 Manual labourers – cooking as a physically demanding task.

Some of these identities enabled the cooks to embrace the work they did and make it an integral part of their self-identity, particularly the first and second. The third and fourth identity positions, on the other hand, tended to involve a certain amount of distancing between the person's self-identity and the role, viewing the job as simply a means for producing profit or a hard 'graft', just like any other manual labourer. However, the cooks were not confined to a single identity position (see Section 3.3.4). Fine also found that cooks used different identities if and when they seemed appropriate in a 'bricolage of identity work' (1996: 112).

More recently, Kitay and Wright (2007) drew on Fine's work to understand the different 'occupational rhetorics' that management consultants used to make sense of their identities. They found that the consultants invoked five different identities – the professional, prophet, partner, business person, and service worker. Kitay and Wright conclude that being a management consultant does not involve a fixed, stable meaning but rather different sets of meanings depending on the situation they were in.

Micro-interactionist perspectives, such as conversation analysis and ethnomethodology (see Chapter 2, Section 2.7), take a different approach to understanding work-based identity as 'multiple'. They view identity 'not as an essential substance [i.e. something we 'have'], but as something that is practically accomplished through action' (Llewellyn, 2008: 785). Conversational analysts do not look for the identity that people bring to an interaction – for example, as a woman or a man, an employee or a manager – but instead focus on how members of the social setting themselves orient towards, account for and display their identities in ways relevant to the interaction in hand. For example, Samra-Fredericks (2004: 1133) shows how the term 'we' is used by a strategist to invoke a sense of collective identity, to suggest that 'we are all in this together', in order to build a sense of commitment to a strategy proposal. This is not read as evidence that the strategist has a well-defined, stable sense of identification with the organization. Rather, it is viewed as a membership categorization device (the social groups we place ourselves and others into, with the kinds of rights, obligations and expectations associated with them) that is relevant to this particular interaction.

On another occasion in Samra-Frederick's study of strategists, an individual refers to himself as a 'simple manufacturing man' (Samra-Fredericks, 2003: 152). CA does not interpret this as evidence of a stable identity as a 'manufacturing' person, or an uptake of a certain subject position made available by a dominant discourse. This individual could well talk about himself in different ways in different situations. Rather, CA asks what the interactional effects of such 'identity labels' are, in the context of what has just been said and what might be said next. For example, describing himself as a 'simple manufacturing man' enables this strategist to question the 'strategy' talk of his colleague and shift the debate into new areas.

4.3 Occupational Cultures and Boundaries

It is not only individuals (see Chapter 3) and organizations (see Chapter 6) that can be understood to have a strong shared sense of norms and values that define 'who I/we are'. Occupations can be said to have their own set of powerful norms, rules and codes – in other words, their own culture. For example, Barley (1983) studied workers in a funeral home in the United States and found that they had a strict sense of rules or 'codes' through which they did their job. These codes were designed to ensure that the mourners experienced the funeral in the most 'natural' and least distressing way, such as the care taken to present furniture that conveyed a 'homely' lounge setting, and the care taken to present the dead body as 'sleeping'. Funeral workers have to perform a certain kind of identity – put on a 'face' – appropriate to the scene (see Goffman's notion of impression management and face in Chapter 2): speaking quietly in a respectful tone of voice, not smiling or laughing, driving the funeral car slowly, and so on.

4.3.1 Turf wars

If occupations can have a strong shared culture that shapes 'how we do things', then these norms and values can be said to exert a strong influence on how members of the occupation see themselves (i.e. their sense of self). Being a 'proper' funeral worker, for example, involves carefully crafting an identity as a respectful, sombre and courteous person, to avoid causing undue distress to mourners. For some occupations, this occupational identity might even 'spill over' into non-work domains. For example, a teacher could find themselves acting in a 'teacher-like' way at home with the family, or when out with friends. Even if the occupational identity is reserved exclusively for the workplace, the norms and values of the occupation are likely to exert a strong influence on a worker's sense of 'who I am'.

Defining 'who I am' also means defining the Other, that is 'who I am not'. In many occupations, workers are keen to ensure that those Others do not enter the occupation, particularly where those Others are thought to be a 'threat' of some sort. This threat could be in the form of Others of a lower social status (e.g. those deemed 'unskilled') whose entry could thereby lower the status of the occupation as a whole. This can have material consequences for the occupation, because reducing the perceived level of 'skill' involved in a job can lead to lower wages. It is therefore not surprising that the 'identity work' (Alvesson and Willmott, 2002: 622) undertaken by workers often revolves around defending the boundary of their occupation. Nelsen and Barley's (1997) study of ambulance workers (see Case Point 4.1) offers a good example of the kinds of identity concerns that emerge when occupational boundaries are contested.

Case Point 4.1   Ambulances and Turf Wars

Nelsen and Barley (1997) studied how a group of emergency medical technicians (EMTs) in the United States tried to create an occupational boundary that excluded unpaid volunteers. The paid EMTs viewed their own identity as 'experts', in contrast to the 'amateur' volunteers. Unpaid volunteers were labelled as 'trauma junkies' who were only interested in the thrill of an emergency medical situation. The paid EMTs emphasized their professional identity by wearing a uniform, identification badges displaying their qualifications and stethoscopes around their necks. By portraying the volunteers as unprofessional and unqualified, the paid EMTs tried to convince legislators, employers and the public that emergency rescue should be a commodity (i.e. paid workers) rather than a charity (i.e. unpaid volunteers). This 'identity work' was important for justifying their remuneration precisely because there was no difference between the medical training, resources and legal status between paid and unpaid EMTs.

4.3.2 Identity, materiality and occupations: the physical aspects of organizational and occupational identity

It has been suggested that identity comprises 'ideational' and physical elements. Some aspects are based on physical elements, which are easy to see, like our gender, our height, our age, the colour of our skin and how we dress. Other aspects, such as our hobbies and interests, our religious beliefs and our family relationships, are not easy to detect from physical appearance.

Work-based identity is in many respects an 'ideational' phenomenon – it is about our ideas about who we are (or who we want to be). You cannot 'touch' or 'see' things like being a professional, being unemployed, being a manager, or being part of a particular department or team. However, this does not mean that physical aspects are unimportant. On the contrary, recent research has suggested that physical and material aspects of work – such as the building you work in, how you dress or the size of your office – play an important role in developing, displaying and affirming our sense of identity.

Parker (2007) found that simply splitting the workforce across two separate buildings can lead to a division of identification among employees. Employees begin to identify with those in 'their' building more than the other, even if they are in different departments and at different hierarchical levels. 'Them over there' are seen as different to 'us over here'. Employees can begin to overemphasize the differences between the employees in the two buildings, simply because they do not interact very often with them. At an office-based party, for instance, the room could literally be divided into two, as people choose to socialize with people they already know (see Chapter 3, Section 3.2). Small issues, such as a lack of water fountains or parking spaces for one building, can lead to inhabitants developing a strong sense of resentment for 'them over there' and further entrench their identification with 'us over here'. Employees might position themselves against people of the same hierarchical grade (e.g. middle management), or the same department (e.g. Marketing), simply because they see themselves as a 'Building One' person rather than 'Building Two'. This identification by physical location is likely to be heightened if the locations are in different parts of town, different cities or countries.

Even small differences in expense of decor, for example, can lead people to make identity-based judgements. For example, something as simple as a more expensive office chair could be interpreted as a signal of the person's organizational status or importance. Indeed, Elsbach (2004) found that apparently 'trivial' aspects of office decor, such as furniture, posters or photographs, act as important signifiers of a person's workplace identity, including their status and rank, and their abilities and values. Her study of middle managers in technology firms in California showed that people interpreted choice of office decor as an expression of a person's (current or 'aspirational') identity. For example, offices covered in humorous posters, such as Dilbert cartoon strips, were interpreted as saying that the person had a sense of humour, but is perhaps also cynical and with a poor work ethic. For those who aspired to get promoted into management, offices were deliberately more conservative, with little indication of the worker's home life, personality, hobbies or interests, beyond perhaps a few family photographs. Industry certificates or achievements were acceptable, but posters or artefacts that were 'jokey' or associated with non-work affiliations were not. Table 4.1 shows some examples of the identity categorizations that the managers in Elsbach's (2004) study placed their colleagues into, depending on their choice of office decor.

Material aspects of an office layout can have strong associations with identities for employees. In some organizations, there are many material manifestations of a person's identity and status (see Figure 4.1). Senior managers might have a large private office (rather than shared open-plan 'cubicles'), their own reserved parking space and more expensive technological 'gadgets' (e.g. company laptop and mobile phone) than other employees. Not surprisingly, employees can have a strong sense of attachment to

Table 4.1 Identity interpretations through office décor

Office décor	Distinctiveness categorizations	Status categorizations
Family photos	Says family oriented, balanced, not work focused	Not a 'player'
Hobby photos, calendar, poster, artifacts	Ambitious, outgoing, well rounded	Unprofessional
Funny, unusual artifacts and conversation pieces	Fun person, joker, off-beat, approachable, lazy, needs attention	Not serious professional

Source: Elsbach (2004: 110)

Figure 4.1　Identity and office space

the physical manifestations of their relative status. For example, imagine that you are a manager and you have an office that is slightly larger than those of other managers, with more expensive furniture and higher specification IT equipment. This physical environment helps to affirm or bolster your sense of status, esteem and importance in the organization. Imagine that you are suddenly told that you are to be moved to a smaller office, equipped with more basic furniture and IT equipment. The new office might be perfectly adequate for you to do your job – there is nothing about it that means you cannot fulfil your work duties – but you are likely to feel a sense of threat to your sense of identity from the change. You may also be likely to resist the change on the basis of its perceived threat to your identity.

Elsbach (2003) found similar patterns of identification with the physical environment in her study of non-territorial work environments ('hot-desking'), where employees share desk space and have a different location each day. She found that problems with the new work space were due to the highly subjective and personal meanings the previous fixed-desk environment had for employees. Employees felt a sense of loss for what was an important marker of 'who they are', such as who they sat near, who was closest to the coffee room, and how they decorated their desks with personal photographs.

The physical appearance of employees can also play an important role in building or communicating identity in organizations. Consider the role of uniforms in work organizations, or think of an organization where managers wear suits and non-managers do not. Here, style of dress acts as a 'marker' of the person's identity and social status. Style of dress can go much further than this, though, and can communicate some fundamental things about who a person is and how they do their work. Pratt and Rafaeli (1997) studied a hospital rehabilitation unit in the United States and found that nurses had two opposing views about what was 'appropriate' dress. One group of nurses thought that traditional hospital gowns and coats were most appropriate for them, and pyjamas or nightdresses were most appropriate for patients. Another group of nurses thought that informal casual clothes for both staff and patients helped them to do their job better on the grounds that patients would then see themselves as getting ready for entering normal life again, rather than feeling like they were 'hospitalized' and 'ill'.

Pratt and Rafaeli (1997) categorize these two distinct identities as the 'rehabilitation identity', which assumed that the nurses' job was to help patients get back to a normal life, in contrast to the 'acute care identity', which assumed that nurses were there to treat ill patients. Style of dress communicated something important about who the nurses thought they were and how their job should be done (treating ill people or helping people feel 'normal' again). A similar logic can be applied to organizational identity (see Chapter 6). Whether intentionally or not, a company that encourages or accommodates 'casual' dress is symbolically communicating to customers and staff it is 'relaxed and friendly', whereas a company that insists on 'smart' dress is communicating an identity as more 'professional and formal'.

4.4 Managerial Identities

What does it mean to be a manager? What sort of an identity is a manager expected to have? Being a manager is not just a neutral, technical set of duties and roles. It is also steeped in assumptions about the identity of the incumbent: what type of person they are and what type of person they are expected to be.

4.4.1 Who and what is a manager?

Does the term manager refer to a distinct group of people with a distinct set of tasks, skills and responsibilities? If so, what would this list of tasks, skills and responsibilities look like? Creating this list would probably be a fruitless and impossible task because no common agreement exists about what managers do (or should do), although numerous vain attempts have been made to 'pin down' managerial work by specifying an exhaustive set of tasks, roles or processes (see Mintzberg, 2011, for an example). However, because there is no clearly defined body of technical knowledge and skills that is required for 'managing', management have been unable to create and regulate themselves as a 'profession' like medicine, law or accountancy (Grey, 1997). You would probably not go to see a doctor or lawyer or accountant who lacked formal qualifications or a professional 'licence' to practise. But you do not need an MBA to become a manager. Nor do you need to be 'licensed' by a particular professional body (Grey, 1997). This can leave the identity of a 'manager' in a somewhat ambiguous and precarious position.

Grey (1999) argues that the label 'manager' was an outcome of a process of separating certain tasks and functions into a 'special' and 'valued' category, ignoring the fact that many supposedly managerial tasks are performed by non-managers inside and outside the organization. To claim to be a 'manager' is therefore to claim to have a particularly special and valued identity: an example of identity work (see Glossary) (Alvesson and Willmott, 2002). When it becomes established, it acts to naturalize (i.e. treat as natural and inevitable) the existing hierarchy and the division of labour (Grey, 1999: 576). Managers are assumed to be 'better' (i.e. more intelligent, qualified, skilled, etc.) than those they manage, although this is not necessarily how the process of moving, for example from a specialist role to occupy a management position, is experienced:

> Becoming a manager is not about becoming a boss. It's about becoming a hostage. There are many terrorists in this organization who want to kidnap me. I used to love my job. People listened to me. People liked me. I'm the same person now but no one listens and no one cares. (Hill, 2003: 261, cited in Mintzberg, 2011: 145)

Grey (1999) notes that recent trends towards empowerment and participation threaten the traditional identity of the manager. Employees are told 'we are all managers now'. For instance, employees are often expected to manage their own time and their own work in an autonomous, self-directing way. Nowadays, more and more people are actually being given the job title 'manager'. Call centre workers are now called 'customer service managers', salespeople are now 'business development managers'. Rarely is the job redesigned to involve more discretion and decision-making power, but the employees are expected to behave more like 'managers' in their daily working lives.

The identity of being a 'manager' is also a contested category. Not everyone who uses the title manager is seen as legitimate (i.e. acceptable and recognized by others). Watson (2008) cites the example of Leonard Hilton, one of the managers in his study of a British engineering firm. Leonard described his reaction following a meeting with a (female) personnel manager, then he added: 'We managers were incredulous and incensed' (ibid.: 138). Leonard constructs an implicit 'them' (i.e. personnel specialists) and 'us' (i.e. managers). He therefore implies that personnel specialists do not deserve to be described as 'managers'. Leonard viewed Personnel as not real managers like him. Being a 'manager' is therefore not just about using the title but also about constructing the legitimacy to be treated with respect for your authority.

4.4.2 Becoming a manager

Becoming a manager can involve a process of 'identity work' (Alvesson and Willmott, 2002), where the manager might have to 'shed' their previous identity in order to take up the new identity as 'manager' (Parker, 2004). Parker (2004) reflects upon his own experience of becoming the manager of an academic department for the first time. He argues that 'being a manager' does not mean the same thing to everyone. Nor is it ever something that is fully achieved or completed. Instead, it must be 'worked at' and 'worked up' in an endless process of 'becoming'. Like a werewolf that is checking in the mirror for signs of hair to indicate the start of the 'transformation' into a werewolf, the novice manager also reflects upon themselves to monitor their own 'metamorphosis' into a manager.

For example, when becoming a manager you might have to come to terms with a new relationship with colleagues that are now 'below' you in the hierarchy. A new set of group identifications and affiliations are created for you (before you were 'one of us', now you are 'one of them'). People you previously counted as a 'friend' might suddenly seem to be keeping their distance, or being more 'business-like' when they talk to you. You might also have to dis-identify with previously strongly held values and beliefs, including perhaps solidarity with peers and being 'anti-management'. You might also feel anxious and insecure about whether you can cope with 'being in charge' – and the 'blame' and 'shame' when things go wrong. Eventually, you might start to have a positive sense of identity from performing the role. You feel like you are becoming a new person, seeing yourself as more confident and competent than others 'below' you. Your 'ego' is massaged by all the praise, respect and status you now seem to attract as a 'manager'.

Becoming a manager means a constant process of having to monitor, control and adapt your everyday performance at work. Down and Reveley (2009) draw inspiration from narrative approaches (see Chapter 2, Section 2.6) and Goffman (see Chapter 2, Section 2.5) to analyze the identity work of a first-line supervisor called 'Wilson', who worked at an Australian industrial company that had recently implemented self-directed work teams (SDWTs). Wilson described the 'identity challenge' he faced as a supervisor, being constantly scrutinized and challenged by his subordinates:

> I'm forever aware that I have to cover my arse, I have to make sure that I have done things right and are whiter than white because … I now have an expectation that some-one down that road is going to f**k me over … and it's not coming from David [the Manager], it's coming from these guys out here. (Down and Reveley, 2009: 391)

Wilson dealt with this constant challenge to the legitimacy of his role by carefully managing his self-image. Wilson saw himself as different to both the people he managed and other supervisors because they lacked his understanding of how to manage people, which he attributes to his previous studies in psychology. This idealized image of himself was displayed not only in the research interviews but also in his daily working life. For example, when the researcher observed Wilson talking to a colleague about a new system they were considering, Wilson was keen to emphasize the importance of the 'people element', stating:

> It's the people that will make this work. Plans mean nothing, because they achieve nothing in themselves, it's the people that achieve things. (Down and Reveley, 2009: 392)

Down and Reveley view this as an example of impression management, a concept drawn from Goffman (Chapter 2). Wilson presents his identity as a 'people expert' in order not only to argue his point, but also to present himself as a particular type of manager, one who knows the value of people. However, as Case Point 4.2 shows, authoring narratives about ourselves is not always a consistent and coherent process, as in the case of Wilson's consistent 'people-person' identity.

🗁 Case Point 4.2   Antagonistic Managerial Identities

Clarke et al. (2009) found many antagonisms in the discourses that managers used to construct narratives about themselves. They studied a group of managers at the British site of a multinational automotive, aerospace and defence engineering company, using a combination of semi-structured interviews, field observations of management workshops and informal conversations in person and by email. The authors categorize the tensions they observed in the narratives they collected into three main antagonisms:

A. Emotional detachment versus engagement

The managers seemed caught up in a tension between being emotionally neutral and detached, and also being warm and responsive to the needs of the people they managed, or 'pink and fluffy' as some called it.

B. Professionalism versus non-professionalism

The managers drew on the notion of being professional, in terms of being 'strong' and adhering to professional values and modes of conduct, but they also acknowledged the need to be unprofessional and act in secretive, underhand and political ways.

C. Concern for the business versus concern for the people

The managers talked about the tension between concern for making the business successful and concern for the people who worked there, especially when the demands of the business had negative impacts on people, such as when restructuring meant redundancies.

(*Source*: adapted from Clark et al., 2009: 332–40)

The authors conclude that identities may not be as coherent as once thought. Competing and contradictory discourses may be incorporated into people's stories of

(Continued)

> *(Continued)*
>
> who they are and what they do. This also creates tensions in knowing how to construct a moral identity. Each of the three antagonisms create competing interpretations of what it means to be a 'good manager'. For example, is a 'good' manager one who is emotionally detached? Or emotionally 'tuned in'? Clark et al. (2009: 344) view this ambiguity as an identity-securing resource rather than a paralyzing problem as it served to provide managers with 'requisite ambiguity … to represent themselves to themselves and to others as morally virtuous in different situations'.

Becoming a manager is not always about expressing your identity at work, like Wilson (see above) expressed his 'people expert' side. It can sometimes involve actively working upon and shaping our presentation of 'who we are' to fit the 'corporate persona' (Watson, 2008: 122) required by the organization. Managers cannot simply 'be themselves' when they are obliged to mould themselves into what is required of them. For example, a person who might normally feel more comfortable being a conciliatory and deferent person might decide to act, or might simply find themselves acting, more authoritatively when filling the role of 'manager'. At the extreme, you may be required as a manager to sack someone whom you consider a close colleague or even a friend. In such cases, there is a tension between the inward-facing 'self-identity' (i.e. my own internal conception of who I am) and the external-facing 'social identity' (i.e. the cultural, discursive and institutional notions of what I should be like) (Watson, 2008: 131). One of the managers that Watson studied, Leonard Hilton, later wrote an autobiography of his experiences as a manager:

> *Now, sat here some 12 years after I retired from industry, I get to feel it is only in relatively recent years I have been able to recognise what happened to that quiet, timid, inoffensive individual who walked through those factory gates 56 years ago, to turn me into an executive manager. (Watson, 2008: 134)*

Leonard describes the process through which his sense of personal identity changed as he took on the social identity as a 'manager': from a quiet and timid person to a ruthless and powerful manager. Leonard goes on to describe how his wife reacted to these changes:

> *My wife did not like what I became … I could sense the characteristics which had endeared me to her when we met had largely gone. (Watson, 2008: 134)*

Becoming a manager, it seems, can sometimes mean 'shedding' an old identity like a snake sheds its skin or of assuming, and even becoming, an identity, such as that of a werewolf.

4.4.3 Gender and managerial identity

The type of identity expected of managers in Leonard's company was also highly masculine: lots of aggression, shouting, swearing and sexist jokes were involved in the everyday 'banter' of the boardroom (Watson, 2008). This gendering of managerial identity can leave women struggling to be accepted as a legitimate source of authority (see

Section 3.2.2). Leonard himself noticed that some women tried to act 'like a man' in order to 'fit in' with the culture, using foul language and aggressive behaviour (ibid.: 138).

Managers are often expected to be rational, authoritative and dominant, which is at odds with the traditional view of women as irrational, emotional and submissive. Watson (2000) relates the story of Caroline, a female Human Resource Manager in a manufacturing firm. She faced an uphill struggle to get her ideas recognized and was constantly referred to in a patronizing and dismissive way, as 'dear' or 'darling'.

Case Point 4.3 shows how female expatriate managers dealt with the identity challenges they faced as both 'women' and 'foreigners'.

🗁 Case Point 4.3   Being a Female Manager in Hong Kong

Westwood and Leung (1994) interviewed 45 female expatriate managers in Hong Kong. The women they interviewed faced a dual 'identity challenge', being both 'strange' because they are female in a male-dominated occupation (management) and a foreigner in the country (Hong Kong). While the majority of the interviewees felt there were equal opportunities for men and women in their own organizations, they still had to learn to cope with the challenges of being 'strange' and trying to establish their authority in a highly patriarchal society where women are normally expected to be subordinate to men.

If a woman is accepted as a legitimate source of authority, however, the predominantly Chinese cultural influences in Hong Kong meant that workers were actually highly deferent and fearful of challenging their superiors. The women had to work hard at 'identity management' (Westwood and Leung, 1994: 77) to gain respect from others, a kind of identity work (see Glossary) (Alvesson and Willmott, 2002: 622) not always necessary for men. For example, they had to make sure they gave off the 'right signals', not draw attention to their sexuality, and work hard to prove their competence in the business results they achieved. They assumed that they would have to work harder and perform better than a man to succeed, just because they were women.

Some women reported feeling belittled by the assumption that they had only moved to Hong Kong because of their husband's career. One woman even reported being mistaken for a secretary, simply because she was female. The gender identity and foreigner identity combined to produce a series of complex challenges in doing the job of 'managing'. Nevertheless, almost all the women interviewed were positive about their experience of being a female expatriate manager in Hong Kong, and enthusiastic about the opportunities their job presented them. The companies they worked for seemed to take a pragmatic approach to gender and management: if the person can get the results they need, then the gender of the person doing the job did not matter that much.

Gendered understandings of what it means to be a manager are also changing, as we noted in Chapter 3. Supposedly 'feminine' traits and styles, such as emotional awareness, participation, consensual communication and empathy, are now being presented as 'superior' to the traditional authoritative style of management (Rosener, 1990), particularly in the 'modern' types of organization that rely on trust-based relationships rather than hierarchy. Garrety et al. (2003) describe a series of 'culture change' initiatives in a large, male-dominated industrial plant in Australia. The traditional 'tough-guy' masculine ethos emphasized hierarchy and respect for authority. People made sure they did not admit their feelings in case they were exposed as 'weak'. Management attempted to introduce a new style that expected people to be reflective about themselves and their relationships with others. They were actively encouraged to discuss their emotions, perceptions and relationships and develop their 'emotional intelligence' (Goleman, 1998). In theory at least, these more 'feminine' management styles assisted in opening up possibilities for women insofar as they were now seen as possessing qualities relevant for becoming credible (and effective) managers (see Section 3.2.3 on this).

4.4.4 National and cultural differences

What it means to be a manager also differs around the world. Managers invoke various cultural resources to make sense of 'who they are' and 'what they do': These include their occupational culture (i.e. the dominant norms and values of the occupation or profession) and popular images and stories drawn from the media (television, advertising, magazines, etc.). Watson and Bargiela-Chiappini (1998) compared the types of discourses about 'being a manager' in the leading personnel management magazines in Britain and Italy. They found that the stories in the British magazine emphasized the personnel manager as a heroic figure, who was driven by an obsession with winning, marketplace success, business efficiency and control. This person was involved in charting dangerous waters (such as employee redundancy programmes and conflict with line managers) and, more generally, was portrayed as an intrepid traveller. The Italian magazine, in contrast, painted a picture of the personnel manager as a caring person who needs to build cooperation and trust in working relationships, with open and transparent communication with staff. Watson and Bargiela-Chiappini interpret these approaches not as reflective of different national forms of personnel management practice but, rather, as different 'story boards' (1998: 285) or 'discursive resources' (ibid.: 300) that shape how managers think about who they are and what they do.

In some cases, managers do not have one single clear picture of what a manager 'is' or 'should be'. Multiple sources of identity definition frequently intersect to create complex and dynamic accounts. Hall (2008) found that Jamaican managers made sense of 'who they are' through a variety of different, not always complementary sources, including discourses of their country's colonial past, discourses of global competition and discourses from Western definitions of leadership. Hall (2008) argues that their identity was constructed by blending elements of the past (what things used to be like) and the future (where we want to go), and the global (what the rest of the world is doing) and the local (what makes sense for us here).

4.4.5 Managers versus leaders

In recent years, increasing numbers of managers are now claiming to be 'leaders', engaging in leadership training and defining their role, identity and practices in leadership terms (Carroll and Levy, 2008). Modern organizations, with their post-Fordist techniques (e.g. teamwork, empowerment) and post-bureaucratic structures (e.g. flat, decentralized, networked), are thought to require more facilitation and coordination by leaders than the types of 'command and control' traditionally done by managers. Although Hales (2002) is sceptical about whether these new types of organizations are as prevalent, popular or productive as they might seem, the shift towards talking about leadership certainly has implications for the identities of those involved.

Table 4.2 Management and leadership compared

Management	Leadership
Dealing with day-to-day activities	Dealing with long-term strategy and vision
Focused on stability and efficiency	Focus on innovation and change
Based upon traditional hierarchical authority	Based upon personality and persuasion
Relies on control and command techniques to ensure compliance with instructions	Relies on inspiration and creation of positive values to ensure commitment to reaching goals

Source: Adapted from Bratton et al. (2010: 361)

What, then, is the difference between a manager and a leader? What sort of personal characteristics and identity is demanded by leadership that is not demanded by managers?

Leadership is often defined in contrast to management, as representing something different to management (Carroll and Levy, 2008). Table 4.2, adapted from Bratton et al. (2010), offers a brief overview of the different ideas associated with both terms.

Leadership, according to this conception, involves a different kind of identity. Managers are assumed to be rule-bound, task-oriented and controlling kinds of people. Leaders are expected to be visionary, determined, forward-thinking, innovative and charismatic sorts of people. Carroll and Levy (2008) argue that developing an identity (who I am) requires developing an anti-identity (who I am not). Carroll and Levy studied senior and middle managers who were embarking on a leadership development programme. They use the concept of 'identity work' (Alvesson and Willmott, 2002) to explore how managers tried to move from their default identity as a 'manager' towards a new, emergent identity as a 'leader'. This move was particularly hard precisely because the qualities and attributes of leadership were so vague and uncertain, compared with the confidence they had in defining what management is about (e.g. mundane, rule following, operational, budgeting, planning). None of the respondents could give a clear definition of what (or who) a 'leader' is, other than referring to what it is not (i.e. not management). Yet the fact that these managers were prepared to invest so much time and money into becoming a 'leader' suggests it has a powerful allure as an identity construct. Carroll and Levy argue that the status and esteem associated with a leader identity – being seen as visionary, inspirational and forward thinking, for instance – helps to explain why the identity is so desirable even though it is so nebulous and ill-defined.

The allure of 'leadership' as an identity construct also helps to explain why the idea of leadership is so popular in spite of the continuities of managerial work. As Hales (2002) argues, most of what so-called 'leaders' do is still the same – monitoring, controlling and directing the work of others. The identity of 'leader' might be attractive because of the positive, almost 'heroic' qualities associated with it (e.g. 'I can make things happen', 'I can transform this business', 'Others look to me for vision and ideas'). But these discourses (see Glossary) of leadership can also have disciplinary effects (see Chapter 2, Section 2.4, for discussion of Foucault's notion of disciplinary power), according to Sveningsson and Larsson (2006). For example, 'leaders' have to retain the 'fantasy' of being in control, being 'transformational' and inspiring others, while the reality of their job gives them very little room to do any of those things. It helps managers to feel special and important while masking the pressure of the work activities they are expected to do.

Ford's (2006) study of leadership identities in a UK public sector organization found many distinct discourses of leadership, some of which conflicted. For example, the discourse of leadership as macho-management (e.g. ideas of leaders being 'tough' and 'in charge') conflicted with the discourse of leadership as post-heroic (e.g. ideas of leadership being more feminine and participative). Ford shows how leaders did not simply adopt one discourse and use that to define their identity. Rather, both male and female leaders drew upon different discourses in different circumstances, even if this meant contradicting previous 'identity positions'. Stein (2007) draws on insights from psychoanalysis to study the December 2001 collapse of the Enron Corporation. He argues that Enron's culture was partially shaped by leaders' childhood relationships with important father figures. This helped foster an 'Oedipal' mindset in top managers, which ultimately weakened their respect for external authorities. This led to ignoring rules governing particular industry sectors, and ultimately the destruction of this firm.

4.4.6 Management, capital and class

Some critical commentators, inspired by labour process theory, have sought to conceptualize management by locating management practice within the wider political economy of capitalism. Managers are then conceived as more or less 'agents of capital' who act to direct and control the labour process of workers in order to ensure that sufficient surplus is generated for shareholders. In this way, managerial work is understood to be shaped by the class structure of society – the class division between those who own the means of production and those who do not – by ensuring surplus value is accumulated by capital in the form of private profit (Willmott, 1997). The term capital refers to any actor who seeks to extract private profit, which could be a single individual owner (in the case of a private limited company) or a institutional investor (such as a pension fund that owns shares in a public limited company).

Willmott (1997) argues that labour process theory has failed to take account of the equivocal and contested nature of managerial work. Managers, he contends, are 'targets' as well as 'agents' of processes of capitalist exploitation. For example, managers face pressures of intensification and insecurity in their work, just like workers, as a consequence of pressures upon them to maintain or increase the return on capital. Like workers, most managers have to sell their labour power to survive: they have no private income and have accumulated little capital. The identity of managers is therefore not reducible to that of passive functionaries who simply execute functions on behalf of the owners of capital. And, for this reason, attention to the role of subjective processes, including managerial identifications, is relevant for understanding what managers do, and why they do it. Willmott draws on Mead's concept of the 'I' and 'me' (see Chapter 2, Section 2.5) to understand how managers are influenced by the need to have affirmation of their self-worth, value and acceptance from 'significant others' such as their colleagues and their superiors. Managers do things not only because of their location in a class hierarchy (as agents of capital), but also because of their own struggle to gain a positive sense of identity and avoid anxiety, insecurity and shame about their sense of self-worth (ibid.: 1345). Indeed, Watson's (1994) study of managers found the same levels of worry, doubt, anxiety and vulnerability as other workers.

Some managers might even identify more strongly with their fellow workers than with the owners of the business. Or they might actively resist attempts to encourage participation, empowerment and involvement in the workplace, even though it could boost profitability by increasing flexibility and reducing unit costs, because it threatens their sense of distinctiveness and importance – for instance, as the only people who can effectively control the 'unruly herd' on the shop floor. This 'subjective' element helps to explain why managers do not simply act as passive functionaries of capital, and may sometimes even resist or subvert such courses of action. According to Willmott (1997: 1347), 'pressures to be responsive to such objectives are mediated and qualified by perceived opportunities for securing or advancing a melee of identity-securing concerns and values' which relate to family and community as well as self-identity. The presence and relevance of such concerns has been challenged by those who argue that 'organizational controls' are pure products of the imperative of capital accumulation. From a stance that is sceptical about the role of identity formation and reproduction in processes of organizational control, the problem is predictably that 'such a theory relies on the improbable assumption … that most managers … react to organizational controls by rejecting the purpose behind them' (Armstrong, 2011: 196).

When existential considerations of identity (re)production are understood to be integral to managerial work, management needs to be studied not only for its technical dimension (e.g. what skills and activities are involved) and its material dimension (e.g. how management facilitates the extraction of profit), but also its subjective dimension (e.g. how their identity is implicated in their work). This subjective dimension, Willmott (1997) argues, is not just a side effect or background 'noise' to the capitalist accumulation of wealth, it is an important medium through which capitalist accumulation occurs, as capitalist imperatives are 'mediated by concerns to secure or enhance a sense of self-identity' (ibid.: 1354).

4.5 Professional Identities

What makes one group of workers a 'profession'? Is it the level of skill, knowledge, experience and training required for the job? How do you measure what 'knowledge' and 'skill' are in the first place? The sociology of professions views professions not as a natural outcome of the skill or knowledge of a group of workers, but rather as the outcome of a 'project' whereby a group of workers construct themselves as an exclusive, valuable and highly paid occupation (Macdonald, 1995). For example, management consultants have for many years been active in trying to get themselves recognized as a legitimate 'profession' (Groß and Kieser, 2006). 'Professions' are therefore simply those groups that have been successful in organizing, defending and regulating the group. From an identity perspective, groups engage in this 'project of professionalization' in part because it helps to secure social and psychological rewards in terms of an elevated social status and sense of self-worth (Macdonald, 1995: 55).

4.5.1 Becoming a professional

How does a worker become a 'professional'? The identity of professional is not something that simply happens when a person enters the occupation, such as lawyer, accountant or teacher. You have to learn to become a professional, through processes of induction, training and socialization. Anderson-Gough et al. (1998) studied trainee accountants in two large UK accounting firms. They found that trainee accountants had to learn how to act, dress and speak in ways that were expected of 'professional accountants'. The idea of a 'professional identity' thereby acts to discipline those who want to attain that identity (Fournier, 1999) – see Chapter 2, Section 2.4, for discussion of Foucault's notion of disciplinary power. A similar idea is put forward by Hodgson (2005), who draws on the work of Judith Butler (see Chapter 3, Section 3.3.5, for more discussion of Butler's work) to examine how some project managers try to put on a 'professional performance' in order to be recognized as a profession, while others seek to resist this move.

Many researchers view talk, in the form of conversations, stories, narratives, etc., as the key site where identities are performed, negotiated and managed (see Chapter 2, Section 2.6, for an explanation of the narrative perspective). Taylor (2006: 96) states that 'talk is understood as the site in which identity is instantiated and negotiated, so the "identity work" of speakers is investigated through the analysis of their talk'. Dyer and Keller-Cohen (2000) examined how two academic professors used linguistic devices such as personal pronouns (like 'I') to present themselves as both experts in a field but also ordinary people, just like their audience. Vásquez (2007) studied the personal narratives of trainee teachers during meetings with their supervisors. Vásquez noticed that the narratives told by the trainee teachers sought to construct them as professionals, for example as skilled, competent and caring in their teaching approach. This theme of tension between being a professional and an ordinary person was also present in a study by Holmes (2005) of identity talk in a senior management meeting. For example, in the way that one of the managers 'Hettie' describes her decisions and actions, she presents herself as having the distance and discipline required of a 'professional', while also presenting herself as a warm and open person (ibid.: 682–4).

4.5.2 Achieving a professional identity

Those with an identity that is different to the 'norm' can often struggle to be seen as a 'professional'. For instance, women may struggle to get themselves recognized and respected as professionals given the prevailing gender assumptions about a 'woman's role'. As we noted in Chapter 3, some women adopt the role of the 'office wife' (Pringle, 1989) or wear masculine business suits (Sheppard, 1989) in order to blend in and feel more accepted. Bell and Nkomo (2001) studied the careers of black and white women in corporate America. They found that black women in particular felt that their authority was often questioned, their ability was challenged and their contribution was not recognized.

Previous research has suggested that gay men have struggled to be seen as 'competent professionals' in occupations such as policing and teaching (Rumens and Kerfoot, 2009: 768). For example, Woods and Lucas (1993, cited in Rumens and Kerfoot, 2009: 769) found that gay men would often try to conceal their sexuality because it was 'unprofessional' to disclose this to colleagues and clients. Heterosexual men and women rarely face this 'identity dilemma' because heterosexuality is often the 'norm' in organizations. Rumens and Kerfoot's (2009) study (see Case Point 4.4) shows how being both 'gay' and a 'professional' can sometimes be an uneasy combination.

📁 **Case Point 4.4   The Gay Professional – An Easy Combination?**

Rumens and Kerfoot (2009) examine how gay men in the British National Health Service related to the idea of being a 'professional'. The research involved in-depth interviews (conducted outside the workplace) with 10 gay men in the NHS who were employed in clinical, managerial and administrative roles. At the time of the research, the organization was developing a lesbian, gay, bisexual and transgender support network and was becoming regarded as a 'progressive' and 'gay-friendly' organization. Many of the interviewees reported feeling more comfortable and open about their sexuality, like Morgan and Dion (both pseudonyms) describe below:

> the world's changed, and even the NHS has tried hard to foster an open environment where I can behave as a normal professional, and be regarded as a professional by others. … I'm appreciative of that … because it's a place where gay men are just accepted in that way. (Morgan)

> Twenty years ago, I couldn't have been seen as professional … I would have been seen as a poof … but employment rights, a more liberal society and better protection from my employer has meant that I can be an openly gay professional. (Dion)

However, tensions also persisted about whether sexuality and professionalism were mutually compatible. When Ciaran wore a T-shirt that read 'It takes balls to be a fairy' on a 'dress-down' day at work to raise money for charity, he got told off by his boss for being 'unprofessional'. The men were careful to wear clothes that set them apart and made them look (and feel) good, but did not play up to the stereotype of gay men as vain, narcissistic and overly occupied with fashion:

> I want to look more edgy than the other guys in the office, especially the straight ones. … But you don't want to overdo it … be seen to be a fashion victim that spends more time thinking about what to wear to work rather than on the job in hand. (Denton)

The idea that 'being professional' meant not bringing sexuality into the workplace was still prevalent: sexuality was a 'personal matter'. Ryan, a hospital doctor, explains:

> The hospital is not ready … for a camp acting doctor … because it brings sexuality into the public eye, and is the workplace the right place to do that?

Ryan views being 'camp' as damaging to the chances of being seen as professional. Certain roles such as management were seen to require 'hard' and unemotional behaviour, dedicated to the 'bottom line' rather than concerned with 'soft' things like 'feelings', which clashed with the supposed 'femininity' of the 'camp' gay man.

According to Rumens and Kerfoot (2009), the dominant masculine and heterosexual 'norm' was still that workplaces should be purely rational and functional, free of sexuality. Their study shows how 'being a professional' is an identity that can be difficult for gay men to achieve and sustain, even in apparently 'gay-friendly' organizations. The men in their study had actively to manage and self-discipline their presentation of 'being gay' to fit with expectations about what professionalism meant.

4.5.3 Professional identity and resistance to change

Professional identities in the public sector in particular have recently begun to come under attack from the rise of so-called 'New Public Management' (NPM). In many countries around the world, hospitals, schools, local councils – even universities – have been subject to changes to introduce more 'private sector' styles of working, including audits, league tables, compulsory competitive tendering, new accounting methods and privatization. In cases where a strong sense of professional identity dominates the industry, these 'managerialist' changes have led to a series of struggles around what it means to be a teacher, or doctor, or lecturer, for example.

In the study of the implementation of NPM in a UK Hospital Trust, Mueller et al. (2004) found that the doctors' sense of professional identity led them to question, challenge and resist the changes being introduced. The doctors saw the changes as undermining their core values of clinical integrity and patient care. This conflicted with the managers' emphasis on meeting targets and the efficient use of resources. The changes threatened the doctors' sense of identity as autonomous professionals who could decide what was best for their patients. This attachment to a medical sense of identity led doctors to refuse to identify with or internalize the pressures of clinical targets (e.g. assessing a patient within half an hour) and resource allocation (e.g. reducing the number of vacant beds). In another study in a medical context, Mueller et al. (2008) found a similar sense of professional identity among nurses who advised patients over the telephone (see Case Point 4.5).

📁 **Case Point 4.5 Being a 'Professional' Nurse**

Mueller et al. (2008) used semi-structured interviews and observations to study the experience of nurses working in two UK NHS Direct call centres that provided telephone-based patient advice services. The nurses felt passionately that being 'professional' meant 'caring for people' and 'showing empathy'. This meant that the telephone conversations were often quite lengthy, as the nurses spent time talking to patients, which contradicted the targets they were supposed to follow regarding the frequency and length of the calls they took. As one nurse put it:

> We're nurses, we care for people, we're supposed to care for people, we're supposed to listen to them, we're supposed to give them the best advice we can. ... I don't think we should be racing to finish a call to get people off the phone.

The nurses did not display empathy because they were instructed to by management (compare, for instance, Van Maanen's 1990 study of the Disney Corporation – see Chapter 5). Rather, they showed empathy for patients because they identified strongly with the values of their profession. The authors conclude that 'empathy and caring are seen as part of one's professional identity, and not the result of managerial coercion' (ibid.: 10).

In a very different context, the patterns of professional resistance to managerialism were notably similar in Mueller and Carter's (2007) study of the privatization of the British state-owned electricity industry. The electricity companies were still dominated by professional engineers with a background in science and engineering, including senior management. The term engineer was regarded with pride, status and prestige and only those who were professionally certified and qualified were allowed to use it. Even managerial positions were described in engineering terms: a regional manager was known as a 'chief engineer' (ibid.: 183), for instance. The introduction of new management and accounting techniques after privatization was fiercely resisted by the engineers because of their attachment to their professional identity, particularly what they saw as an encroachment on their professional autonomy, skill and discretion.

Kosmala and Herrbach's (2006) study of auditors employed by one of the Big Four audit firms in France and the UK uncovered resistance to the 'professional identity' encouraged and enforced by the firm. The authors draw on Foucault's notion of 'technologies of the self' (see Chapter 2, Section 2.4) to understand the way in which the firm attempted to control how the auditors saw themselves and their work. They found that the auditors identified with some elements of the identity attributes of 'professionalism', but also distanced themselves from other attributes. Auditors are caught up in the interplay of three, sometimes competing, logics: the need to serve the public interest; the need to deliver good client service; and the need to protect the financial interests of the firm. One of the auditors they interviewed expressed cynical distancing from the espoused values of the firm:

> The firm had the value charter 'People, Knowledge, Clients'. … In theory it worked well because it looked good. But practice is different than theory; it does not always work as well as it looks on the paper. You could challenge the manager and tell this is not within our values, but not much would have been changed! (Interview quote from Kosmala and Herrbach, 2006: 1405)

Many auditors dealt with their dis-identification (see Glossary) with the values of the firm by replacing it with identification either with the profession as a whole (i.e. 'the audit profession') or with a subsection of the firm (e.g. their office or team). Some also justified their commitment to the job in terms of the benefit it gave themselves, in terms of their sense of 'being a professional':

> For me, being dedicated to my work is only evidence of a strong professional conscientiousness. I give importance to my designated responsibilities because I like my job to be done well, not because it is beneficial to the firm. (Interview quote from Kosmala and Herrbach, 2006: 1406)

Kosmala and Herrbach (2006) argue that the auditors distance themselves from the firm but retain a belief in the virtues of professionalism itself. Ironically, this actually makes them complicit in protecting the interests of the firm, because it makes them into highly motivated and hard-working employees. Minor instances of 'bending the rules' or sarcastic jokes about management, for example, give people a sense of freedom, pleasure and self-esteem, but do nothing to disrupt the workings of the firm. Apparently dysfunctional attitudes actually make employees feel more in control and inadvertently help the organization to work. Thus, processes of dis-identification are not always bad for the firm but can sometimes be part and parcel of furthering its interests. We discuss the issue of identification, resistance and organization control in more detail in Chapter 5.

4.6 The Dirty, the Deviant and the Degrading

How do you maintain a positive sense of identity when your work is dirty, deviant or degrading? This is the challenge faced by people who do jobs such as coal mining, sewage maintenance and garbage collection. Ashforth and Kreiner (1999) studied how people in 'dirty' occupations used downward social comparisons to present themselves as superior to a lower status occupation, for example 'at least I am not cleaning toilets'. In a study of Finnish underground miners, Lucas and Buzzanell (2004) found that the miners gained dignity by valuing their *sisu* (meaning 'inner determination').

The classic work of Sennett and Cobb (1972) shows how working-class men often view work as distinct from, and irrelevant to, their core identity. Because it is often dirty, difficult and low paid, work is viewed simply as a sacrifice they have to make to provide for their families. They gain their sense of worth and self-respect from being the 'head of the household' at home with their families.

4.6.1 Dignity, gender and ethnicity

The dignity associated with a job is often infused with gender meanings. For example, Tracy and Scott (2006) found that corrections officers working in a prison viewed some aspects of their work as more 'feminized' (e.g. feeding inmates, providing care) and therefore less 'valuable', in the macho prison environment that valued tough masculinity.

Ethnicity is also a key factor in a person's ability to secure 'dignified' work. Zlolniski (2006) studied Mexican immigrants working in Silicon Valley in the United States. The immigrants worked in low-status, low-paid jobs such as janitors who cleaned the offices of high-tech companies. Zlolniski explores the agency (i.e. ability to act) of the immigrants as they organized rallies and meetings to form unions that would help them to challenge their exploitative work conditions. From an identity perspective, the formation of a collective sense of identity (i.e. Who are we? What do we want?) was an essential component of the immigrants' drive to improve their working conditions.

4.6.2 Dignity and sex work

People who work in so-called 'deviant' occupations such as prostitution often experience a challenge to their sense of identity precisely because their work is viewed as degrading and immoral. This prompts intensive identity work (see Glossary) in order to restore their sense of normality, dignity and status. For example, prostitutes attempt to build a positive sense of identity and maintain self-respect by describing their work as a service to society which helps to avoid rape and sex crimes, save marriages and provide psychological counselling for men (Watson, 2005: 229).

Grandy (2008) found that exotic dancers who worked in gentlemen's clubs in the UK viewed the customers they performed for with 'disgust'. Grandy argues that this enables the women to maintain a critical distance from their jobs, which in turn helps to minimize the stigma of their work and secure a positive sense of self. Brewis and Linstead (2000) found that some of the prostitutes in their study used drugs to help them to 'perform' the roles demanded by clients and keep their 'work' distanced from their 'real' self. Similarly, kissing was often avoided because it suggested a level of intimacy and affection that comprised their sense of separation between their work self (i.e. 'sex for money') and personal self (i.e. 'sex for love').

Sanders (2005) found that the sex workers in their study viewed their work as 'acting' in order to separate their sense of self, in spite of the physical and emotional work involved in the job. Goffman's notion of 'front-stage' is relevant here (see Chapter 2, Section 2.5). By creating a 'manufactured identity' that was performed to clients, the prostitutes ensured they only sold a 'service' rather than their 'selves'. Natasha, one of the prostitutes in the study, explained that she was able to perform the 'fantasy' image for clients while being 'very aware that it is not me' (ibid.: 335). Outside work, their sense of self was very different. They did not see themselves as 'exploited victims' but rather as independent, intelligent and resourceful women. For example, some of the women were also studying for a university degree, while others chose prostitution to support their families without relying on state benefits.

4.6.3 The emotional self

This manufacturing of identity observed by Sanders (2005) is not exclusive to so-called 'deviant' occupations. Increasing numbers of occupations require forms of 'emotional labour' (Hochschild, 1983) – the careful display of emotions at work – in order to craft the correct identity for doing the job. Think of the warm smiles and helpful demeanour of air stewards and stewardesses, and the carefully crafted happiness and 'fun' portrayed by workers in Disneyland (Boje, 1995). The occupations where emotional labour is required are often explicitly or implicitly 'feminized' ones such as nursing (Pullen and Simpson, 2009). Emotional displays are not always fake acts designed to 'con' customers. In some cases, workers can become so caught up in their manufactured self that they no longer view it as phoney or alienating (Hochschild, 1983: 136).

4.7 Unpaid Work and Unemployment

Most of this book focuses on issues of identity when people are doing a job they get paid for. Yet identity is also important when people are unemployed and out of work. In fact, identity is a crucial issue when you are not in paid work precisely because paid work is awarded such an important role in modern society – with its emphasis on personal advancement, material wealth and social status.

4.7.1 Identity and unpaid domestic labour

The tasks of housework, childcare and eldercare are 'work' just like any other form of work, in the sense that they involve skill, physical exertion and cognitive capabilities. However, in many societies the people that do these tasks are not offered the same identity status as those involved in paid labour. These people are most often female, given that women are still expected to be responsible for the majority of housework in many societies (Burchell et al., 2007). In some countries, these tasks are not actually seen as 'work', but instead viewed as part of the normal duty of women and the expression of their love for their families (Luxton, 1997).

In general, remuneration levels (i.e. pay) are closely associated with the level of prestige, status and honour ascribed to a job. Therefore, women often struggle to secure a positive sense of self when they are 'just a housewife'. In fact, since 1985 the United Nations has committed to 'valuing and measuring' the unpaid work of women's family care-giving (Luxton, 1997). For example, the UN calculates how much women's unpaid labour would cost if those same services were 'bought': childcare, cleaning, cooking, ironing, etc. Placing a monetary figure on the value of women's domestic labour, some feminists believe, will help to offer women a better deal in terms of their social status and material position (Luxton, 1997).

The gendered identity associated with unpaid domestic labour poses an acute identity challenge for those men who are so-called 'house-husbands'. How can men secure a positive sense of identity when their role as house-husband departs from the commonly held expectations about men as the 'breadwinner'? Wentworth and Chell (2005) found that it was seen as less acceptable for a man to be a house-husband than for a woman to be a housewife. They also found that both roles were viewed negatively, with little status and respect given to the task of home-making. This leaves male home-makers with an 'identity crisis', with few cultural resources for feeling proud of 'who they are' and 'what they do'.

4.7.2 How do people deal with becoming unemployed?

The dominant 'ideology of work' (Grint, 1995b: 37), particularly in Western societies, is that 'work' refers to exclusively paid work outside the home. This ideology has many repercussions for the identities of people who are unemployed. In particular, the masculine nature of this ideology has serious consequences for men who find themselves outside the paid labour market. A sense of 'masculine pride' is often bound up with the role of 'breadwinner' and 'provider'. This damage to a man's sense of self could in fact be linked to the rise in levels of depression, suicide and criminal convictions among redundant men (Pritchard, 1990). Case Point 4.6 explores how redundancy was linked to dominant notions of masculinity in Walkerdine's (2009) study of the closure of a steel plant.

📁 Case Point 4.6   Masculinity, Redundancy and 'Men of Steel'

Walkerdine (2009) argues that men's sense of 'identity crisis' when they lose their jobs is not only about losing their 'masculinity', but also about the fear of being 'too close' to the 'feminine'. Walkerdine studied a South Wales community after the local steel plant, the town's main employer, closed down. She found that the unemployed men were most concerned with the loss of distance from the 'feminine' space of the home. The steel factory was an exclusively male preserve where men were 'in charge', whereas women were expected to be 'in charge' of the domestic sphere. The men who were made redundant resented being forced to stay at home all day, viewing the home as an 'unmanly' place.

The closure of the steel plant also affected the identities of boys who were still in school and yet to even enter the workforce. Teenage boys feared that they would never become 'proper men' if they were unable to leave their mothers and 'prove' themselves as being tough and independent. They longed for a chance to prove themselves to be

(Continued)

(Continued)

'manly' enough to cope with the heavy physical labour of a job in the steel industry. A sense of dignity and pride was attributed to 'getting dirt under your nails'. Boys leaving school were ashamed about being seen as 'soft' because they had to stay at home with their mothers, or take alternative jobs in 'unmanly' industries. Walkerdine's study therefore shows how the closure of one steel plant has effects on the identity of men throughout the generations, even years after the industry first declined.

However, Walkerdine was surprised to find that the workers in her study did not decide to move to find alternative jobs. Their sense of community remained strong and families wanted to stay in the area to build a better future for everyone in the community. The residents identified passionately with their town and their sense of self was rooted in the place they came from. This sense of identification led in turn to a sense of belonging and a sense of commitment to the community.

While many studies have focused on the experience of working-class men, unemployment can of course affect anyone. Redundancy is increasingly common thanks to the popularity of de-layering, downsizing and restructuring in organizations, which includes managerial and professional workers – see Figure 4.2. In fact, de-layering is specifically targeted at reducing the number of layers in the hierarchy and creating a 'flatter' organizational structure, with less 'red tape' and fewer chains of authority supposedly making the organization quicker to respond to the needs of customers and changes in the business environment. This often means making whole groups of managers redundant in a single restructuring exercise.

Middle-class anxiety and insecurity?

In recent years, organizations have begun to adopt a more flexible approach to the employment contract. What this means is that, increasingly, organizations attempt to outsource work that is not seen as 'core' to their activities. The idea is that through being 'leaner' in structure, firms can be more flexible and can respond quicker to changes in the marketplace and competitive environments (Heckscher, 1994). Interestingly, this approach has also been applied to staff. The preference is for

Figure 4.2   Outsourcing

shorter term contracts rather than a 'job for life' and this has effects on traditional stable career paths. As Case Point 4.7 shows, even traditional middle-class professional occupations are increasingly risky, and this can have profound effects on how people at work see themselves.

Case Point 4.7   Bait and Switch: An Assault on the Middle-Class Professional Identity

In the book *Bait and Switch*, Ehrenreich (2006) shows the challenges of middle-class workers in today's employment market. Even those who have done 'everything right' in their careers, gathering college degrees and developing the right skills for the job market, are increasingly vulnerable. In the move towards 'flexible working', organizations have been laying off 'expensive' permanent employees who may not be core to the organization's functions, instead hiring people to do the same work on a short-term contract basis. This places the middle-class professional worker in an increasingly fragile situation, unsure of where their next job might come from. Ehrenreich goes 'undercover' to pose as a public relations and event planning professional. Her story is, having been freelance for years, she is now seeking a stable corporate position with regular benefits, and is ready to move anywhere. The book traces her adventures in job seeking, career coaching, recruitment fairs, personality tests and image makeovers.

At one point, Ehrenreich describes her experiences with Kimberley, who charges $200 per hour for telephone coaching. In their session, Kimberley tells Ehrenreich that she must begin to think of herself as a brand, a product to sell. Referring to Ehrenreich's adopted career she enthuses, 'You sell things, and now you're going to sell yourself!' Ehrenreich describes her response to this:

> Looking down at my sweatpants and unshod feet, all of which is of course invisible to Kimberly, I mumble about lacking confidence, the tight job market, and the obvious black mark of my age. This last defect elicits a forceful 'Be really aware of the negative self-talk you give yourself. Step into the take-charge person you are!'

In the face of this dubious advice and encouragement to rebrand herself, Ehrenreich reports that the session leaves her feeling drained.

Overall, the study is an account of continual challenges to her sense of self and well-being as she struggles to succeed in a precarious job market that celebrates the young and the energetic. The rich, first-person account shows how people can find themselves alienated in this 'twilight zone of white-collar unemployment', where there are precious few social supports and little acknowledgement of the frightening position that the disposable middle-class worker can find herself in. In terms of identity, this leaves middle-class workers with an insecure sense of self.

In discussing this phenomenon, commentators such as Boltanski and Chiapello (2006) point out that such people are actively encouraged to see their careers as flexible 'life projects' and to view the ability to move between potentially interesting projects, and perhaps from location to location, as a great advantage. In some senses, workers are encouraged to have no fixed identifications: to be whatever the market wants them to be. Others join in critiques of this 'mobile worker' identity, arguing that it acts as an illusion masking the fact that today's world of work is increasingly precarious, and despite gaining qualifications and experience, the professional employee suffers as a result.

Workers nowadays are expected to embrace positively the end of the traditional 'job for life'. However, when a person's identity is anchored primary on their occupation, this might be hard to achieve. Garrett-Peters (2009) used participant observation to study four support groups in the United States for people who had just lost their job. The study found that most people saw job loss as damaging to a valued aspect of their self-concept. Not only in North America but also around the world, paid work is a key source of positive appraisal by the self and others. People often have a sense of pride and self-worth tied up with what they do for a living. The study found that the groups acted collectively to help members to repair the damage to their sense of identity. However, not everyone is likely to react in the same way to job loss. While some people might view unemployment as 'losing' their sense of self, others might view it as an opportunity to 'find' themselves or be 'truer' to themselves, without the constraints of their old job to hold them back. The study by Gabriel et al. (2009) (see Case Point 4.8) is a good example of the range of responses to the 'identity challenge' of losing your job. Their study shows how a group of unemployed managers and professionals reconciled the experience of losing their job with their self-image and sense of identity.

📂　**Case Point 4.8　Dealing with Redundancy**

Gabriel et al. (2009) use a form of narrative methodology (see Chapter 2, Section 2.6) to analyze their interviews with 11 men and 1 woman, from professional and managerial occupations, who had lost their jobs through either redundancy or dismissal. The authors propose that the type of narrative the respondents used to tell their life story has implications for their sense of self-identity.

The authors argue that losing your job can mean that an important part of your identity is also lost: the image, status and reputation that a managerial or professional job brought you. You might have seen yourself as 'somebody', 'important', 'successful', 'gifted', 'respected' and 'valuable'. Losing your job can leave all of these self-images in doubt. It can also make you start to doubt the very person you are: 'Am I good at my job?', 'Is there something "wrong" with me?', 'Am I to blame for what has happened?'

This said, job loss can also prompt the formulation of a new sense of 'who I am'. Losing your job can sometimes lead to a new 'realization' about yourself. Bill, one of the respondents, said that being made redundant from the accounting firm he worked for helped him to reflect on who he was and what he wanted. Perhaps he did not want to be an accountant after all? Heather also reconsidered whether being a manager was really suited to the type of person she was. She saw being a manager as suiting someone

(Continued)

(Continued)

who is quite 'hard' and with a 'strong streak' about them, which does not fit with who she thought she 'authentically' was.

Gabriel et al. (2009) categorize the responses of their interviewees into three main types of narratives:

A Job loss as a temporary event with hope for a successful future career.
B Job loss as a cruel and unjust event (others are to blame) or a sign of failure (I am to blame), from which there was no hope of resuming a meaningful career.
C Job loss as due to forces outside my control, with a pragmatic attitude towards the future involving different sorts of activities, including unpaid work, temporary work, studies and other creative activities.

The narratives we use to make sense of job loss matter because they affect how we view our identity during traumatic life-changing events. A person adopting Narrative A views their identity as unchanged by the experience of job loss: 'I am still a successful person and will soon get another good job'. Narrative B, on the other hand, views job loss as undermining the person's sense of self-worth, having 'lost' their previous identity for ever: 'I will never be a successful person again'. Narrative C enables the person to be more pragmatic: 'I am still the same person with the same skills, but I might have to change what I do temporarily'.

4.8 When I Grow Up I Want To Be …

Work-based identity does not start when you get your first job. The shaping of who we are (or want to be) and what we should do (or want to do) for a living starts as soon as we are born. Chapter 3 showed how being born as a man or woman, for instance, has a huge influence on what job you are likely to do as an adult. Men are statistically more likely to become a mechanic, engineer or senior manager. Women are statistically more likely to enter occupations such as teaching, nursing or hairdressing. This 'clustering' of certain social groups into certain occupations (known as horizontal segregation) and certain levels of the hierarchy (known as vertical segregation) – see Section 3.2.2 in Chapter 3 – does apply not only to gender, but also to other identities we are born with or grow into – such as our race, ethnicity, religion, sexuality and class.

The job your parents do (or did) tends to have a significant influence on who you think you are, and what you wanted to do when you were 'grown up'. Children of professional working parents, such as lawyers, teachers or accountants, are much more likely to join their parents in the professional classes when they are older. Children of parents with blue-collar and manual jobs, such as plumbers, cleaners and hairdressers, are much more likely also to get a working-class job when they grow up. It does not always work out in this simplistic way, of course, and there are many other factors influencing occupational choices. Yet this is how class-based identities are formed and the class structures of society are reproduced.

4.8.1 Working-class lads

The classic study by Willis (1977) showed how working-class boys in the UK developed their own 'counter-culture' in school which rebelled against the education system. To attract the attention and approval of their peers, the lads would cause trouble in class, 'talk back' to the teacher and play truant from school. This 'lad' culture ensured that the boys failed to achieve their potential at school. In turn, they secured their place at the bottom of the occupational hierarchy when they left school without qualifications and determined to seek out jobs that would affirm their laddishness (so, not hairdressing, for example). The 'lads' developed a counter-culture of rebellion as it offered them an immediate, positive sense of identity within their subgroup. They were 'cool', 'hard', 'macho', etc., and, in their eyes, these qualities made them superior to the other conformist students – the 'ear oles' who compliantly listened to authority (teachers). The 'lads' also sought to gain status and respect by copying adult behaviour – for example, by smoking, drinking and using sexist and racist language. Ultimately, however, the lads' counter-culture meant that most of them ended up failing at school and becoming stuck in low-paid, shop-floor jobs (or unemployed). So, unwittingly, their rebellious actions helped to reproduce, rather than challenge, the class structure of society as it led to their filling low-status, low-income, dead-end jobs.

4.9 Conclusion

The job that we do, or the lack of a job at all, is profoundly important for our sense of identity. It is often the very thing that people you meet for the first time expect when they ask: 'Tell me about yourself'. Imagine the different reactions that you could get if you replied with: 'I am a CEO of a multinational corporation', 'I am a stripper', 'I am a house-husband' or 'I am on benefits'. Having said that, not everyone relates their identity to their job in the same way or regards their job as what defines them or is of central interest to them. Nonetheless, for many people, their job is an important, and sometimes the most important, aspect of their self-identity. In this case, losing that job could lead to an intense sense of loss and despair, and not just to a crisis of personal finances. A senior female manager, for example, could find it hard to adjust to being 'reduced' to a 'housewife'. For others, though, their sense of identity is held at a distance from their job. A part-time cleaner or indeed an executive could view their job as just a 'means to an end' – a way to pay the bills while the dreams of becoming a rock star or a novelist, for instance, are realized.

There may of course be material elements to a lack of identification with occupations. Jobs that are viewed as dirty, monotonous, low paid and subject to intense surveillance are probably less likely to inspire a sense of identification than jobs that are regarded as skilled, interesting, highly paid and enjoy lots of 'responsible autonomy'. Other people might even feel a sense of dissonance between their sense of self and their job. A manager might feel that making staff redundant is at odds with a sense of themselves as caring and compassionate. What this chapter has shown is that our understanding of what our job or occupation is, and how we see ourselves in relation to it, plays an important role in the formation of our identity – in our own eyes and in the eyes of others. More specifically, we have shown how important identity can be for issues of motivation and resistance to change.

Suggested Reading

Kirk, J. and Wall, C. (2010) *Work and Identity: Historical and Cultural Contexts*. Basingstoke: Palgrave Macmillan.

O'Doherty, D. and Willmott, H. (2001) 'Debating labour process theory: the issue of subjectivity and the relevance of poststructuralism', *Sociology*, 35 (2): 457–76.

Watson, T. (2006) *Organizing and Managing Work* (2nd edn). Harlow: Pearson. Ch. 3.

Watson, T. (2008) *Sociology, Work and Industry* (5th edn). London: Routledge.

Sample Exam/Assignment Questions

- Explain the role of identity in shaping the meaning people attach to the job that they do.
- Critically assess the importance of identity for understanding the experience of being without paid employment.
- Discuss the identity issues that arise in dirty, deviant and degrading occupations.

Identity and Organizational Control

5

The 'Disney' Person

Single, white males and females in their early twenties, without facial blemish, of above average height and below average weight, with straight teeth, conservative grooming standards, and a chin-up, shoulder-back posture radiating the sort of good health suggestive of a recent history in sports ... facial hair or long hair is banned for men as are aviator glasses and earrings ... women must not tease their hair, wear fancy jewellery, or apply more than a modest dab of make-up. Both men and women are to look neat and prim, keep their uniforms fresh, polish their shoes, and maintain an upbeat countenance and light dignity to complement their appearance – no low spirits or cornball raffishness at Disneyland. (Van Maanen, 1990: 59–60)

5.1 Overview and Introduction

The description of the 'ideal' Disney theme-park person above, written by John Van Maanen, shows how important worker identity was to the corporation. Disney recruiters were interested not only in the skills or competencies of the person – for example, whether they could wait on tables, or operate the rides – but also, and mainly, in the very person they were. Disney wanted to have control over all details of their employees' physical appearance, personal dispositions and character. In other words, their identity as a person had to 'fit' the ideal Disney model. Disney might be a somewhat unique case as personal appearance and manner are so important for the hospitality and entertainment business. But the idea that employers want to have strict control over the type of person they hire increasingly applies to diverse industries and sectors of the economy.

Identity is not just something that people 'bring to' work, however. Organizations do not just hire people who they think 'fit'; they also actively try to shape their employees' sense of identity after they join the organization. Recruiters have begun to recognize the potential of 'managing identities' for shaping how people behave in the workplace, the idea being that identity holds the 'key' to unlocking employees' inner motivation. According to Knights (2002: 585), 'employees work productively and efficiently partly because their identity is tied up in so doing'. The issue of identity thus lies at the heart of understanding 'how individuals relate to the groups and organizations in which they are participants' (Brown, 2001: 114). In this chapter, we explore how employers have sought to control the identities of staff by striving to enlist and manage their deeply held attitudes and values.

5.2 Bringing Identity to Work

For some commentators, identity is something that is relatively fixed, perhaps established during their childhood. From this viewpoint, a person's 'personality' affects how they do their job and interact with others. As an example of this approach, Sosteric's (1996) ethnographic study of workers in a 'trendy' nightclub in Canada looks at what happened when the normally 'high-trust' labour relations (referred to as 'responsible autonomy') were replaced with an authoritarian management approach (referred to as 'direct control'). Previously, staff had been relatively free to decide among themselves who should do which job, and how fast they would work. The new management regime introduced surveillance, performance measurement and job rotation. Sosteric saw the earlier 'responsible autonomy' phase as allowing workers to express their genuine, authentic 'personality'. The imposition of 'direct control', in his view, repressed and alienated the expression of the workers' identities.

O'Doherty and Willmott (2000) have criticized Sosteric's interpretation. Drawing on insights from Foucault (see Chapter 2, Section 2.4), it is argued that the nightclub employees did not simply 'bring their identity to work', only to be repressed and alienated by the imposition of 'direct control' following the change of management regime. Rather, employees actively negotiated their self-identity through their social relations with colleagues, customers and management, even during the 'responsible autonomy' period. For example, forms of surveillance and discipline were evident even during this phase, including peer surveillance during informal 'after-work' gatherings of co-workers. O'Doherty and Willmott observe that the workers were being disciplined by their own sense of self-identity even before strict management controls were introduced.

5.3 Managing Culture

The popularity of the concept of 'corporate culture' sparked a surge of interest in employee identity (Kunda, 1992). The idea of 'managing culture' – also referred to as socio-ideational control (Kärreman and Alvesson, 2004) or normative control (Kunda, 1992) – involves attempts to shape employee identity (who workers are) as well as employee behaviour (what workers do). The assumption is that controlling the former is an effective way of managing the latter. From a managerial perspective, it is hoped that employees will act in the best interests of the organization not because they are physically coerced, but because they are driven by a strong identification (see Glossary) with company goals (Willmott, 1993; Legge, 1994; Watson, 1994).

Management 'gurus' Deal and Kennedy (1982: 15) claim that firms can get an extra two hours of productive work per day from employees who identify strongly with the culture of the company. The popular book by Peters and Waterman (1982) *In Search of Excellence* claims that 'excellent' companies are distinguished by their successful shaping of the norms, beliefs and emotions of the workforce. Employees who have internalized the corporate values into their very sense of 'who I am', they contend, are unlikely to require formal supervision. Instead, these 'strongly identified' employees are more likely to be self-managing and to undertake their jobs with passion and enthusiasm. For the 'gurus' who advocate the creation of a strong corporate culture, managing the thoughts, feelings, attitudes and values of the workforce is seen to provide an effective way of ensuring commitment to corporate goals. Put simply, workers are more likely to do what the organization wants if they view it as part of 'who they are'.

5.3.1 Critical perspectives on managing culture

More critical commentators, however, have highlighted the power and control involved in managing culture. Alvesson and Willmott (2002: 621) argue that identity is 'a significant, neglected and increasingly important modality of organisational control'. They view culture as something that is not neutral or benign. Kunda (1992) studied how a US high-tech firm called 'Tech' (a pseudonym) tried to 'engineer' a strong corporate culture. The culture espoused by management presented the firm as a humanistic, non-hierarchical and loyal 'community'. However, Kunda views 'Tech' culture as an attempt to exercise power over employees by seeking to control their 'hearts and minds'. One of the employees in Kunda's study described the organization's culture as a kind of 'religion' (ibid.: 6), requiring a passionate belief and commitment to the values of the company. Kunda views the culture as a form of 'ideology' (ibid.: 52) – a set of ideas that aim to serve the interests of a particular group, in this case the interests of the company. Figure 5.1 explores how new forms of management – based on a strong corporate culture – can act as a form of organizational control.

Critical work challenges the ethics of corporate culture (see box on p. 103) but it has also begun to question whether managing the norms and values of the workforce actually works. While subjective self-discipline (see Chapter 2, Section 2.4, for a discussion of Foucault's ideas around self-discipline) can be a more effective form

Figure 5.1   Corporate culture

of control than coercion; it also has its limits and points of resistance (Knights and McCabe, 1998). Alvesson and Willmott (2002: 621) argue that management is not 'omnipotent' in defining employee identity, nor are employees 'passive consumers of managerially designed and designated identities'. It is also important not to marginalize the potential for resistance against managerially defined identities (Thompson and Ackroyd, 1995). Employees are not 'cultural dopes' and the workforce is not an 'empty vessel' into which senior management can pour their desired values (Grugulis et al., 2000). Senior management are not the only voice within an organization, and the corporate culture that is often shared by senior management might be one of several subcultures within an organization (Legge, 1994). Management certainly cannot assume that the re-engineered culture will necessarily be internalized by employees. Perhaps what Legge (1994) terms 'resigned behavioural compliance', or what Willmott (1993) describes as 'instrumental compliance', is a more likely outcome? The box below explores in more detail the debate about whether managing the 'hearts and minds' of employees is ethical.

Is Identity Management Ethical?

Critical work has also begun to question whether managing the norms and values of the workforce is an ethical thing to do. Ackers and Preston (1997) have criticized the efficacy and ethics of attempts by employers to capture the 'soul' of employees as a process akin to religious conversion. They argue that, unlike religious conversion, identification with corporate goals is not a voluntary and wilful commitment. This calls into question not only whether cultural control is likely to be effective in 'winning souls', but also whether it is morally defensible.

Willmott (1993) draws parallels between modern corporate culture programmes and George Orwell's novel of a totalitarian future *Nineteen Eighty-Four*. Willmott illuminates the 'dark side' behind these programmes, drawing attention to the way in which they seek to regulate the conscious and unconscious thoughts and feelings of employees. Employees are encouraged to discipline themselves through being guided by the desire to embody the values prescribed by the organization, along with the guilt, shame and anxiety of falling short of these values.

Although these 'strong culture' organizations typically have less bureaucratic types of control systems, such as strict rules and hierarchical authority, control is certainly not absent. On the contrary, cultural control seems to offer the opportunity for an even more complete and effective form of power, by controlling the 'insides' of the employees. Failing to recognize this as an exercise of power, according to Willmott, means that employees are less likely to find ways to 'emancipate' (or 'free') themselves from these types of 'subversive' control mechanisms.

 Thinkpoint

Think about if you were in charge of human resource strategy in a large organization. What kinds of culture management programmes would you advocate, if any? What kinds of culture management programmes would be ethically unacceptable?

Figure 5.2   Being an 'intra-preneur'

5.3.2 The Foucauldian perspective

Many commentators have drawn on the work of Michel Foucault (see Chapter 2, Section 2.4) to analyze the power and control involved in attempts to create a strong organizational culture. Du Gay (1996a; 1996b) draws on this perspective, among others, to examine the effects of what he calls 'enterprise discourse'. Enterprise discourse refers not only to the reconstruction of organizations (including the public sector) along market principles of 'enterprise' and the importance of being 'customer focused', but crucially also to the reconstruction of the identities of individuals as 'enterprising subjects' – calculating, autonomous, responsible, self-regulating individuals (du Gay, 1996a).

Du Gay (1996a) examined how these new 'enterprising' selves were created in several retail sector firms in the UK. Organizations, he argues, increasingly attempt to 'simulate conditions in which employees of large organizations are made to act a bit more like they were in business for themselves' (du Gay, 2000: 174) – what he calls an 'intra-preneur'. Figure 5.2 explores the idea of employees acting as if they were intra-preneurs who 'in business for themselves'. In other words, the employee is reconstituted as 'an entrepreneur of the self' (du Gay, 1996a: 72). The values of self-realization, personal responsibility, ownership and accountability are presented as not only economically desirable but also personally attractive and virtuous characteristics. The British sociologist Nikolas Rose has been a particularly influential commentator on the more general shift in responsibility onto individuals, as the box below details.

The 'Responsible' Organizational Citizen

Some commentators have been interested in the general shift of responsibility towards the individual in society at large, not just in organizations like du Gay (1996a) describes. The British sociologist Nikolas Rose has been particularly influential in this area. Rose draws on the work of Foucault (see Chapter 2, Section 2.4) to analyze how a person's sense of self is shaped in modern 'advanced liberal' society. The field of 'governmentality' was established to study the way in which power is exercised over a person by attempting to change their understanding of themselves and their identity. Rose argues

(Continued)

(Continued)

that modern liberal societies try to move responsibility onto individuals, a process known as 'responsibilization'.

In modern businesses, similar trends – noted by du Gay (1996a), for example – are also evident. In modern work organizations (both public and private), employees are actively encouraged to be more 'responsible' in many ways. This is particularly associated with so-called 'post-Fordist' and 'post-bureaucratic' techniques that aim to make the workforce more flexible, creative, innovative and responsive to customers. Organizations no longer focus solely on directing the movement of the body – for example, by making people work harder. Modern management techniques also aim to direct people's minds: their thoughts, feelings, judgements and values. Rose (1990) calls this 'Governing the Soul'. For example, employees might be encouraged to do the following things:

- Taking the initiative rather than waiting for your boss to tell you what to do.
- Coming up with ideas and innovations that can benefit the organization, and taking responsibility for implementing them.
- Being 'close to the customer' and 'putting the customer first' in everything you do.
- Having the same passion, commitment and drive to succeed as if it was your own business, set up with your own money.
- 'Going the extra mile' to exceed the expectations of customers and meet targets, such as working evenings and weekends to finish an important project (because you care about it, not because you will get paid overtime).
- Wanting to 'be the best' and succeed at work – your achievements at work reflect your value as a person.

Case Point 5.1 discusses Casey's study of identity control in a high-tech firm. Casey draws on Foucauldian theory to analyze the responses of the employees in her study to a culture change programme. While the Foucauldian perspective has been quite influential, particularly in European scholarship, it has also attracted some criticism, as the box below illustrates.

Criticisms of Foucauldian Perspective

There have been several criticisms of the Foucauldian approach to understanding the 'regulation' of identity in modern organizations. Newton (1998) criticizes Foucauldian work for overemphasizing the 'fragility' of the self, relying too much on the concept of 'stability' and paying too little attention to the 'material' relationships that workers are part of (see also Thompson, 1990). Newton asks:

- Are workers really so 'fragile' that they are vulnerable to having their identities defined by managers?
- Do workers really desire this sort of 'stability' of identity?
- Does identity really matter if material conditions, such as inequality and exploitation, seem to be more important than our sense of self?

(Continued)

(Continued)

Fournier and Grey (1999) have criticized du Gay's analysis (described in this section) in particular. First, they argue that du Gay claims 'too much' for the power of the enterprise discourse he describes. Second, they argue that du Gay's analysis places 'too little' emphasis on resistance and alternative discourses. Third, and finally, they argue that by reiterating his argument 'too often' he is implicated in constituting the power and 'factuality' of the very discourse he purports to describe.

📁 **Case Point 5.1   Identity Control in a High-Tech Firm**

Casey (1995) was inspired by the work of Foucault, along with a range of psycho-analytic writers, in her study of corporate culture in a US high-technology firm called 'Hephaestus' (a pseudonym). Hephaestus tried to establish a strong corporate culture where particular traits, values, attitudes and behaviours were encouraged, while others were discouraged. Casey found that employees reacted in different ways to these attempts to shape and fit their sense of self to the requirements of the firm. For some employees a 'colluded self' was constructed, which was compliant with the requirements of the new 'designer employee' and was eager for recognition and ambitious for promotion within the company. For others, a 'defensive self' was constructed, where small-scale resistances, retreats and blockages were attempted in response to the confusion, ambivalence, fear and anxiety brought about by the changes in working life. The most common strategy, however, was the formation of a 'capitulated self': employees negotiated a pragmatic or reluctant settlement of relative subjective stability from the 'family-like' bonds of the team, which provided a measure of compensation for the experience of assault upon their self under the corporate culture.

5.4 Managing Identities

Employees are often the 'public face' of an organization and, as such, are crucial for expressing and reinforcing the identity attributed to their organization (see Chapter 6 for more on this topic). For customers, their interactions with employees – when they are buying food from a supermarket, eating a meal in a restaurant or a passenger on an airline – actively shape their view of what the organization stands for. It is not surprising, therefore, that organizations are keen to control 'impressions' that their staff give off to customers.

5.4.1 Creating the desired identity

There are many ways in which organizations try to manage the identities of their workforce. We will look at five aspects:

1 Controlling (ensuring the employee's identity fits what the organization wants).
2 Concealing (hiding unwanted aspects of the employees' identity).
3 Exploiting (profiting from an aspect of employees' identity).
4 Faking (asking employees to portray a 'false' identity).
5 Shaping (trying to change the employee's sense of identity).

Controlling identities

Customer-facing employees might be subject to tightly controlled rules about how they express their identity at work, to make it fit with the desired 'image' of the company. These rules typically cover:

- Style of dress (perhaps including a company uniform).
- Hairstyles, earrings, tattoos and body piercings.
- 'Scripts' to follow governing interactions with customers.
- Wearing of religious dress or symbols.

How we choose to dress, how we style our hair and how we talk to people are normally very important for expressing our 'unique' identity to others. Organizations with strict rules seek to govern and control the expression of our 'individuality' by making sure it conforms to the managerially sanctioned organizational identity. Employees are expected to change (e.g. their 'punk' hairstyle) or conceal (e.g. their 'biker' tattoos) aspects of their identity to conform to the preferred organizational image. In certain cases, an employee might even be refused a job because their identity does not 'fit' with the identity desired by the organization. For example, a candidate who attends an interview with tattoos visible on their face, an expression of their identity as a 'rebel' or 'rocker', might be passed over on their visible identity alone.

The 'norms' of a particular occupation or profession can exert powerful influences over a person's identity, in the absence of any explicit managerial control objective. Occupational and professional groups often have established norms dictating how a person should behave and how they should dress, as Section 4.5 in Chapter 4 on professional identities showed. Sumara and Luce-Kapler (1996) describe how newly appointed teachers had to learn what was appropriate and inappropriate for their new 'teacher' identity, including wearing more conservative clothing, having more conventional haircuts and removing earrings.

Concealing identities

The case of the British Airways employee Nadia Eweida (see Case Point 5.2) shows how tightly some organizations seek to control the image given off by employees, such as religious symbols like a necklace with a Christian cross. Although Eweida ultimately lost her case against the company, the case fuelled a debate about the extent to which companies should be allowed to control the expression of employees' identities, including their religion.

> ## 🗁 Case Point 5.2   The Case of the Necklace with a Cross
>
> In October 2006, a British Airways employee called Nadia Eweida left her job on unpaid leave in protest at being asked to cover up her necklace with a Christian cross. BA's uniform policy stated that jewellery, including those with religious symbols, should be worn under the uniform. Eweida attempted to sue the company for religious discrimination, stating that 'It is important to wear it to express my faith so that other people will know that Jesus loves them.'
>
> *Source*: BBC News, 20 November 2006
>
> http://news.bbc.co.uk/1/hi/england/london/6165368.stm (accessed 18 February 2010)

Exploiting identities

In other cases, there are attempts to encourage and exploit a particular identity. A rock music nightclub, for instance, might actively welcome the candidate for a bar job who sports visible facial tattoos as they express the very image the nightclub wants to portray. A candidate with a smart suit, sensible haircut and polite manner might find themselves rejected precisely because they dress conventionally.

Pettinger (2005) found that the women employed in clothing retailers in the UK were actively encouraged by the firm to cultivate a sexualized feminine appearance. Staff were usually expected to buy their work clothes from the store from their own wages, albeit at a discounted price, in order to display the products they sold – a form of 'aesthetic labour' (ibid.: 473). Sales assistants were expected to 'embody' the brand and image of the company (Warhurst and Nickson, 2001). This might also involve being assessed to be adequately 'slim' and 'pretty'. The companies studied by Pettinger (2005) seemed to capitalize on employees' desire to look 'beautiful', 'feminine' and 'stylish' – precisely the image they sought to 'sell' to their customers. Selling clothes actually relied on (and shaped) the gender identity of the workers.

Religion and spiritual belief is one of the most intensely personal aspects of our identity. It is also often one that is most passionately held. McGuire's (2010) study of staff in a religious boarding school found that the organization sought to 'commodify' its spirituality by placing normative pressure on staff to live up to certain standards of behaviour, as laid down by the religious code of the sponsoring church. Specifically, staff were expected to 'embody' and 'enact' its core values as this was a potent means of inculcating these values into the children.

Where codes and norms are informally transmitted and enforced through peer surveillance and pressure from colleagues, this is often described as 'concertive control' (Barker, 1993). That is because such control emanates from within a group of workers who are part of a 'concertive' team effort, rather than 'from above' by dictates from management. McGuire (2010) reports that staff who failed to live up to these 'spiritual' expectations were disciplined, or in some cases faced losing their job or being transferred to another post. Drawing directly on Foucault's notion of the panopticon (see Section 2.4), McGuire shows how this 'spiritual commodification' becomes a 'totalizing' form of control. This is comparable with what Goffman (1961) called a 'total institution', where members have all aspects of their lives administered by some form of authority and are largely cut off from the outside world. Control becomes 'total' in the sense that staff have few spaces where they can escape the 'watchful eye' of others.

Faking identities

Boje (2003: 41) tells the story of his experience as a diner at a 'French' restaurant in the United States. Every half an hour, the waiters and waitresses performed a French dance and song routine. The staff were trained in enough French phrases to give off the impression of a Parisian restaurant. When one of the customers in Boje's party ordered their meal in French, the waitress confessed that she did not speak any French beyond the few stock phrases she had been taught during her company train-ing. David Boje asked the waitress whether her real name was actually 'Angelique', to which she replied that her real name was Angela.

In this example, the organization sought to fabricate a new identity for its employ-ees to convey the impression of being a French restaurant. The staff were obliged to change their names to accommodate the Parisian theme. While this may be an extreme example, many more subtle tactics are used to achieve a similarly 'fabri-cated' identity for the employees. For example, customer-facing staff (such as super-market checkout staff and airline flight attendants) are often expected to act out a script, to smile and approach customers in a warm and friendly manner, regardless of whether they are feeling happy, warm and friendly inside – a process known as emotional labour (see Chapter 3, Section 3.2). In such ways, management contrives to control the most inner and private aspects of our selves – our feelings.

 **Thinkpoint**

Can you spot a fake?

Think about your own experiences of shopping at a supermarket, telephoning a call centre or eating in a restaurant. When you get warm, friendly or helpful service, do you think it is a result of the staff responding as they feel fit, or an outcome of organization control strategies?

When the checkout assistant at the supermarket asks you if you would like help packing your bags, do they genuinely want to help you due to spontaneous altruism (kindness)?

When the call centre agent ends the conversation with 'Have a nice day', is that because you have developed such rapport in the course of your conversation that they are now concerned for your welfare?

When the waiter or waitress asks you if you enjoyed your meal, do you think that their enquiry is motivated by a concern for your opinion of the food?

If customers can easily spot when an employee is 'faking', what does this suggest about the effectiveness of identity regulation as a management technique? What impression are you left with when you recognize that your experience of an organization is manufactured?

It is obvious that managers believe that the manufacturing of 'fake' identities can help an organization to improve its organizational identity and image. It is anticipated that, for example, customers will receive an impression of a warm, happy, friendly and helpful organization if employees greet customers with a warm smile. Yet, in some (many?) cases, customers do 'see through' this identity regulation (Alvesson and Willmott, 2002) and recognize the 'fake' nature of the employees' performance. And, indeed, managers may themselves recognize that customers are not deceived, yet continue to believe in engineering the deception. In Boje's (2003: 41) story of the 'French' restaurant, his friend in fact commented: 'It is the Las Vegatisation and Disneyfication of Paris, this is fake Paris.' Take a look at the Thinkpoint above and reflect on whether you normally interpret customer service interactions as 'genuine' or 'fake'. Of course, we need to be careful about the idea of there being a 'fake' identity and a 'real' or 'authentic' identity. As Goffman pointed out (see Chapter 2, Section 2.5), all social interaction is to some extent a 'performance' we put on. This perhaps goes some way to accounting for why managers may persist with impression management when they suspect that customers are not deceived by it.

The study of Indian call centre workers by Mirchandani (2004), discussed in more detail in Chapter 7 (Section 7.6), is a good example of how organizations train and pressure employees into presenting 'fake' identities. Because the customer and employee are physically separated, communicating over the telephone, the customer might not even be aware of what country the employee is based in. Mirchandani (2004) uses the term location masking to describe how the call centre sought to mask the real nationality of the workers – for example, by pressurizing staff to adopt a more American accent. Staff literally had to put on a 'fake' identity when they were at work, pretending to be American citizens when they were actually residents of New Delhi, India.

Shaping identities

In the section on organizational culture above (see Section 5.3), we discussed the trend towards organizations actively seeking to change not only employees' behaviour, but also their sense of 'who I am' in order to meet organizational goals. This means changing emotions as well as behaviour. In fact, the idea of 'emotional intelligence' (Goleman, 1998) has sparked a huge interest in the idea that management can (and should) be developing and managing the inner 'thoughts and feelings' of their workforce.

Garrety et al. (2003) studied a culture change programme in a large, male-dominated Australian manufacturing company. Previously, the company was very 'masculine' in its ethos, where strict hierarchical lines of authority were respected and emotions were suppressed at all costs. Employees were expected to be 'tough' and 'manly'. The company then wanted employees to be more flexible and more 'in touch' with their emotions and the emotions of others. The company hired consultants to lead a series of management development workshops, including role-playing scenarios, brainstorming sessions and personality questionnaires. The authors draw on the Foucauldian notion of disciplinary 'technologies of the self' (Foucault, 1988) – discussed in Chapter 2 (Section 2.4) – to make sense of how tools such as personality tests shaped employees' understanding of 'who they are' and 'who they want to be'.

To understand the responses of the employees to the culture change programme, the authors draw on the symbolic interactionist perspective put forward by Mead, which was also discussed in Chapter 2 (Section 2.5). Some employees were disconcerted to find that their supposed 'personality type' was no longer valued in the new regime. For example, those that were labelled by the personality test an 'IJ type' of person, who is introverted and bases decisions on rational judgement and seeks order in their life, were not valued as much as those who were labelled an 'EP type' of person, who is extrovert and embraces ambiguity and uncertainty. Some employees felt a sense of 'loss' that their identity was no longer prized by the organization, which led to resistance, distancing and cynicism towards the new regime. Others, however, felt a sense of self-validation, as their previously 'deviant' or 'misfit' identity was now being recognized and valued.

Each 'personality type' came with a list of strengths and weaknesses. Employees were encouraged to understand and manage the 'weaknesses' associated with their personality 'type'. Garrety et al. (2003) argue that these 'technologies of the self' (a term from Foucauldian theory – see Chapter 2, Section 2.4) control employees by outlining what is acceptable and unacceptable – in terms of thoughts, feelings and behaviours, and thereby encourage employees continually to self-monitor and self-evaluate against these qualities. It could be argued that the company contrived to exploit employees' capacity for reflexivity – that is, their ability to reflect upon themselves and make adjustments to their behaviour – to its advantage.

5.4.2 Methods of identity management: before (and beyond) corporate culture

As we discussed in the previous section, much of the literature on identity control focuses on the role of organizational culture as a control technique, where efforts are made to shape the dominant 'norms' ('the normal way of doing things') and 'values' (sense of right and wrong) of the workforce. Culture is, however, only one of many methods of managing and regulating identity. Table 5.1 summarizes Alvesson and Willmott's view of the different ways that organizations can try to control the identity of the workforce.

Although the topic of 'corporate culture' has recently generated much debate among academics and practitioners, the idea that organizations could (and should) try to manage the identities of their workforce is hardly new. Interest in the realm of employee subjectivity – the thoughts, feelings, beliefs and desires that comprise our self-understandings or self-identity – has a long heritage. The so-called 'human relations' movement of the early twentieth century was influential in highlighting the importance of the psychological and social needs of workers. In Chapter 1 (Section 1.3) we discussed how the Hawthorne Experiment led researchers and managers to see the managerial potential of addressing subjective elements, such as identifications with a group and a sense of self-esteem and recognition. In other words, workers were thought to be motivated by a positive sense of identity as an individual (e.g. feeling 'valued' and 'special') and positive identification with a group (e.g. feeling like 'part of a team').

Even as far back as the Industrial Revolution, long before the Hawthorne Experiment, the more paternalistic employers expressed a concern about the social and moral as well as physical well-being of the workforce. For example, Sir Titus Salt, the business-owner and philanthropist from the north of England born in 1803, established a series of houses, bathhouses, institutes, hospitals, almshouses and churches at his own expense around his wool factories. In Goffman's terms, he sought to establish a 'total institution' where everything was provided in a form that disseminated and reinforced Salt's totalizing worldview. Salt was concerned not only with the psychical reproduction of his labour force, but also with their mental, spiritual

Table 5.1 Methods of managing identity in organizations

Method of regulating identity	Summary	Example
Defining the person directly	Explicit reference is made to characteristics that distinguish a person from others	'To be a manager in this company requires the type of tough and fearless person who is not afraid to make big decisions'
Defining a person by defining others	Indirectly defining the identity of one person (or group) by defining the characteristics of specific others	'Women are far too sensitive and emotional to be able to deal with the challenges of being a manager'
Providing a specific vocabulary of motives	A particular interpretive framework is promoted by management attempts to define what is important and natural for a person to do (or want to do)	'We don't want to employ people who do not love their job, we are only interested in people who want to be here and want to make å difference'
Explicating morals and values	Management attempts to instill a particular sense of right and wrong, good and bad	'You can't let the team down'
Knowledge and skills	Claiming to have certain knowledge, skills or professional status is important in framing who one 'is'	'They are not really professionals, they have not even been to university'
Group categorization and affiliation	Social categories are developed that divide 'us' (towards which the person identifies) and 'them' (towards which the person dis-identifies)	'We are not like those people at Head Office, who don't understand what it's like to be on the front line'
Hierarchical location	The level of superiority in the hierarchy, with associated status, influence and resources, is important in who we think we are	'I am not trusted to make any decisions, I am told I'm just a supervisor'
The rules of the game	Established ideas and norms about the 'natural' way of doing things in a particular context shape who we think we are	'I never talk disrespectfully to customers, however rude they are to me, because the customer comes first'

Source: Adapted from Alvesson and Willmott (2002: 629–33)

and emotional condition. His aim was to create a community that actively wanted to be decent, honest, law-abiding and hard-working. In other words, he wanted to shape 'who they are' as well as 'what they do'.

John Cadbury, the founder of the Cadbury chocolate and confectionary firm, had a similar paternalistic and philanthropic concern for each of his employees as a 'whole person', rather than just being interested in their capacity for work. Cadbury was from a religious Quaker family and provided more than a 'job' for his workforce by providing a 'total package' of accommodation, health care, education and moral guidance, particularly for young women, at a time when none of these things were provided for by the state. The soap factories established around Merseyside in the north-west of England by the Lever Brothers, which went on to become the Unilever Corporation, are another example of a paternalistic concern for employees' emotional and moral, as well as physical, well-being – a concern that was intended to coincide happily with a more reliable and productive workforce.

Religion seems to be a common theme underlying many of the early attempts to manage employees' sense of self, rather than just viewing workers as bodies that could provide labour. Weber's classic study of the 'Protestant ethic' can also be understood in relation to the formation of identity. Protestant religious groups, notably Calvinists, believed that success in business activity was a sign of God's favour, and an indication that they would be chosen to enter Heaven. As a result, their identity as Protestants and the strength of their faith are seen by Weber to lead them to embrace a strong 'work ethic'. Who we are, including our religious affiliations and spiritual faith, is in such ways intricately linked to our orientation to work. Notably, Weber believed that the custom and practice of traditionalism – where there was no expectation of working harder than tradition required – was overcome by the Protestant work ethic. As he observed with regard to the suitability of workers with a 'religious, especially a Pietistic background':

> by far the best chances of economic education are found among this group. The ability of mental concentration, as well as the absolutely essential feeling of obligation to one's job, are here most often combined with a strict economy which calculates the possibility of high earnings, and a cool self-control and frugality which enormously increase performance … the chances of overcoming traditionalism are greatest on account of the religious upbringing. (Weber, 1992: 62–3)

5.4.3 Identity regulation and management control: other perspectives

Work-based identities are not wholly controlled by organizations. Nor are they always productive for organizations. Identities can also be formed apart from, or in conflict with, management's goals and objectives. In this section, we examine ways in which identities work outside of (and against) management.

The literature on organizational culture sometimes gives an impression that management are the only (or at least the primary) source of identity definition for employees. Management are often portrayed, within the 'managerialist' literature at least, of being the 'givers' and 'controllers' of identity. Yet – as we saw in Chapter 4 – occupational and organizational groups can develop their own sense of 'who we are' without management intervention.

Burawoy (1979) found that workers in a factory created their own 'games' to give themselves a feeling of being 'in control' of their work and break the monotony of the working day. The game of 'making out' involved shop-floor workers competing with each other to exceed their production targets, by finding ingenious ways to speed up their production and maximize pay in the piece-rate system. In terms of identity, this game can be understood in two ways. First, it was important for the workers' sense of identity within the social group. Playing the game meant having a positive sense of attachment to others from being 'one of us'. Second, the piece-rate system, in which workers were paid a set amount for each 'piece' completed, helped to create a sense of control and autonomy, albeit over a very limited area of activity. A sense of autonomy, however 'manufactured', can be valued for the positive identity it offers. Workers who feel 'in control' are also more likely to have a sense of pride and dignity in their work, in contrast to those who feel like they are being controlled by others. A piece-rate system can enable workers to feel that it is their choice whether to work hard or to have an 'easy day' and forfeit the wages. The resulting sense of identity, through group belonging and the sense of personal freedom, led workers to consent actively to their own exploitation, according to Burawoy. The game-playing, involving choice and control, is seen to deflect potential resistance against owners and managers who, arguably, were the principal beneficiaries of the piece-work system.

◻️ Case Point 5.3   Life in the Slaughterhouse

Most people would expect working in a slaughterhouse to involve little from workers' identities. From the literature on 'dirty work' that we reviewed in Chapter 4, it would be reasonable to expect slaughterhouse workers to distance their sense of self from such a dirty and gruesome job. Beyond those few individuals who gain sadistic enjoyment from death and dismemberment, who could possibly derive a sense of identity from this type of job?

Ackroyd and Crowdy's (1990) participant observation study showed how identity was a crucial factor in how working-class men working in a slaughterhouse developed a strong sense of pride in their work. The job of 'sticking' – severing the arteries of the stunned animal – was reserved for the most senior man. Others aspired to this role because of the status it was afforded in their 'gang', despite the fact that it was one of the most messy and gruesome tasks. There was also very strong peer pressure to work hard. Those who were not 'fast' enough according to the 'norm' set by the group would have animal carcasses flung at them to pressurize them to speed up.

Case Point 5.3 describes some of the findings of a study of working in a slaughter-house, where animals are killed and dismembered ready for packaging. Two important identity aspects are illuminated. First, it was the desire to 'fit in' and be respected by peers – the drive for a positive social identity in the group – that supported a highly efficient and productive work process, not any deliberate control strategy invented by management. Fear of 'losing face' among peers seemed to be at least as important as any fear of reprisal from management. Second, masculine identity was an important factor: the slaughtermen saw the most physically demanding and dirty jobs as the most 'manly' and therefore the most desirable. From the outside, we might well expect that workers in a slaughterhouse would find their job dirty, degrading and monotonous. Yet these two aspects of their work (group identity and masculine identity) meant that the men had a largely positive attachment to their work and a relatively high level of motivation.

The idea that management can and should create a strong set of norms and values rests on the assumptions that identity offers potential as a managerial tool and that managers are in a position to apply the tool at will. The assumption is that identity, if appropriately managed, will help organizations to achieve their objectives and improve their performance. This is not the whole story, though. Identity can also work against the achievement of organizational goals. Ezzamel and Willmott (1998) studied a factory that made goods for a global retailer. Management decided to replace the traditional production line and piece-rate system with self-managing teams. The intention was that a new found sense of autonomy and a desire to avoid 'letting the team down' would increase worker motivation and generally improve quality and efficiency. Management fully expected that such 'concertive control' (Barker, 1993) would be more productive than a more traditional, hierarchical supervision. Things did not work this way, however. The workers were very reluctant to put pressure on 'slower' members of the team because they saw themselves as 'mates'. The idea of 'telling off' a friend went against their sense of identity and group affiliation. Ezzamel and Willmott (1998) conclude that employees' sense of self-identity can make them resistant to the practice of teamwork. Identifications may prove hard to 're-engineer', in which case a sense of (communal) identity that is comparatively unchallenged by individualized, line-work may frustrate the introduction of new, group-work processes and thereby impede the realization of management objectives.

5.4.4 Managing identity in knowledge-based and creative industries

The recent interest in methods of 'identity-based' control has gone hand in hand with the rise of more flexible, de-layered and 'post-bureaucratic' organizational structures. Modern firms are thought to boast a 'flatter' hierarchy, to empower workers and use self-managing teams to break free of the rigid, rule-bound hierarchy of traditional bureaucracies. These post-bureaucratic forms are thought to generate a more agile, adaptive and innovative organization. Post-bureaucratic organizations are thought to rely on a strong set of norms and values to bind everyone together, in contrast to the formal plans and rules typical of bureaucracies. Knowledge-intensive firms such as consultancies are thought to rely heavily on these new identity-based forms of control (Robertson and Swan, 2003).

However, in their study of a large, multinational consultancy firm, Kärreman and Alvesson (2004) found that bureaucratic systems, such as a hierarchical chain of command, standardized work, formal appraisals and performance measurement were still used by the firm. The authors noted a strong presence of traditional bureaucratic forms of control, which they call 'technocratic', alongside new forms of control that they call 'socio-ideological control', which involve managing the 'values, meanings, and ideas, including identities' of employees (ibid.: 171). They conclude that new forms of identity-based control have not completely replaced existing forms, but rather tend to supplement the traditional forms of management to create a kind of 'hybrid' of control systems (see Willmott, 2011b).

People who apply high levels of complex knowledge or creative talent in their work can pose particular challenges for managers. The principles of control built into classical theories such as scientific management (see Chapter 1, Section 1.3) are ineffective as such methods depend on managers knowing exactly what the worker is doing (i.e. the movements of the body). Creative and knowledge-based workers, such as architects, management consultants, lawyers, accountants and graphic designers, are engaged in the manipulation of largely invisible symbols and often work together to share knowledge and creative ideas. In some cases, the employee is the product that the firm is selling, because the customer or client will choose the firm based on their experience of interacting with the employee. This is also the case in service indus-tries, such as advertising and design (Andriopoulos and Gotsi, 2001) where customers' experience of front-line staff is crucial for building the relationship with the customer. Their work is not easily standardized, not are they readily 'watched' to make them work faster or better. In general, firms within any industry that rely on creativity, initia-tive and drive from employees are more strongly obliged to rely upon forms of control that are based on aligning employees' sense of self with the organization.

Robertson and Swan (2003) argue that complex, knowledge-intensive environ-ments are associated with a heavier reliance on normative and cultural forms of control, such as defining norms around 'who we are' and 'what we stand for', rather than traditional bureaucratic systems of hierarchy and structure. Their study of an 'expert' consultancy business revealed that the firm created a highly ambiguous cul-ture, where many different roles and identities were accepted (or even encouraged). This, it is argued, served to develop a committed and loyal workforce as it enabled employees to combine multiple identities, simultaneously identifying themselves as 'experts' and 'consultants'.

Workers in creative industries might like to see themselves as free-thinking, pas-sionate about their 'art' or 'craft' and able to break away from traditions and restric-tions by innovating. Yet, they work in firms where they have to defer to the demands of clients, work within budget limitations and meet tight deadlines. Gotsi et al. (2010) conducted comparative case studies of product design companies and found that workers struggle to cope with the conflicting demands of being both an 'artist' and a 'consultant', while the company tried to integrate the two identities by encour-aging employees to see themselves as 'practical artists'.

In the creative industries sector (such as advertising, architecture, fashion, art and design) front-line employees have to establish a profile and reputation that will attract future clients. In many ways, therefore, the staff are the 'brand'. It then becomes even more critical that employees identify strongly with the values required by the company, and enact them in their day-to-day work activities; or, at least, that they successfully manage the appearance of doing so. Case Point 5.4 shows the methods that two creative firms used to encourage staff to identify with, and embody (i.e. not just 'believe in' but also 'act out' in their daily work), the desired values of the firm.

▱ Case Point 5.4   Embodying the Company

Andriopoulos and Gotsi (2001) studied the way in which employees identified with their organization's desired identity in two 'creative' firms based in London (England) and Glasgow (Scotland). Their methodology involved a combination of semi-structured interviews, observations and documentary analysis. They found that the firms used dif-ferent methods to encourage employees to identify with and embody (i.e. signify with their very actions and bodies) the values and behaviours the firms wanted to project – such as creativity, innovation and collaboration.

Andriopoulos and Gotsi (2001) outline the three key methods through which the com-panies encouraged employees to identify with the values desired by the organization:

(Continued)

(Continued)

- 'Bonding' – encouraging employees to bond with colleagues and the company:

  o Company networking events where employees meet other colleagues and clients.
  o Company cafeteria where employees from different disciplines interact over lunch, creating a 'community spirit'.
  o Open-plan office layout, encouraging employees to communicate freely with others.
  o Coaching and mentoring systems where senior staff help junior staff.
  o Accepting people for their individuality, making everyone welcome regardless of their diverse backgrounds.

- 'Inspirationalizing' – inspiring employees to identify with the values and behaviours desired by the company:

  o Hiring senior managers who have a personal sense of passion and belief in the values of creativity and innovation, to inspire passion in their 'followers' by acting as good 'role models'.
  o Reinforcing the core values in management decisions and actions, such as putting creative flair above the 'bottom line'.
  o Employing people whose passion for their industry 'spills out' into wider projects, including academic papers and books, speeches at conferences, TV documentaries, etc.

- 'Breaking new grounds' – inspiring belief that the company is doing important and groundbreaking things:

  o Actively encouraging and rewarding employees with praise and awards.
  o Giving employees a sense of control and direction in their work.
  o Providing employees with the material and symbolic resources needed to 'excel' in their work, such as time, money, professional memberships, conference fees, etc.
  o Allowing employees to fail without fear of punishment – not all groundbreaking work is a business success first time.
  o Encouraging employees to 'break the mould' and try new ideas.

Source: Adapted from Andriopoulos and Gotsi, 2001: 149–52

5.5 Identification and Dis-identification

The term identification refers to the extent to which a person attaches themselves to an organization and the degree to which individuals define themselves as organizational members. Complete identification means that an individual shares all the values of an organization and sees themselves as belonging to the organization. For example, when a person uses the term 'we' rather than 'they' when they talk about the organization they work for, or when they feel personally insulted and leap to the defensive when their organization is criticized, they probably identify strongly with the organization (Ashforth and Mael, 1989). This is, of course, how most managers would like all their employees to be. A strongly identified employee is more likely to work harder, perform better and be more committed to the organization. However, the literature shows that most organizations typically have a range of levels of identification within their workforce, ranging from those who completely feel 'at one' with the organization, to those who feel completely detached and distanced, or 'dis-identified' (Dutton et al., 1994).

5.5.1 Variations in identification

Humphreys and Brown (2002) offer a useful set of categories for understanding this variation in levels of identification. They argue that all organizational members have the capacity to resist and rewrite the identity preferred by those in powerful positions. As a result, identification is often a complex and incomplete process. While some people may identify strongly with the organization, others can experience dis-identification, schizo-identification and neutral identification:

- *Dis-identification refers to a strongly negative connection with the organization.*

- *Schizo-identification refers to the process of both identifying and dis-identifying with different parts of the organization.*

- *Neutral identification refers to an impartial stance, where the person feels neither attached to, nor detached from, the organization. (Humphreys and Brown, 2002)*

A similar set of categories has been put forward by Collinson (2003). He argues that three main types of subjective response are typically found in organizations that attempt to survey and shape their members' identities. First, 'conformist' selves are those who strongly identify with the organization and want to be valued by those in authority, actively 'self-disciplining' themselves to do what the organization wants them to do. Second, 'dramaturgical' selves are those who recognize the need to be seen to be the 'right' type of person. Like Goffman's notion of impression management (see Chapter 2, Section 2.5), these people are skilled at manipulating the impressions they give to others, even if they are contradictory. The difference is that the 'dramaturgist' experiences a more distanced and cynical level of attachment to the organization than does the 'conformist', and so tends not to view their identity performances as necessarily reflecting their 'real self'. In other words, they might 'toe the company line' but not truly identify with it. Above, we gave the example of staff in creative industries who 'are the brand' but do not necessarily identify themselves with it, but nonetheless manage the appearance of doing so when interacting with clients (and probably their bosses, too). There is nothing directly equivalent to this orientation in Brown and Humphreys' levels of identification but it might involve elements of each of them. Third, and finally, 'resistant' selves are those who strongly oppose and contest the identity preferred by the organization, perhaps creating an alternative, transgressive sense of identity. This might not always take the form of direct confrontation and conflict. Employees could act indifferently or ironically towards organizational initiatives, follow company rules rigidly to expose their failings, refuse to engage in attempts to gather their input, anonymously 'blow the whistle' about bad practices within the firm, or just make sarcastic jokes about senior management (Ezzamel et al., 2004).

5.5.2 'Authenticity': emancipation or control?

Employees often develop ways of challenging and subverting pressures to identify with the requirements of the 'managerially prescribed' identity. Tensions between what employees conceive to be their self-identity and what is championed and rewarded by their employer are often driven by a desire to preserve a sense of self-esteem and personal authenticity in the face of its organizational erosion. Employees can 'hit back' at employers by engaging in minor or sometimes major acts of sabotage that can be difficult for employers to detect or manage. These acts of subversion can be understood as attempts to retain a sense of 'freedom' in the face of control attempts and a sense of 'being true to yourself' in the face of identity-prescription attempts.

Aside from acts of sabotage, employees may strive to distance themselves from what is conceived as (organizational) role playing. Distancing through humour, cynicism, irony and so on can enable employees to retain a sense of unique selfhood and dignity as they undertake tasks and participate in relationships that are personally not engaging, demeaning or even morally degrading. Distancing themselves from what they are required to do – including displays of identification or loyalty – can help people to feel less 'fake' and less 'controlled'. Recognizing that such outlets can be functional for employee self-respect and morale, some employers may actively tolerate or accommodate some expressions of dis-identification. The incorporation of such 'patterns of indulgency' (Gouldner, 1954) into organizational life can, paradoxically, serve to improve performance by allowing staff to 'vent' their concerns about being controlled, stopping them from being manifest in other ways, such as resistance, industrial action or sabotage.

If this form of 'indulgency' is to be effective, however, the employee must have and hold on to a sense of authenticity (the 'real me') that is distanced from the self required by the organization. What, then, if the sense of authenticity is eroded when extensive and sophisticated efforts are made by corporations to acknowledge, accommodate and exploit it? Some organizations claim to allow space for a variety of different types of people, allowing everyone the freedom of expressing their 'real selves'. Fleming's (2007) study of sexual identity in the Sunray call centre (see Chapter 3, Case Point 3.3) is an example of this. Is this a form of liberation, or a form of control? Some critical commentators view notions of celebrating difference and encouraging authentic displays of the 'real me' as attempts to exploit employee identity. After all, expressing the 'real me' is normally only permitted within the limits and rules laid down by management and restricted to those aspects deemed productive for the organization. A nudist might be told they are not allowed to come to work naked, for example. A person who wants to have a sex change could face problems if management thought their new identity was 'bad for business'.

When management seek to control what this 'real me' is allowed to be, dis-identification becomes swallowed up, as it were, by the 'corporate' self. Costas and Fleming (2009) call this 'self-alienation' – the experience of losing your sense of self (see Case Point 5.5). This experience, it is suggested, takes employees beyond dis-identification into a 'space where the boundary between the narrated imaginary of authenticity [the stories we tell ourselves and others about 'who we are'] and corporate defined identity is difficult to sustain' (ibid.: 360).

> 📁 **Case Point 5.5   'Self-alienation': Working at 'Y-International'**
>
> Paul regarded Y-International as a 'good place to work' but he also described the work as 'quite limiting and constricting … I describe it as being "brain-rotting"'. Paul is especially concerned that working for Y-International is turning him into a different person. He feels that it is gradually draining him of any sense of an authentic self. Paul senses that he is fighting a losing battle as he struggles to hold on to the idea that there is a 'real self' existing beyond, or currently buried beneath, the person he has become as a consequence of working for Y-International.
>
> Feeling a growing tension between his sense of who he was and the work he was doing at Y-International, Paul volunteered to become a member of the company's corporate responsibility team, believing that this would 'make him feel more integrated within'. In the event, however, this voluntary CSR work only compounded Paul's 'self-alienation' as it was found to 'function like a business within a "large corporation"'.
>
> *Source*: Based on Costas and Fleming, 2009

In the mainstream literature, it is assumed that identification with an organization is functional and unproblematic so long as it does not become counterproductive – in the form of excessive identification (where the ability to change and adapt is impeded) or extreme dis-identification (where cynicism turns into hostility and subversion). It might be thought that complete identification with an organization would be regarded as unequivocally beneficial – it makes work supremely meaningful for the employee while maximizing effort and productivity for the organization. Surely, obtaining the unwavering devotion and loyalty of employees must be managerially desirable? Think about the Honda worker who 'on his way home each evening, straightens up windshield wiper blades on all the Hondas he passes. He just can't stand to see a flaw in a Honda' (Peters and Waterman, 1982: 37). Certainly, advocates of 'strong corporate cultures' are inclined to believe that 'excellence in performance has to do with people's being motivated by compelling, simple – even beautiful values' (ibid.). Advocates of strong cultures, in which employees are required to 'buy into their norms or get out' (ibid.: 77), set aside the ethics of this totalitarian view (see Willmott, 1993) and disregard the business risk that over-identifiers will engage in over-exuberant wrongdoing, or cover up corporate misdemeanours in their dedicated efforts to advance or to defend the organization. They also tend to overlook or downplay 'how the ability of organizations to learn from experience depends at least in part on individuals' willingness to doubt and question the organization and its actions and claims' (Dukerich et al., 1998: 253).

5.5.3 The pathologies of identification

Dukerich et al. (1998) suggest that there are four different 'dark sides' or pathologies arising from the degree of identification and dis-identification with an organization – see the box below. The four types of identification that Dukerich et al. identify may be more or less conscious so that, for example, a person may believe that their investment is minimal and yet struggle to tear themselves away or feel at a loss when they leave as a consequence of retirement or redundancy.

Four Types of Identification

'Apathetic identification'

Definition: Minimal buy-in to any identity attributed to the organization.

Pathology: Under-identification, which may lead to employees being unconcerned about quality issues, for example. From the employees' perspective, this stance may be entirely functional for retaining a degree of dignity by refusing to devote their energies to producing or delivering of work they view as 'trash' or 'trivial'.

'Focused identification'

Definition: Individuals are keenly identified, whether consciously or unconsciously, with certain attributes of the organization.

Pathology: Over-identification, such as the example of the Honda worker who cannot pass a Honda car without straightening its wipers. Reluctance to part with the current identity of the organization, which may become necessary or desirable in response to shifts in customer preferences or technologies, for instance.

'Conflicting identification'

Definition: Individuals are attracted by some aspects of the organization but repulsed by others, or both attracted and dissatisfied by the same attribute. For instance, a relaxed atmosphere may give employees a sense of low stress and good work-life balance, but cause frustration at the slow pace at which things happen.

Pathology: Schizo-identification, a kind of love–hate relationship, with continuous swings from identification to dis-identification, leading to unpredictable responses and behaviours, such as 'whistleblowing' (see Chapter 1). In the case of Paul (see Case Point 5.5), Y-International was regarded as a good employer but, at the same time, he did not enjoy working for the organization. Yet, he continued to work for it.

'Focused Dis-identification'

Definition: The identity of the employee and the attributes of the organization are experienced as polarized opposites. Different to 'apathetic identification' because the employee actively distances themselves from the organization. Irony and humour are typical expressions.

Pathology: Over-dis-identification, where every possible occasion is found to demonstrate how bad or wrong the organization is, and how deluded, misguided and floundering everyone else is.

Source: Adapted from Dukerich et al. (1998)

Understood in this way, employees like Paul (Case Point 5.5) make the assessment that any sense of authenticity has been 'strangled' by his collusive participation in the organization's 'brain-rotting' activities. Paul's case is not easy to place in the

Dukerich et al. matrix (see box above). Paul was not seeking to dis-identify with or condemn Y-International and, indeed, describes the company as a 'good employer'. Nor was his identification 'apathetic' in the sense of being purely instrumental or simply 'going through the motions'. Despite his disaffection with his job, he was apparently continuing to do it conscientiously and effectively. His experience is perhaps closest to 'conflicting identification' as he is positive about Y-International as an employer but is negative about the organization as a place (for him) to work.

A psychoanalytic approach can help us to understand such complexities. For example, Hoedemaekers (2010) explores identification in a public sector organization and shows how, in interviews, workers drew on images of what an 'ideal' employee meant to them. By paying attention to the various breakdowns, slips and inconsistencies that occurred in how people identified with these ideals, the author argues that there is considerable space for resistance as people identify with such images.

5.6 Conclusion

In this chapter, we examined the phenomenon of identity from a perspective that foregrounds organizational control. For those in charge of organizations, identity is recognized as an important means for motivating employees, for example by creating a strong organizational culture in which people feel that they belong. It is clear that whether one works at Disney or British Airways, a sense of self that somehow coheres with the image and values sanctioned by management is important.

We have pointed to ethical ambiguities inherent to the idea of 'identity management', referring to studies which understand such strategies and techniques as subtle and insidious forms of domination. The topic is complex, however. While highlighting the impact of identity 'regulation' on employee domination, authors also point to instances of resistance, where people manage to evade such techniques, or engage with them on their own terms. These processes are not straightforward, however, since even 'resistant identities' can feed into the goals of those whose interests are closely aligned to those of the organization.

Another instance of complexity in this topic relates to the novelty of the idea of 'identity management'. Such initiatives appear to be features of recent changes in contemporary working, with 'knowledge work' and customer-focused service sector employment both on the increase. But a historical perspective suggests that some form of interference in employees' selves has long been in place, as far back as early industrialization. Given these complexities, it is likely that questions around 'control' and 'identity' will continue to be central to the future development of both managerialist (e.g. new human relations thinking) and more critical accounts of the techniques, processes and ethics of control at work. Clearly, people are complex, unpredictable and capable of engaging with managerial strategies in a multiplicity of ways, and so it is impossible to anticipate precisely how the practice and study of organizational control will evolve. What we can say is that the future holds many interesting twists and turns for both management practitioners and scholars of the significance of identity for processes of control. We therefore invite you to reflect upon how your identity is invoked and enrolled within organizations as you progress through your working life.

Suggested Reading

Alvesson, M. and Willmott, H. (2002) 'Identity regulation as organizational control: producing the appropriate individual', *Journal of Management Studies*, 39 (5): 619–44.

Casey, C.J. (2002) *Critical Analysis of Organizations: Theory, Practice, Revitalization.* London: Sage.

du Gay, P. (1996) *Consumption and Identity at Work.* London: Sage.

Dukerich, J.M., Kramer, R. and Parks, J.M. (1998) 'The dark side of organizational identification', in D.A. Whetten and P.C. Godfrey (eds), *Identity in Organizations*. London: Sage.

Willmott, H. (1993) 'Strength is ignorance; slavery is freedom: managing culture in modern organisations', *Journal of Management Studies*, 30 (5): 515–52.

Sample Exam/Assignment Questions

- Critically assess the ethics and effectiveness of approaches to managing identity through corporate culture.
- Explain the different ways in which organizations seek to control, conceal, exploit, fake and shape employee identity.
- Discuss the range of identification responses that might be expected from modern forms of organizational control. What kinds of functional and dysfunctional outcomes could these generate?

Organizational Identity   6

6.1 Introduction

'Who do you work for?' Your response to this question – whether it produces a positive reaction or a glazed response – enables you, as well as other people, to define or affirm a sense of identity. In this chapter, we examine 'organizational identity'. This refers to the idea that it is not only what we do (see Chapter 4) but also the organization that we work for which contributes to forming our identity. For example, people who work for companies with a 'good' reputation and 'strong' brand, such as Apple, might feel very differently to people who work for a small components factory in China that manufactures Apple products. The former could be proud to be called an 'Apple employee', whereas the latter could be somewhat indifferent about their employer's identity, simply feeling that 'it's just a job to me'.

An alternative response to 'Who do you work for?' might, of course, be 'I am self-employed' or 'I am between jobs'. But the same general point applies – our response to the question 'Who do you work for?' defines us in relation to the existence (or the absence) of an organizational identity. Of course, in cases where people are not formally employed by an organization, they may well be 'working' in a voluntary capacity – for example, as a member of a church or a local charity from which they also derive a sense of identity.

This chapter will consider what organizational identity is, why it matters and how it is constructed, maintained and contested. As we will see, 'organizational identity' is a contested concept, with debates over whether 'identity' is best conceived as a property of organizations or as a set of beliefs (for overviews, see Ravasi and van Rekom, 2003, and especially Porter, 2001). We begin by considering the widespread appeal of 'organizational identity' and the diverse ways in which it has been conceptualized and explored. We then examine two dominant approaches to its analysis: a 'realist' tradition that considers organizational identity in terms of its properties; and a 'constructionist' tradition that examines organizational identity in terms of beliefs that people hold about it. The following section addresses how organizations define their identity, and explores the types of identity they attempt to construct. We bear in mind that this can be an evolving, ongoing process that is often laden with power and conflict. The next section tackles the issue of power and control head-on, by delving into the 'managerialist' proposition that high levels of identification among the workforce can (and should) be attained.

6.2 Organizational Identity: What Is It and Why Does It Matter?

One of the major problems faced by anyone wanting to study organizational identity involves the different ways in which 'organizational' and 'identity' are defined and then combined. Van Rekom et al. (2008: 184) note that students of organizational identity deploy 'different philosophical, epistemological and methodological perspectives', and observe that this is confusing when it is not recognized and taken into account. The widespread appeal of the concept 'organizational identity' has led to its adoption by researchers from diverse specialist backgrounds including 'organizational behavior, marketing, strategy, psychology, organization theory and corporate communication' (ibid.).

Some commentators even doubt whether an organization can justifiably be said to have 'an identity' at all. After all, are organizations not simply aggregates of many individuals, each one of them having a distinct identity? Figure 6.1 looks at the debate between those who think organizations have an identity and those who want to reserve the term identity for individuals.

Can Collective Entities have Identities?

Some scholars have questioned whether it is legitimate to ascribe an identity to 'organizations', arguing that the concept of identity should be reserved for individuals. The claim is that a person exists, and can therefore be sensibly identified, in a way that an organization – at best, a legal fiction – does not. From this point of view, a collective enterprise, such as an organization, is only legitimately viewed as an aggregation of individuals. From this perspective, it makes no defensible sense to suggest that an identity, unified or plural, is shared by persons because this compromises or distorts their individuality. We believe that there is some merit in this position as it helps to remind us that 'organizations' do not have 'goals' or 'purposes' like people do. When we say that, for example, Organization X 'has focused its strategy', what we probably mean is that a limited number of senior people within X have decided to divest elements which they have assessed to be marginal to the 'core' business. The point is that Organization X did not make this decision. Rather, some of its members made it: individual human beings.

Czarniawska-Joerges (2004) is particularly critical of the idea that organizations can have an 'identity' because of the many questionable assumptions the notion relies on. First, as we have noted, it assumes that organizations can (and should) be treated as 'superpersons' (Czarniawska-Joerges, 2004): large aggregates of people that are said to have the same properties as individuals including the capacity to think, feel, learn, decide, act and so on. Second, it relies on the idea that organizations are largely consensus based and 'unitaristic', with everyone agreeing what the organization is, what it should do and what it is for. Third, it assumes that organizations can be allowed to (and be expected to) behave like persons. Since the invention of the corporation as a 'legal person', it can now do most of the things a person can: own land and property, buy and sell its assets, be punished for acting illegally, etc. (ibid.: 409).

A counterargument is that the unity supposedly attributed to persons does not itself withstand close scrutiny. Persons are themselves not unified or bounded except in a physically reductionist

(Continued)

(Continued)

sense (i.e. a single body). Of course, this argument flies in the face of a common-sense view that persons are individuals who have distinctive personalities and recognizably consistent ways of behaving. The response to this defence is that persons come to exist as seemingly unified 'individuals' by using symbols (e.g. language) – which include the term individual as well as organization and identity. In this process, a complex, multi-faceted and dynamic sense of identity is assigned a sense of unity by invoking the term individual or organization. Just as there is a risk that the identity of a person is reduced to one or two key features (e.g. male, manager), there is a danger that the identity attributed to the collective activity that comprises 'organization(s)' assumes the status of a thing rather than being recognized as a context-contingent construction devised and deployed in particular circumstances. Sometimes, this thing-like status is actively sought and promoted – for example, in efforts to define a corporate identity for purposes of external or internal marketing. Notably, branding is generally intended to convey a specific, comparatively stable and unified sense of identity or image – of companies as well as products.

Following Czarniawska-Joerges (2004), organizational identity might be better viewed as a social construction – that is, the outcome of the meaning-making and narratives told by actors about 'who we are'. When, for example, a person (e.g. manager or customer) tells a story about the organization to others, the identity of the person and the identity of the organization are being simultaneously constructed. Those listening are also influenced by the meaning bound up in the story. A manager might tell a story about the future vision of the company, with a view to encouraging staff to abandon their old ideas of the company as 'old-fashioned' and 'conservative' and embrace a new identity as 'modern', 'innovative' and 'cutting edge' (see e.g. Hatch and Schultz, 2008). Of course, the staff may respond by reaffirming their identification with the familiar identity of the company and dis-identify from the one envisioned by the manager. And, of course, what the manager says to their partner about the 'cutting edge' vision may be a very different story (e.g. they may be sceptical or even contemptuous). So, it is not just about organizational identity being 'socially constructed', it is also about which 'constructions' are voiced and are made to 'stick'.

Overlaps of terminology are another source of confusion. Identity, image, reputation and brand all seem to be related, but in what ways? What these terms mean is, obviously, a matter of convention; their meaning can and does change over time and in relation to context. Nonetheless, offering a basis for distinguishing between them, as Brown et al. (2006) do (see Table 6.1), can help.

In some situations, it is relatively easy, or at least plausible, to distinguish between the five elements presented in Table 6.1. Consider a highly diversified corporation such as Unilever – producing everything from Persil washing detergent to Ben & Jerry's ice cream – that has a range of branded products associated with different images that convey distinctive meanings. At the time of writing, a new 'concentrated' form of Persil washing liquid has been launched that aims to reduce environmental impact. This associates the product and the company with an intended image of corporate social responsibility. For some consumers, however, who are suspicious of big brands and big companies, this move is more likely to be greeted with some (unintended) scepticism – perhaps as yet another example of 'greenwashing' (this time, literally as well as metaphorically!). Hence, the reputation of the company could be different to the intended image and brand message. Ben & Jerry's ice cream,

Table 6.1 Distinguishing identity, image, reputation and brand

Term	Key question
Identity	Who are we as an organization?
Image (intended)	What does the organization *want* others to think about it?
Image (construed)	What does the organization *think* others think about it?
Reputation	What do others *actually* think about the organization?
Brand	What attributes and images do we want others to associate with a particular product/service?

Source: Adapted from Brown et al. (2006)

on the other hand, is identified, or marketed, by associating the product with passion and fun. Potential consumers who remember (or are attached to) the original, 'hippie', handcrafted product are, again, more likely to avoid it when Ben & Jerry's countercultural reputation is branded and marketed by a huge, 'soulless' corporation. Nonetheless, the point to be noted is that there are many different products, with different images and reputations, that can form part of the same organization.

In many cases the five terms defined by Brown et al. are closely related and overlap. The identity, image, reputation and brand of Apple, for example, are comparatively closely intertwined. Each product/brand – such as the iPod, iPhone and iPad – articulates, and contributes, to Apple's identity as a world leader in innovation and design. The 'i' now effectively signifies Apple. In turn, the external reputation of the company helps to reinforce the identity perceived by employees about 'what we stand for' and 'who we are'. Unilever employees are probably more likely to identify with a particular product line, such as Persil, whereas Apple employees are more likely to identify with the company.

 Thinkpoint

What impression (and sense of identity) does 'I work for Unilever' convey, compared with 'I work for Apple'? What does this tell you about organizational identity?

In this chapter, we are focusing mainly on organizational identity – the equivalent of Apple or Unilever. The other terms considered by Brown et al. – image, reputation and brand – tend to be studied more closely in other fields such as marketing, public relations and corporate communications. Here our concern is with the identity attributed to the organization as a whole (rather than particular products or brands) as understood primarily by those within the organization (as opposed to consumers, shareholders, suppliers, regulators or indeed the general public).

In order to offer an overview of the issues explored by students of organizational identity whose focus is primarily upon members of the organization, we refer to a list prepared by van Rekom et al. (2008) in which a number of the questions that researchers have asked about organizational identity are listed (see Table 6.2). In this chapter, we touch directly, or in passing, upon most of these questions and explore a number of answers to them. It will be helpful to keep them in mind when reading the following sections.

Table 6.2   Research questions in the organizational identity field

Research question	Example
What is organizational identity?	Albert and Whetten (1985)
Under what conditions do identities change?	Dutton and Dukerich (1991)
Is organizational identity more or less enduring?	Corley and Gioia (2004)
Where do identities originate from?	Glynn (2000)
How does organizational identity relate to knowledge and practices within the organization?	Nag et al. (2007)
What is the nature and impact of identity threats?	Elsbach and Kramer (1996)
How does organizational identity relate to wider institutions?	Whetten (2006)
How and why do organizations have multiple identities?	Pratt and Foreman (2000)
What is the relationship between organizational identity and image?	Gioia et al. (2000)

Source: Adapted from van Rekom et al. (2008: 184)

6.3 Organizational Identity – Properties or Beliefs?

One of the most influential, but also ambiguous, definitions of organizational identity is provided by Albert and Whetten (1985) in an article that effectively 'kicked
off' the contemporary academic study of organizational identity. Albert and Whetten
view organizational identity as what members believe to be the central, enduring and
distinctive characteristics of their organization. Those influenced by this definition
have, accordingly, tended to emphasize the 'enduring characteristics', or properties,
of organizational identity or, alternatively, have stressed 'what members believe …'.
At the heart of their definition, then, is an ambiguity about how to make sense of
organizational identity. In short, it can be said that Albert and Whetten's definition
points in two different directions:

- properties of organizations which are then more or less adequately reflected in
  members' beliefs; or
- a set of beliefs that ascribe central, enduring and distinctive qualities to their
  organizations.

Why does this matter? One significant reason is that, depending upon what we assume
about the nature of organizational identity, we will favour very different ways of
researching it, and very different kinds of knowledge will be made available (or not).

These competing views of organizational identity exemplify two broad traditions
within the social sciences and within the study of management and organization.
These traditions have been given a variety of names but here we characterize them as
realist (advocated by Whetten and others, although seemingly not the later work of his
co-author, Albert) and constructionist (commended by Gioia and others). It is perhaps more helpful to regard these traditions as positioned at ends of a continuum as

this allows for ambiguities at its centre, rather than as diametrically opposed. At the realist end of the continuum, the features attributed to organizations are understood to comprise actual properties resident within them. At the other end are constructionist accounts that suggest that whatever features or properties an organization is considered to exhibit, we cannot know these features themselves, we can only know what people believe, or claim to know, about them. In other words, from a constructionist position, the features are more credibly understood as an articulation of how people make sense of the organization, and not as a direct representation of the properties themselves.

Constructionism places in question the realist claim that organizational identities are sensibly conceived as comprising specific properties (see also the exchange between Cornelissen, 2002, and Gioia et al., 2002), as contrasted with different frameworks or narratives developed by organizational members (and academics, of course) for making sense of the organization. From a constructionist perspective, then, the realist understanding of organizational identity is simply one of those narratives that is distinguished by its lack of reflexivity about the relativity of its own framework. Conversely, from a realist perspective, constructionism is viewed as 'idealist' in the sense that it considers only the narratives about organizational properties, and not the properties themselves. To appreciate differences of orientation to organizational identity, Table 6.3 summarizes these two approaches.

Which of these two positions is correct? Although we authors of this book have our own preferences, which makes us lean towards the constructionist position, the key point is that they lead us to view (and research) organizational identity in different ways. The realist position leads us to research identity using scientific methods, in the search for the most 'reliable' and 'unbiased' knowledge of the properties of organizational identity. As Whetten notes, realist analysis drives the researcher towards scientific approaches of 'model building, hypothesis testing, and empirical measurement' (2006: 229). For example, imagine two employees who give different accounts of their organization's identity. The realist analyst would set about discovering which view is more truthful, accurate and unbiased. The constructionist viewpoint, on the other hand, would not search for this ultimate 'truth' position. Rather, it would look at how and why different people construct different interpretations of the organization's identity.

So, if you favour a realist standpoint, you will design research that is geared to uncovering the 'real' properties of the organization, perhaps using a questionnaire survey. The data generated by the survey will then enable you to identify the dominant properties reported by respondents. If you view organizational identity as a set

Table 6.3 Realist and constructionist conceptions of organizational identity

	Realist	Constructionist
How organizational identity is understood	Property or asset	Set of representations articulating beliefs
How organizational identity is studied	Analysis of empirical phenomena measurable through scientific investigation	Analysis of sensemaking processes whereby meanings are constructed in context-contingent ways by different actors
Example	Elstak and Van Riel (2004)	Gioia and Thomas (1996)

of beliefs, you will design your study to show how people make sense of, or construct, their organization in the stories and narratives they tell, perhaps using open-ended interviews. When considering the results of the questionnaire survey undertaken by the realist researcher, you will view the disclosure of 'dominant properties' as the expression of one popular narrative and might then ask the question of how and why it has come to be so widely embraced (at least for the purpose of responding to a questionnaire). Conversely, when considering the results of the research based upon open-ended interviews, the realist might challenge the scientific basis of such work – which hypothesis is being tested, what was the sample size, how representative was it, etc.?

A good example of a realist perspective is the framework provided by Soenen and Moingeon (2002) (see Table 6.4). Soenen and Moingeon take a realist position when they describe their 'five facets' as different parts of a 'common underlying empirical phenomenon' (2002: 17). For them, the facets are actual properties or 'assets' of organizations, made up of five interconnected parts that can be uncovered through scientific investigation. A constructionist position, on the other hand, would view these facets as narratives developed by different groups – managers, employees, consumers as well as academics – that actively make up (construct) the identity of the organization in different ways, depending on the mobilization of particular values and beliefs.

The constructionist position appreciates that particular, culturally contingent, transient constructions do become hardened or 'reified' into what seems like 'properties' that exist outside of the human realm. For constructionists, it is this process that accounts for why a majority of respondents to a questionnaire identify many of the same properties. What the constructionist perspective aspires to avoid is the (realist) reification (treating things that are socially constructed as real) of the constructions (e.g. concepts) into separate things or 'variables' that then become the targets of model building, hypothesis testing and measurement. Constructionism emphasizes the importance of appreciating how meanings – such as those attributed to organizations in the form of 'properties' – are created and mobilized within a particular culture (i.e. group of people with particular norms, values and beliefs).

Table 6.4 Five facets of organizational identity

	Definition	Example
Professed identity	What a group or organization professes (claims) about itself	Mission statement
Projected identity	What elements an organization deliberately uses to present itself to specific audiences	Advertising
Experienced identity	The experiences and collective representations held by members within an organization	Current norms, rules, values, rituals
Manifested identity	The elements that have been associated with the organization for a period of time	Well-established and enduring structures, strategies, myths, taboos
Attributed identity	Elements that are ascribed to an organization by various audiences outside the organization	Media reports

Source: Adapted from Soenen and Moingeon (2002: 17)

For example, in a study of the Port Authority of New York and New Jersey, Dutton and Dukerich (1991) report how the Authority's corporate image became tainted when homeless people began to shelter in its bus and train stations. The Authority responded initially by denying the problem, then moving the homeless out. This 'cleansing' policy was interpreted, especially by its employees, as discrepant with the Authority's generally positive public image – an image that was valued by its staff who identified with it. The discrepancy between the positive reputation enjoyed by the Authority and its treatment of homeless people was felt by employees to reflect badly upon them. In turn, this led employees to demand that the Authority address the discrepancy by closing the gap so as to restore their positive sense of organizational identity. This pressure brought about a change of policy that restored its damaged public image and reinstated its members' preferred organizational identity.

This example of the Port Authority illustrates how a work culture (set of shared norms, values and beliefs) fostered a particular sense of organizational identity, as a responsive public service organization. Employees were so identified with this collective sense of identity that they pressed their employer to change its policy by building drop-in centres, thereby acting as a kind of advocate for the homeless. In this regard, work culture is understood as 'a symbolic context within which interpretations of organizational identity are formed and intentions to influence organizational image are formulated' (Hatch and Schultz, 1997: 360). It is the medium through which contents (both positive and negative) of organizational identity are developed, media reports are interpreted, and efforts to repair the image are mobilized. Some of the dynamics of this process are presented in Figure 6.1.

The basic idea is that organizational identity is embedded in organizational culture, and that it shapes but is also shaped by members as well as the vision and leadership of top management. So, for example, organizational identity has been held to be important in conditioning and screening how people interpret events (Gioia and Thomas, 1996), share knowledge (Empson, 2001), identify their core competencies (Glynn, 2000), inform their decision-making processes (Fombrun, 1996) and shape

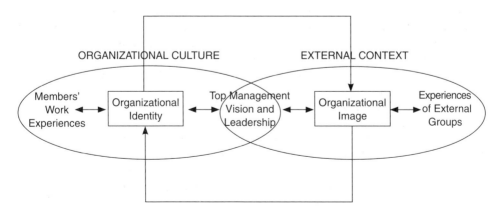

Figure 6.1 A model of the relationships between organizational culture, identity and image

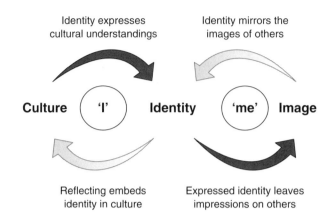

Figure 6.2   Relationship between culture, identity and image

corporate governance (Golden-Biddle and Rao, 1997). An issue, then, is how 'work culture' or 'organizational culture' is established and shaped. Is it something that develops through a spontaneous consensus among organizational members? Or is it something that is contested, and so the norms and values which emerge as dominant are the outcome of ongoing struggles between groups who favour divergent images and narratives of the organization? If it is the latter, then 'culture', whether it is associated with the immediate context of work or the broader organization, becomes 'hardened' or 'reified' (see earlier) within relations of power where some individuals and groups are in a better position to shape its form and content. This is perhaps most apparent in how the connection of organizational image with the experiences of external groups as corporate identity is predominantly influenced by top management and the PR consultants employed by them. The images of the organization generated by such groups are understood to form part of the external context of organizations but are also significant for the formation of organizational identity (as indicated by the top right hand grey arrow in Figure 6.2). Hatch and Schultz (2004) – from which Figure 6.2 is drawn – use Mead's conception of identity (discussed in Chapter 2, Section 2.5) as the interaction between the 'I' and the 'me', to understand how identity, image and culture are linked. The bottom right hand black arrow in Figure 6.2 indicates how the view of external groups is also informed by their knowledge or evaluation of members' sense of organizational identity. For example, when you shop at your local supermarket, your interaction with the staff at the checkout – such as how friendly and helpful the staff were – will inform your image of the organization.

Constructed beliefs can become so taken for granted that they can appear natural, inevitable or self-evidently 'real' objects. When a moment of 'crisis' occurs, such as the announcement of a cut in research funding in a university department (see Case Point 6.1), efforts are then made to make sense of what is experienced as a significant and disorientating event or development. In this process, a particular notion (or narrative) about 'who we are' or 'who we should be' can emerge which enjoys plausibility and extensive appeal, at least for some groups. Hence, a particular version of 'who we are' can be treated as if it was real. From a constructionist perspective, though, any such version is no more than a (narrative) construction (Czarniawska, 1997) that has become 'hegemonic' (accepted as 'natural' or 'right'). For example, in Case Point 6.1, we can see how one seemingly authoritative identity construction (e.g. a 'research-focused' university) displaces or unifies many other particular identities that have been or could have been attributed to the organization. The constructionist perspective invites us to understand the (re)production of social realities, including the properties attributed to organizational identity, as power-invested processes of struggle through which an account of reality becomes institutionalized as its values and beliefs become so widely taken for granted as to appear natural. By opening up the process of enacting realities, the constructionist position may also prompt us to ask 'who benefits from a particular construction of organizational identity?'

Let us look in more detail at the example of the funding cuts at the University of Illinois analyzed by Whetten (2006) (see Case Point 6.1 below). Research adopting a realist perspective (see Table 6.3) might well argue that, because the University enjoyed increased funding for research for many years, this explains why this 'property' (i.e. 'research') is regarded as (comparatively) central, enduring and distinctive. A constructionist would not deny that funds had been flowing into the University during those years. Crucially, however, it is not the funds per se but the meanings and beliefs that surround such funding that, from a constructionist standpoint, is of key importance. Members of another university could attract the same amount of funding but view teaching, rather than research, as more central to their organization's identity. The significance of any event is always a matter of interpretation, not a given.

📁 Case Point 6.1   Budget Cuts at the University of Illinois

In 1979, David Whetten was working at the University of Illinois when it suddenly had its budget cut by 2 per cent. This cut was unprecedented but it was not accompanied by any devastating consequences – such as shutting down departments, firing faculty or downsizing core academic programmes. Nonetheless, according to Whetten, the cuts were regarded by many faculty at the University as posing a 'profound threat to the organization and their membership in it' (1998: vii). Whetten found this reaction deeply 'puzzling'. Contemplating this puzzle led him to 'realize that concerns about identity are just as profound as concerns about survival' as they involved 'the anguishing personal and collective examination of members' taken-for-granted assumptions about what was core, enduring and distinctive about an American research university and the University of Illinois in particular' (ibid.: vii). That is to say, at the moment of the cuts, it became evident that the identity of the University was incompatible with a budget cut as such a cut delegitimized its claimed and distinctive status as a research university. In other words, at this moment, it became clear, at least from Whetten's properties-centric definition of 'organizational identity', that a central, enduring and distinctive property of the University of Illinois, as a research university, is maintenance of the funding that enables this identity to be sustained.

Source: Whetten (2006)

The University of Illinois example also illustrates how beliefs about an organization's identity may be so ill-articulated, poorly defined and/or simply taken for granted that they are hard for members to recognize or describe explicitly, prior to encountering something that is sensed to pose a challenge to their implicit beliefs. It was only when the threat of cuts was understood to loom over the University that faculty interpreted their significance in terms of ascribing to the University a research-based identity. Likewise, in Pratt and Rafaeli's (1997) study of a rehabilitation unit, it is argued that elements of an acute care identity were deeply embedded in nurses' practices but these were latent. They did not become manifest until some changes, notably in the patient population, led to nurses interpreting the acute care identity as more salient. A similar story occurred in a study of change in the German Police Force, by Jacobs et al. (2008), outlined in Case Point 6.2 below. To repeat, from a social constructionist standpoint, these examples do not demonstrate that, for example, the articulation of organizational identity is contingent upon a challenge to implicit understandings about it. Rather, the constructionist perspective consistently privileges processes of interpretation whose contents can never be reduced to the operation of a contingent set of factors.

Case Point 6.2   Organizational Identity in the German Police Force

Jacobs et al. (2008) studied how changes in the German Police Force threatened the prevailing view among police officers about their collective identity. The research involved two stages. First, semi-structured interviews were conducted with 98 students from the German Police University, which trains officers for senior ranks, focusing on their project experiences over the previous two years. Second, 50 in-depth interviews were conducted with officers from five different police forces at all hierarchical levels, about their experiences of change in the last decade.

The study found that the introduction of new public management 'modernization' changes, such as budgeting, management by objectives, contract management, performance assessment, cost accounting, quality management and benchmarking, was at odds with the collective organizational identity held by the police officers.

The following two quotes illustrates how the members interpreted the change:

> They made us sit there talking about management concepts while all hell was breaking loose out there in the streets. (Police Lieutenant)

> I remember how we left the room after this information meeting. I said to my colleague: I can't believe this. I always thought we were police! We're not selling anything! We're not a business! I wish they'd stop this management bullsh...! (Police Officer)

Jacobs et al. (2008) argue that the change was resisted by the police officers because they interpreted it as a threat to what they saw as central to their organization's identity. Their intense emotional reactions suggested that the members felt very strongly about 'who we are'. The new 'managerial' and 'entrepreneurial' initiatives were considered to be at odds with the established identity of the organization as 'crime fighting'. The authors themselves note the similarities between their case and the strong emotional reactions following the cut in budget at the University of Illinois in Whetten's case (see Case Point 6.1).

6.4 Types of Organizational Identity

In this section, we expand upon questions, touched upon above, of how the identity of organizations is defined, what this identity consists of, and whether identity is a singular and relatively coherent whole. In doing so, we will refer to what 'organizations' do. But it should be born in mind that 'organizations' invariably comprise shifting factions who will not necessarily agree on their primary purpose, or will mean different things by it. Therefore, the process of (re)defining 'who we are' is likely to involve conflicts between factions, and may even exclude certain people from this process.

6.4.1 Defining 'who we are' and 'who we are not'

The most obvious way in which an organization is defined is through explicit statements, visions and symbols prepared by consultants and/or senior managers that portray, to members and outsiders, 'who we are'. The mission statement or strategic plan of an organization is a good place to look for written statements of what the organization – or, more credibly, what the architect(s) of the statement or plan – thinks it is, wants it to be, or wants others to think it is.

Symbols and material aspects are often central to defining organizational identity. Logos, for example, are intended to symbolize visually what the company stands for. Adverts on the Internet, on television and in newspapers and magazines attempt to portray a particular visual image of the organization. Material dimensions such as the decor and layout of the Head Office building are also symbols of the intended image the organization wants to portray (Elsbach, 2004) (we discuss the identity dimensions of office layout and decor in Chapter 4, Section 4.3.2.) The way that employees dress can also send out a strong signal about the ethos and values of the organization (Pratt and Rafaeli, 1997).

 **Thinkpoint**

Consider your own experience of working for an organization or of being a new customer. What was your image of that organization prior to becoming an employee or a customer, and how had the image been acquired? Then, how was your sense of the organization's identity elaborated or changed as you became an employee or a customer, and what enabled that process to happen?

A more subtle, but equally important, way of defining identity is by comparing the organization with 'who we are not' (Elsbach and Bhattacharya, 2001). Alvesson and Empson (2008) argue that organizations often define their identity in comparison with others, especially competitors. Identity is often about distancing and distinctiveness, often with negative comparisons of others ('we are different to them', 'we are better than them'). For example, one consulting firm studied by Alvesson and Empson defined itself as 'elite' by referring to competitors as 'the McDonald's of consulting' (2008: 7), using a negative downwards comparison ('we are better than them') to imply their superiority.

6.4.2 Hybrid identities

The view that organizations have distinct and enduring 'properties' leads us to assume that organizations have a single, relatively coherent and consensual identity that can be precisely pinpointed and defined. But do all organizations have (or even strive to

Table 6.6 Terms associated with multiple organizational identities

Term	Definition
Mono-identity	Organizations that have a *single, coherent* identity
Hybrid/dual-identity	Organizations in which members incorporate *two or more* distinct (and possibly conflicting) dimensions or types simultaneously
Ideographic identity	Organizations in which different *units* of the organization exhibit different dimensions of the organization's hybrid identity
Holographic identity	Organizations in which *all* units exhibit *all* dimensions of the organization's hybrid identity

Source: Adapted from Albert and Whetten (2004: 95–6) and Golden-Biddle and Rao (1997)

have) a distinct and well-defined identity? What about organizations in which there are diverse, conflicting and contradictory views about 'who we are'? We will address these questions in turn.

The term hybrid identities (Albert and Whetten, 1985) has been developed to describe organizations in which members incorporate two or more distinct (and possibly conflicting) dimensions or types of purpose for the organization. For example, universities typically present themselves as simultaneously being about teaching, research and service or engagement of some kind (to industry, society, public policy and others) (ibid.: 95). On some occasions, these activities may be grouped into different units, known as an 'ideographic identity' (see Table 6.6). For example, a unit of staff might be dedicated to teaching (e.g. Teaching Group), another to research (e.g. Research Centre), and another unit dedicated to service to wider society (e.g. Public Policy Think Tank).

On other occasions, the three competing areas of activity will be exhibited by all units, which are tasked with doing all three things at once, known as a 'holographic identity' (see Table 6.6). While the holographic approach invites greater synergy and transfer, it may also provoke increased tensions and role conflicts for external stakeholders as well as members. Students, for example, may find that teaching effectiveness suffers because their lecturers are focusing on consultancy activities with companies or advising policy-makers. Some universities may try to address their hybrid identity by elevating one element: 'we are excellent at teaching' or 'we are a research-focused university'.

The Atlanta Symphony Orchestra studied by Glynn (2000) is an example of an ideographic organizational identity; some members identified the organization as being devoted to artistic excellence, whereas others identified it as a business. But few identified it as both. The non-profit organization studied by Golden-Biddle and Rao (1997) is an example of a holographic organization identity in which every member is reported to have held two paradoxical views of the organization's identity: as a group of friends and as an administrative unit that required tight financial controls. Such conflicts over organizational identity, and the meanings and priorities that are assigned to it, are commonplace. It is not unusual, for example, for those who are responsible for financial matters to come into conflict with others who are directly responsible for winning orders, producing goods or providing after-sales service. Hence, different people – organizational members, customers, suppliers, etc. – may construct different properties and purposes for the organization, as they devise and mobilize their own favoured narratives.

Do some organizations claim not to have an identity at all? One of the consultancy firms studied by Alvesson and Empson (2008) claimed exactly that. The consultants rejected the very idea that their firm had, or needed, an identity. As one senior manager explained:

> Our MD sees the consulting organization as a collection of individuals who have very little in common except for the fact that they share an office space. (Alvesson and Empson, 2008: 12)

Unsurprisingly, the culture of the firm is characterized by Alvesson and Empson (2008) as individualistic, tough and macho. They report that, for the members of this firm, any suggestion of a common identity was seen as 'fluffy' and 'wimpy'. Consultants did not care about whether any common sense of identity bound them together; they only cared about themselves as individuals. They defined their sense of self not through organizational membership (and so expressed an extreme form of dis-identification perhaps?) but in relation to symbols of their individual status and success – such as winning prestigious clients, beating the competition and being able to afford expensive cars. Alvesson and Empson (2008) interpret this hostility towards identity as their organizational identity, a kind of 'anti-identity' identity. Other organizations that employ large numbers of part-time, temporary and agency staff may also generate little sense of collective identity: their staff view the organization instrumentally as no more than a source of 'a job' rather than affectively as forming some part of 'who I am'. In other cases, professional (e.g. as a lawyer) or occupational (e.g. as a plumber) identities are more salient than the organization per se. Chapters 4 and 5 look in more detail into how individuals come to identify (and dis-identify) with a particular organization or occupational or professional group. Alvesson and Empson's (2008) study of four consulting firms (see Case Point 6.3) shows the different kinds of 'characteristics' that management consultants used to distinguish what their firm 'stood for'.

🗁 Case Point 6.3   The Case of Consulting Firms

Alvesson and Empson (2008) conducted a comparative study of four consulting firms. Their study illustrates four different dimensions (Table 6.7) that were important in defining 'who we are':

- What is known about the way their members work (e.g. work processes).
- How the organization is managed and how the members relate to the favoured approach (e.g. ideals and motivation).
- How the members regard themselves in that organizational context (e.g. morality).
- How they see others and how they are seen by them (e.g. image of clients).

Alvesson and Empson's findings highlight the ambiguity concerning whether characteristics such as 'intellectual creativity' were (1) actually referenced by organizational members in their day-to-day interactions; (2) invoked only when interviewed by the researcher(s); or (3) refer to the properties of the organization or to the beliefs of the employees. Interviewees could have been regurgitating the 'company line' when they were interviewed, without actually believing or 'living' these ideas (e.g. being 'free' and

(Continued)

(Continued)

'creative') in their everyday working life. It is also possible that alternative kinds of con-structions were present within the firms (i.e. did some people think differently?) but not shared with the researchers.

Table 6.7 Organizational identities of four consultancy firms

	Consultancy A	Consultancy B	Consultancy C	Consultancy D
Work processes	Organizationally codified	Highly personalized, emphasis on intuition	Highly personalized, emphasis upon intellectual creativity	Highly personalized, emphasis upon autonomy
Ideals and motivation	To deliver promised benefits to clients	To make a difference to the lives of clients	To develop intellectually creative solutions	'To beat the shit out of the competition'
Morality	Mutual support and enthusiasm	Good-doers, ethical, values-driven	Pursuit of academic 'truth'	[Not identified by members]
Image	Pragmatic, reliable, cultish	'Classy, sexy'	Elitist, intelligent, academic	Individual, not organizational

Source: Adapted from Alvesson and Empson (2008: 7)

Alvesson and Empson (2008) point out that accounts of 'who we are' can sometimes serve to boost members' sense of importance and value, making themselves appear 'better' than their competitors. Such self-serving accounts may also act to protect or 'shield' against negative characterizations. In the case of Consultancy A, its members are reported to have reconstructed outsiders' (pejorative) use of the McDonald's metaphor to characterize the firm's positive key features. Employees at Consultancy A apparently embraced the idea of being the 'McDonald's of consulting'. This identity signified, for them, 'efficiency, reliability, value for money and world-wide success' (ibid.: 15). This has parallels with the way in which workers in dirty, degrading and deviant occupations tend to deny or reformulate the negative connotations associated with their work (see Chapter 4, Section 4.6).

Others have sought to extend this line of thinking by introducing a psychodynamic perspective to organizational identity research. Driver (2009) uses psychoanalytical theory, specifically the ideas of Jacques Lacan, to examine organizational identity as an illusion or fantasy. Driver argues that the answers that we provide to questions about 'who we are' are imaginary because they are always based on our desire to be a certain thing. A subconscious 'lack' is understood to fuel this desire – a lack that arises when our joyous, non-neurotic sense of non-separateness is dislocated by the emergence of self-consciousness. In (unconsciously) striving to restore this feeling, we repeatedly develop pleasurable identifications, such as those provided by the properties attributed to organizations. As these imaginaries are unable to fill the original lack, we are continuously disappointed and then feel compelled neurotically to enhance or change the properties, but resulting in the same, disappointing outcome. According to Lacan, the only escape from this neurotic cycle is to abandon the process by 'traversing the fantasy'.

6.5 Power in (and of) Organizational Identity

It has been suggested that contemporary organizations are increasingly concerned with identity and image (Alvesson, 1990), not just survival. As a consequence, managers are receptive (and vulnerable) to being persuaded (e.g. by consultants) that a strong and positive identity, or even perhaps a multiple identity with facets appealing to different stakeholders (see above; Pratt and Foreman, 2000), will improve performance (see Fiol, 2001, for a review). Is it right, though, to equate the identity of an organization with any one group's (e.g. executives') representations of it? Does this privileging of one representation tend to 'pave over individual diversity embedded within its boundaries, particularly that predicated on social categories of race, gender, religion, class, or age' (Glynn et al., 2000: 731)?

We have noted how, for those who favour a 'realist' position, 'organizational identity' is a comparatively descriptive and neutral concept that captures key properties of an organization (see Table 6.3). If we take a constructionist position, on the other hand, the question is not what these properties are. Instead the question is: what do such (realist) claims about the central, enduring and distinctive properties of the organization do – that is, what power effects do they have? For example, in Whetten's (2006) example of the budget cuts at the University of Illinois (see Case Point 6.1), the faculty seemed to share a strong sense of their University as a 'research' institution. This identification as 'researchers' might well act as a potent means of securing employees' dedication and commitment to research activity. In turn, this commitment to being 'excellent at research' could enable the University to extract more 'discretionary effort' from faculty – effort, that is, which is supplied by employees at little or no material cost to the organization (e.g. without the inducement of overtime pay, bonuses, etc.). This kind of effort is often expressed as the degree of care and pride taken in work, or the exceptional level of customer service provided, where workers go 'the extra mile' for the customer or their colleagues. Saying that identification is a medium and outcome of power relations is not to imply that such identifications are negative, or to signal disapproval. A strong, even obsessive, identification with the exacting demands of research activity is frequently a component of path-breaking scientific work or technological innovation that can, in principle, be widely beneficial. That said, we need to understand how and why such power effects operate, and also to ask who benefits and who is disadvantaged by strong identifications, such as the identity of being a 'researcher' in a 'research-intensive' university or being a Honda worker who obsessively straightens the windscreen wipers on every Honda they pass when returning home from work?

The 'managerialist' perspective views things like organizational identity, branding and corporate culture as media and instruments for managing the organization more effectively. Hatch and Schultz (2008), for example, contend that having a clear and well-aligned strategy, culture and identity that are led by senior management through 'corporate branding' can improve competitive advantage. Of course, this effect relies on employees interpreting positively the images conveyed by management and identifying with the meanings communicated. Kärreman and Rylander (2008) studied the process of corporate branding in a Swedish IT consultancy firm. The corporate brand of the firm emphasized high performance, with services delivered on time and to a high quality, using the idea of a famous sports star to conjure up images of a 'winner', someone who is the best in their league. Taking a critical perspective on the managerial use of corporate branding, Kärreman and Rylander argue that branding is not simply a marketing tool, aimed primarily at customers but involves a broader process of 'meaning management' through which the firm attempts to control the meanings about organizational identity (Who are we? What are our core beliefs and values?) among a wider range of stakeholders, including employees. For them, branding involves 'systematic efforts from top management to influence and shape frames of reference, norms and values among organizational members' (ibid.: 108). Branding, from this perspective, is not a neutral process of associating a company (or product) with certain positive attributes, but also a power-laden managerial tool of internal marketing that is influential for the workforce. This theme of understanding power and control is explored in more detail in Chapter 5.

From a constructionist perspective that is also critical in orientation, the narratives constructed by those in power can enable their position to be consolidated in comparatively covert, ostensibly benign and often rather effective ways. As a consequence, what organizational members believe to be central or enduring to the organization may have less to do with their 'own' thoughts and beliefs, and more to do with the success of internal propaganda, such as internal communications. In other words, organizational members may come to view and adopt, at least partially, managerial propaganda as their own beliefs. In such a 'managerial translation of the "organizational identity" metaphor, an overarching set of values and beliefs is presumed to exist and to transcend individual members of the organization … with the aim of giving them some sense of purpose' (Cornelissen, 2002: 266).

Humphreys and Brown's (2002) study of 'Westville Institute' (a pseudonym), a further education college in the UK, illustrates how managers make attempts to control the taken-for-granted definitions of 'who we are' in order to influence, subtly and invisibly, what they should do. When senior management decided that they wanted the Institute to become research active and strive for university status, certain established identity narratives (that emphasized teaching skills and student learning) were deleted or dismissed. Reflecting upon these developments at Westville College, Brown and Humphreys (2006: 231) argue that definitions of organizational identity amounted to 'hegemonic "moves" in an ongoing struggle for control over the organization as a discursive space'. Not everyone has the same power to make these moves, or have their voice heard. As Brown and Humphreys (2006) point out, given their hierarchical position of power, senior managers often have the most say in defining what the organization 'is' or 'should be'. However, to be effective in a hegemonic sense, staff must be willing to reject, or at least suspend, their own definitions as they embrace those of management.

As we saw in Chapter 5 (Section 5.5), high levels of identification with the managerially approved organizational identity is not always possible. Nor, indeed, even from a managerialist standpoint, is it necessarily desirable. The obvious risk for management is not just that staff will over-identify with the 'organizational identity' to the point of resisting change. Case Point 6.4 below illustrates this dilemma using the example of a steel worker.

📂 **Case Point 6.4   Organizational and Personal Identity: The Case of a Steel Worker**

[A] man who works for many years in a steel company is likely to develop a sense of himself as a steel worker. Hence attempts [by management] to de-emphasize steel in that company are likely to trigger emotional stress in such individuals. By clinging to a definition of their organization as a steel company instead of learning to regard it as, say, a manufacturing-services company, they preserve their personal identity and their emotional equilibrium. At the same time, they reinforce the steel-company identity of their employing organization. Add up all such employees and other stakeholders and you have a major potential roadblock to transformation. (Bouchikhi and Kimberley, 2003: 21; see also Fiol, 2002)

Identification can be a managerial problem for organizations in one of two ways. If members fail to identify with the organization, it is unlikely that they will be fully committed to its goals and motivated to achieve them. Identification can also be a managerial problem if members are too strongly identified with the identity attributed to the organization, and refuse to let go of those beliefs. Brown and Starkey (2000) adopt a psychoanalytical perspective to analyze how organizations (or, better, members of organizations) develop 'ego defenses', where stigmatizing events are denied, rationalized or idealized in order to maintain collective self-esteem and protect their established sense of 'who we are'. These types of defensive responses can stop the members of an organization from learning about themselves and asking questions such as 'what did we do wrong?' and 'how should we change?'. Pathological adherence to existing notions of 'who we are' can be dysfunctional as they limit the capacity of organizational members to engage in 'critical self-reflexivity' (ibid.: 102).

6.6 Conclusion

It is likely that 'organizational identity' will continue to be a popular topic for students of management as it resonates with issues pursued across a number of its specialisms, including human resource management (HRM), marketing and communications. In an era where the image of an organization is significant for consumers and investors, and not just for employees, efforts to manage organizational identity are set to intensify and become more sophisticated. In turn, this emphasis is likely to accelerate where managerial worries about staff commitment and loyalty – and its knock-on effects for product quality and service delivery – are most acute. So, paradoxically perhaps, where there are increases in temporary work and high rates of staff turnover, interest in organizational identity and identification is likely to increase in an effort to compensate for less job security and poorer terms and conditions by engineering loyalty and commitment through 'culture'. There are few industries where some form of understanding of, and identification with, the managerially preferred sense of 'who we are' and 'what we do' is not important. Only perhaps in sectors where staff are viewed as wholly unreceptive to developing any significant identification with their employing organization, or where their replacement is comparatively easy and costless, is the notion of organizational identity less relevant.

At the same time, wherever there are efforts to target-manage organizational identity in order to motivate or retain employees, it is likely that staff will become increasingly savvy and sceptical about such developments. Indeed, the inclusion of these issues in undergraduate textbooks at once reflects and stimulates both kinds of development. Employees will become more aware of how attempts are being made to manipulate them and may respond in various, perhaps unpredictable and unexpected ways. Some may embrace such efforts, insofar as they are received as a welcome source of meaning, pride or pleasure. Others may strongly dis-identify with efforts to regulate their activity and view them as insidious ways of squeezing from them the 'extra mile'. Their response may be psychological withdrawal and/ or hostility. Efforts to 'glorify' and 'worship' the identity of the organization may be greeted with counterproductive disbelief and disaffection that (further) discredits the authority of management. The challenge for managers is to develop a narrative that employees find plausible as well as attractive so that resonates with, rather than jars against, their own sensibilities and fantasies. For those more critical commentators, attempts to impose a narrative and appeal to fantasies are inherently imbued with power that is exercised to suppress resistance.

Suggested Reading

Hatch, M.J. and Schultz, M. (1997) 'Relations between organizational culture, identity and image', European Journal of Marketing, 31 (5/6): 356–65.

Hatch, M.J. and Schultz, M. (eds) (2004) Organizational Identity: A Reader. Oxford: Oxford University Press.

Humphreys, M. and Brown, A.D. (2002) 'Narratives of organizational identity and identification: a case study of hegemony and resistance', Organization Studies, 23 (3): 421–47.

Schwartz, H. (1992) Narcissistic Process and Corporate Decay: The Theory of the Organization Ideal. New York: New York University Press.

Whetten, D.A. (2006) 'Albert and Whetten revisited: strengthening the concept of organizational identity', Journal of Management Inquiry, 15 (3): 219–34.

Sample Exam/Assignment Questions

- Can the term identity be applied to organizations? Discuss.
- Does organizational identity refer to a property of an organization or a set of beliefs about an organization? Critically evaluate the relative merits of the realist and constructionist perspectives on organizational identity.
- With reference to a range of examples, critically assess the power relations involved in the process of constructing organizational identity.

Virtual Identity   7

7.1 Overview and Introduction

One of the most significant changes in people's working lives over the last 20 years has been the extent to which ICTs (Information and Communication Technologies) mediate our activities. Social networking sites (SNSs) like Facebook and Twitter, email available on our mobile phone devices, and the increasing prevalence of wi-fi Internet in places that previously remained 'disconnected' – all promise to alter our working lives in both subtle and obvious ways. For identity scholars, the concept of 'virtual identity' is becoming increasingly important.

The notion that we are in an era of 'information revolution' has occupied commentators for many years. Just as technological advancements in manufacturing, energy and transport transformed society during the Industrial Revolution, so, some people argue, ICT is transforming contemporary life (Castells, 1996). The idea of the so-called 'network society' is that time and space have been compressed, if not 'demolished', by ICTs: individuals and organizations who might previously have been separated by physical space are now connected instantaneously, regardless of where they are.

These changes affects people's working lives too, with ICT mediating relationships with and between an increasing number of organizations: banks, suppliers, partners, colleagues and customers. All sorts of interactions are now 'virtual'. Automated call centre technology, for example, has enabled banks to answer customer queries from anywhere in the world. Distance learning programmes enable students to study a course without ever setting foot on the university campus. While it would be simplistic to argue that such changes in technology lead to predictable and universal social effects, it is vital to ask how identity is implicated in these important changes (Woolgar, 2003). We focus in this chapter on what 'virtuality' means for the world of work and organizations.

7.2 Competing Perspectives: Technological Determinism and Social Constructionism

Before embarking upon a discussion of virtual identity, it is important to be clear about how we understand the role of ICTs. Technological determinism and social constructionism represent two distinct approaches to the understanding of technology (Table 7.1).

Table 7.1 Technological determinism and social constructionism compared

Technological determinism	Social constructionism
Technology is an autonomous force that lies outside society	Technology is created by society
Technological change is driven by forces of logic and rational progress	Technological change is driven by the society in which it is created and used
Technology has a predictable 'impact' on society	Technology does not have a predictable impact, it depends on how it is created and used
Essential features and capacities (i.e. what a technology can do) determine the impact of the technology	No essential features; what a technology can 'do' depends on interpretations of different social groups
Technology is neutral and apolitical	Technology is loaded with political and economic interests

> The distinction between technological determinism and social constructionism also par-
> allels the discussion of realism and social constructionism in relation to understanding
> organizational identity, outlined in Chapter 6, Table 6.3.

Determinism rests on the assumption that technology is an autonomous force that lies outside society, with a logic of its own that drives it forward – such as the forces of 'science' and 'progress'. Technology is thought to have certain features that cause a particular 'impact' on society. For example, certain historians attribute the rise of feudal society, with its aristocracy enforced by horse-mounted knights, to the invention of the stirrup (a foot-hold for the rider) (MacKenzie and Wajcman, 1999: 4; Vurdubakis, 2007: 412). Before the stirrup was invented, fighting on horseback was difficult because lunging with a sword or lance would often cause the rider to fall off the horse. The stirrup was considered to have sparked a reorganization of society designed to develop the stocks of horses, armour and training required to organize a horse-mounted battle 'machine'. A feudal society, with land-rich aristocrats, is seen to be driven by this technological 'leap' in progress. The idea that society is 'driven' by advances in science and technology is popular. Notably, the 'Stone Age', the 'Bronze Age' and the 'Iron Age' are defined by the predominant technology used to make tools and weapons. More recently, the invention of the telegraph, the telephone, the steam engine, the jet engine, the contraceptive pill, the microchip and the Internet are all commonly associated with 'causing' huge changes in society.

Social constructionism, on the other hand, views technology as created by society, rather than an autonomous force that lies outside society (MacKenzie and Wajcman, 1999). What technologies we develop, and how we subsequently use them, depends on a range of social, political and economic influences, and especially upon the worldview of those who are developing and using technologies. Society does not simply have to adapt to technological change, its members actively shape it. For example, the Internet was originally designed for military purposes, then used by computer programmers for developing software, largely within the US university system, and is now harnessed for a multitude of different uses: by governments to monitor and control the population, by hackers to steal our personal information, by companies to advertise their products to consumers, by teenagers to chat to their friends, and by activists to 'leak' corporate and government secrets and deceptions. The technology itself does not have a predictable impact, it depends on the way it is used by different social groups. Facebook and Twitter are good examples of this. Twitter can be used to make, maintain or break friendships, to organize anarchic protests by a social movement group, or by relatives to keep in touch with loved ones. All these groups utilize the available features of the technology in different ways. There is no way of predicting what it might be used for in the future.

Social constructionists view technological change as shaped by society rather than supposedly 'rational' forces of progress. The Betamax video format was considered by most people to be technologically 'superior' to the VHS format, but VHS 'won' the format war for video-recording devices in the 1980s due to a range of economic and social factors, such as advertising and retailing strategies. As we write this, a similar case can be seen in ongoing battles between Blu-ray and HD-DVD formats. To take another example, the male contraceptive pill had been 'technically' possible for decades, but it has not been widely developed or used largely due to social norms about who should be responsible for contraception and whether men are deemed 'reliable' and 'trustworthy' enough to take the pill. To make a new technology 'work', it is necessary to do more than just 'engineer' the technical components. It is also necessary to 'engineer' social, economic and political relationships so that the technology is relevant and appealing.

7.2.1 How is identity implicated in virtual technologies?

The kinds of virtual technologies being considered in this chapter – including email, mobile phones, websites and Internet-based virtual communication sites (blogs, Twitter, Facebook, Second Life, etc.) – can be understood differently from determinist and constructionist perspectives.

A determinist, for example, might argue that Internet communication sites cause certain effects on a person's identity, such as compelling people to 'play' with their identity in new ways (by pretending to be someone they are not, for instance), as Case Point 7.1 on postmodern identity play suggests. A constructionist, in contrast, would argue that the technology itself does not cause the effect. The effect of a technology depends on how it is designed (by society) and used (in society). A group of teenage boys using Second Life might well 'play' with their identity and pretend to be a woman. However, an employee that is using collaboration software to communicate in a global virtual team is unlikely to 'play' with their identity because this would probably be seen as inappropriate and unprofessional. The firm context, and how this is constructed, plays an important role here because the organization employing the 'virtual team' wants to control it to ensure that it is used in a 'corporately responsible' manner which is, for example, consistent with raising productivity.

⬛ Case Point 7.1　Cyberspace: An Arena of Postmodern Identity Play?

When forms of Internet-based communication software were first emerging, long before the advent of MSN Messenger, Facebook and Twitter, many commentators were keen to speculate on the possible impact of these new types of online communication. Van Gelder (1996) tells the story of a user of the first ever online chat system, CompuServe CB Simulator. 'Joan' was a disabled woman who had been disfigured in a serious car accident involving a drunk driver. Joan made a lot of friends on the CB network, and was particularly pleased to have these 'cyberspace buddies' because she still struggled to speak and walk following the accident. Many of Joan's 'cyber friends' were inspired by her story and felt a strong personal connection with her, despite the fact that they had never met in person. They were all enthralled by her stories of her struggle to get people to accept her disabilities, and her work as a psychiatrist. They were particularly delighted when she got married to a local police officer and sent them all postcards from her honeymoon.

When some of Joan's online friends started to notice how far-fetched and inconsistent her stories were becoming, they confronted her about her identity. Joan revealed that she was not a disabled woman, but was instead 'Alex' – a male psychiatrist. Alex confessed that he had started to pretend to be a woman when one user accidentally mistook him for a woman and started to 'open up' in new ways. He enjoyed this new sense of insight and connections when passing as a woman, so decided to create a 'false' identity as 'Joan'. Many of 'Joan's' cyber-friends were not so happy about the deception, describing their experience as 'identity rape'.

Some postmodernist commentators have described cyberspace as ushering in a new era of postmodern identity play – where we can 'play' with our identity and pretend to be whoever we want to be (see Case Point 7.1). Postmodernist perspectives on identity emphasize its fluid, fragmented and constructed nature. Cyberspace is seen as an inviting place for people to change and shape their identities in new ways. Turkle's (1995) exploration of identity on the Internet highlights this aspect of identity freedom. Turkle studied how people interacted while engaging in role-playing games on the Internet. She argues that this new technology encourages people to create new, postmodern ways of being and knowing. The idea is that because a player realizes that the online game is merely a set of surface-level simulations, the game of 'real life' comes to appear in the same way. Players eventually might come to see themselves as more open to multiple, non-traditional ways of being. Whitty and Carr (2003) study the phenomenon of online flirting, comparing it with 'traditional' flirting. Somewhat in contrast to Turkle, they argue that the distinction between 'real life' and its virtual counterpart becomes blurred when people 'play at love' in this way. The authors emphasize in particular how people reconstruct their bodies online. Far from being absent, bodies are played with and presented in different ways as part of flirting online (see also Whitty, 2003).

Modern companies such as IBM see great potential in 'virtual worlds' such as Second Life for helping organizations to learn and innovate. Particularly in multinational corporations spanning the globe, virtual worlds enable people to interact without being physically co-present. Companies use virtual worlds for things like 'brainstorming', collaborative project work or staff training. People enter the virtual world using an 'avatar' to represent themselves. In some companies, play and fantasy are actively encouraged because it is thought to encourage innovative thinking. A male employee, for example, could choose to represent themselves as a woman, a frog or an asexual mythical creature. The normal identity-markers of hierarchical status can be inverted or dissolved in these virtual worlds. Employees might feel that they can communicate more freely, without inhibition, if they are unaware that the 'frog' they are talking to is the CEO. However, in other companies, such identity-markers might be more visible, with senior managers perhaps being given certain labels (such as their avatar being larger) to 'mark' their status. From a social constructionist perspective, it is not the essential properties of the technology that causes certain effects, such as an increase in innovation or collaboration, but the way they are interpreted, configured and used by people.

Van Gelder (1996) sees 'cyberspace' as an inherently egalitarian and liberating arena. Because visible aspects of your identity – such as your age, gender, appearance, disability and race – are not always visible to others, people are less likely to pre-judge you. Instead, they make judgements based solely on how you come across in what you write: your personality, charm, sense of humour and friendliness.

 ## Thinkpoint

Have you ever pretended to be something or someone you are not online? (This could include minor things like exaggerating an aspect of your identity, as well as major things like pretending to be someone else.)

When using SNSs like Facebook and Twitter in particular, do you engage in identity play of any kind, when you know that work colleagues are watching?

The Internet can be used by members of the same organization in radically different ways. Within the Royal Mail, for instance, it is used to post official documents and information about the postal service, but also by ordinary workers to 'blog' (write diary entries online) about their grievances. One such example is given in Case Point 7.2.

🗁 Case Point 7.2   Roy Mayall

A well-known workplace blogger is 'Roy Mayall', an anonymous postal worker who reports from 'inside' the Royal Mail UK's sorting office. His blog posts are simple anecdotes and insights into what working life is like, and 'Roy' is often critical of his employers. In response to recent moves by the UK government to privatize the Royal Mail, for instance, Roy writes:

(Continued)

(Continued)

> It's been a bad few weeks at our delivery office. First of all Vince Cable [British Minister] announced that the Royal Mail was going to be privatised. Then, at one of our weekly 'Work Time Listening and Learning' meetings, the line manager announced that our delivery office is going to close. We are going to have to move to the main sorting office in the next town, seven or eight miles away. He couldn't say when this was going to happen. All he could say was that 'plans are underway'. (Mayall, 2010a)

A few weeks later, Roy's diary notes:

> Unite, the trade union for Royal Mail managers, is balloting its members over the threat of compulsory redundancies. Up to 1,500 jobs are at risk. This was the subject of a great deal of hilarity in the smoking shed at work this morning.
>
> 'What would happen if Unite went on strike?', I asked.
>
> 'I'd laugh,' said Dennis. 'I'd come into work and I'd fuckin' laugh.'
>
> 'Let 'em,' said Les. 'I won't be going on strike for them, that's for sure. They came into work and broke our strike.'
>
> 'Yes,' said Jerry, 'they cheerfully took their bonuses and implemented all that shit. They can go whistle.'
>
> 'Compulsory redundancies?', said Dave. 'It's because there's too many of 'em, that's why. They're right to be shifting managers out. Sometimes there's half a dozen of 'em in there, wandering about doing sweet FA.'
>
> There's not a lot of sympathy for the managers. (Mayall, 2010b)

In the example of Roy Mayall, the Internet is used as a source of resistance against particular aspects of an organization. We can also imagine how it could be used as a form of control – for example, if Roy's managers were to discover his identity and sanction him for these posts. Many companies attempt to forbid employees writing about the organization on social media sites like Facebook and Twitter for fear of damaging the organization's identity and reputation (see Chapter 6). Figure 7.1 illustrates how companies use 'virtual control' to protect the organization's public identity. Research in 2009 suggested that 54 per cent of companies banned the use of Facebook and Twitter at work (Computerworld, 2009). However, as the case of Roy Mayall demonstrates, it is difficult to police. Moreover, such outlets can be useful to senior management if they draw attention to problems and issues that have been withheld from them by middle managers. In effect, people like Roy can act as valued internal whistleblowers.

Gossett and Kilker (2006) discuss the rise of 'counter-institutional' websites, noting that they are valuable in enabling workers to discuss issues that are normally discouraged in the workplace. The anonymity in which people post affords them a fearless position from which they may speak out. The authors examine and

Figure 7.1 Social media at work

analyze one such site, RadioShackSucks.com, in order to theorize about the ways these technologies grant a voice to those who would not otherwise be able to articulate certain issues: These examples show how virtual technologies enable us to control our identities, but can also be used to control us, in turn. Some criticisms around these approaches have emerged in recent years, and these are taken up in Chapter 8.

7.2.2 Face-to-Face Interactions and Identity

In Chapter 2, we discussed the ways in which a person's sense of identity is said to be influenced by our interactions with others and with society, for example (1) as we construct our sense of self in relation to dominant discourses, as Foucault suggests; (2) as we perform our self for others, as Goffman reminds us; and (3) through our membership of, and interaction with, different social groups, as theorized by SIT scholars. The idea is that we develop our sense of who we are through our interactions with the people around us. If this is the case, then what happens when these interactions are mediated by ICTs?

Authors studying virtual work and dislocated teams tend to argue that face-to-face contact is vital for building a sense of solidarity, interpersonal trust and meaningful relationships between people. There appears to be something unique about being physically present with another person, which is difficult to replicate in other media (Rudy, 1996). Exploring this aspect of social interaction, Hallowell (1999) argues that an 'authentic' psychological encounter between two people requires that they share the same physical space, as well as emotional and intellectual connections. Without these 'true human moments', as Hallowell terms them, the authentic encounters that form the building blocks of social life are thought to be disrupted.

For Musson and Cohen (1999), the kinds of 'mundane, everyday talk' that takes place when we encounter people informally around the workplace (such as in the office corridor or canteen) is fundamental in how people develop shared and meaningful perspectives on organizational life, for example their sense of identity at work: 'who am I' and 'how do I fit in here'? If we follow the importance of physical co-presence for the development of authentic relationships, then, for authors like Hallowell (1999) at least, workers who find themselves 'virtualized' can feel undervalued and out of touch. Perhaps, therefore, mediated relationships impact upon workplace identity in a way that hampers social bonds. Workers might not identify with the organization if they only interact with others virtually. Alternatively, they might identify in different ways: with those they feel a strong 'virtual' bond with, as opposed to people in their same department, or at the same hierarchical level, for instance. The identifications typical of an office-based environment (see Chapter 1, Figure 1.4) are likely to be very different in virtual work environments.

As a specific example of this, Gilmore and Warren's (2007) study of how tutors experienced online class interaction is very interesting. The authors discuss how student behaviours seemed to change in this new environment, in particular opportunities for shame were reduced, largely because elements that 'ground' these feelings in everyday life – the body, physical cues and other embodied aspects of face-to-face contact – were missing. Whereas, in a classroom, students may feel too shy or embarrassed to admit they do not understand something, for fear of losing 'face' (see Chapter 2, Section 2.5, on Goffman), online the sense of anonymity meant this did not happen. This tended to skew the normal ways in which feelings were managed and presented in a classroom setting. One outcome was that students appeared to feel more comfortable about 'speaking out'. This could possibly lead to better opportunities for learning in this case, because the students might feel more able to admit if they do not understand something they are being taught. In this article, Gilmore and Warren draw on psychoanalytic theories of emotion in order to conceptualize online identity in this way.

For some people, virtual interaction can feel more 'free' and people feel that they can express themselves more authentically, without the inhibition of worrying about what others might think about them. Some commentators therefore believe that virtual environments can help us to express our 'real selves' more than face-to-face situations. This could be seen as a good thing, where people feel able to 'be themselves'. But it can also lead to some negative things, especially when people do not feel the normal sense of inhibition and courtesy in face-to-face contact. For example, would you feel comfortable about making personal criticisms or racist remarks to someone face to face? Would you be more likely to do this by email or an SNS? The term flaming refers to the tendency for people to send more aggressive and insulting messages electronically than in face-to-face interaction. The Thinkpoint below invites you to reflect on how your own forms of expression might be altered by being 'anonymous'. Anonymity enables people to feel that their sense of identity – including their social status and reputation – will not be affected by what they say.

 **Thinkpoint**

Imagine that your course tutor has set up a virtual student discussion board through the Internet. What sort of things (about yourself or about the course) would you be likely to 'post' on the discussion board if you were allowed to post anonymously, compared with what you would post if your name was identified?

Some authors take the view that face-to-face and virtual interaction are not in opposition to one another. They argue that carefully designed ICTs can go a long way towards simulating face-to-face encounters. Studies of the impact of computer and Internet-mediated communication on interactions between people show that 'richer' media can be used to enable different social 'cues'. These cues can let a communication partner know more about the person contacting them, such as their race, gender and age (Rudy, 1996). They can also work to convey what people are 'really' feeling or thinking, through allowing people to hear voice inflections, or see facial expressions (Daft and Lengel, 1986). For example, even in basic text-only media, people often use symbols such as a 'smiley face' in SMS or email messages to give a 'cue' about the emotion they want to portray. Overall, the idea is that in the right context, with certain forms of technology, interactions between people need not suffer, and can be enhanced. For subscribers to this 'media richness' school of thought, the quality of communications and interactions depends on the richness of the medium and the reliability of the medium in question: Internet connections must not be erratic, for example. It must be noted that since these studies were completed, the richness of media has improved vastly, with technologies like Skype and online chat creating opportunities for richer interpersonal engagement online. Anonymity is therefore relatively rare in modern virtual interaction. Many standard laptops have built-in webcams nowadays, which has not always been the case. The opportunity for 'identity play' (see Case Point 7.1) may be limited. However, such technologies are not enabled everywhere, as the digital divide between richer and poorer areas worldwide has meant vast differences in the quality of information and communication technologies available to people (Castells, 2003).

In line with the discussion presented above, it appears important to resist taking a determinist stance on the impact of ICTs on social bonds and resulting identity work. For example, Castells discusses this topic, drawing on studies that link increased use of the Internet to a decline in people's interactions with other household members, a reduction in one's number of social acquaintances and increased feelings of isolation and depression (2003: 387). However, he argues, we must remember that these findings are based on certain studies and that, in fact, online interactions are complex and varied and so their outcomes are difficult to predict. One instance of such complexity involves the fact that new forms of negative social 'cues' have emerged with new ICTs. For some, email actually invites conflict in organizations, at times enabling disrespectful, insulting forms of communication, known as 'flaming', along with more manipulative behaviour (Markus, 1996). Email is seen as a forum upon which anger can escalate more easily, largely because the sender and the receiver appear somewhat depersonalized to each other. Markus notes that workers can often use ICTs such as email deliberately to avoid particular face-to-face interactions, to create a barrier between themselves and people with whom they had a problematic relationship, or simply dislike (ibid.: 494). The same 'media richness' that is lauded elsewhere can sometimes lead to negative interactions.

 ## Thinkpoint

List the relationships in your life that are largely mediated by ICTs of various kinds: phone, social networking sites, online messaging, blogs and email.

How do these media affect:

- The nature of your relationships with other people?
- The kind of identity you present to others?
- The kind of identification you have with other people or social groups?

In summary therefore, when considering the effects of ICTs on face-to-face inter-action, we cannot assume in advance that relationships will be strengthened or weakened depending on the richness of the media or some other technological attri-bute. Technology can be understood, experienced and used in a variety of ways in different contexts. What this demonstrates, alongside the above discussion on determinism and constructionism, is that ICT mediation has no predictable impact upon people's identities that can be 'read off' from the properties of the technology. All we can do is try to understand the many and complex ways in which this plays out, in different settings, with different technologies. The following sections explore some of these ways.

7.3 New Connections and Identity: Online Communities

If we depend on those around us for a sense of identity, as argued in Chapter 2, then new forms of media vastly increase the number of people 'around us'. A recent special issue of the academic journal *Organization Studies* focused on the phenomenon of online com-munities, drawing together insights from the first 20 years of these groups' existence. The editors note how the Internet has changed 'the scope, boundaries and dynamics of social … interactions' (Sproull et al., 2007: 278). Virtual identity is discussed in an article by Ross (2007), who shows how trainee London cabbies use an Internet discussion group to stay in contact with each other during training, and share experiences of studying for the gruelling 'Knowledge' examination which requires them to have a detailed knowledge of a six-mile (ten-kilometre) radius of the centre and 320 key routes. Interestingly, the online site provides something of a back-stage (drawing on the concepts of 'front-stage' and 'back-stage' developed by Goffman, see Chapter 2, Section 2.5), where cabbies can discuss the 'grey areas' of cab driving (see Case Point 7.3).

Case Point 7.3   Back-stage with the Knowledge Boys and Girls: Goffman and Distributed Agency in an Organic Online Community

Ross (2007) reports on an online community that emerged organically among trainee cab drivers. Members were studying for the Knowledge, an exam that prospective taxi drivers must pass before becoming qualified to run a cab around London. These trainee cabbies were known as, and called themselves, the 'Knowledge Boys and Girls'. On the message boards, trainees posted frank, informal and somewhat confessional accounts of their experiences as they trained for the exam, which enabled members to understand more about other trainees and to share their own situations. It also allowed for friend-ships to emerge, and helped trainees ready themselves for the upcoming test, which is famed for its difficulty and high-stress testing environment. The key here appeared to be

(Continued)

(Continued)

the pseudonyms that forum contributors adopted – they were allowed to remain anonymous and so felt that they could contribute honest and frankly without compromising their professional image.

To study this community, Ross analyzed the content of the online message boards, along with carrying out interviews with participants on this Internet forum. The study focused upon what benefits people felt that they gained by being part of such a community. Ross draws on Goffman's ideas (see Chapter 2) in order to conceptualize the online community as a safe, protected 'back-region' in which people did not have to feel that they were on show, and did not risk embarrassment. Where Goffman talks about how his crofters in the Scottish Highlands depend on such a back-region, Ross shows how cabbies retreat to their online space to confide, for example, about riding a motorcycle in the bus lane. The idea is, for Ross, that the 'online self' presented in such virtual communities helps people to deal with the offline world and its problems (see also Turkle, 1995).

Other studies show the importance of online communities for forming social ties around issues that are important to people, developing a sense of group identity (i.e. shared sense of 'who we are') and identification (i.e. sense of attachment and belonging), particularly where they find few people to talk with in their 'physical' location (Putnam, 2000). For example, the Internet offers opportunities for breast cancer sufferers to gather and share experiences (Lieberman and Goldstein, 2005). Maloney-Krichmar and Preece (2005) note that when online contributors engage in this kind of interaction, the off-topic, informal tangents that online chatting frequently takes allows people to disclose aspects of their private lives and build friendships. Ren et al. (2007) use ideas from social identity theory (see Chapter 2, Section 2.2) and bond theory to discuss how this plays out in online communities, and discuss the prevalence of new SNSs such as Facebook and Myspace. The idea is that a common identity can form around a shared problem (e.g. the identity of 'breast cancer sufferer'). The perception of a shared fate feeds into this identity, which originates from social categorization. In relation to this, Whitty (2002) reports on a study that aimed to examine how emotional support was made available to members in Internet chat rooms. She also wished to find out whether people tended to be more honest, or otherwise, in these online spaces. Over 300 people responded to her 'Chat Room Survey'. She finds that people who took part in chat rooms tended to be more open in relation to themselves and their thoughts, and enjoyed greater emotional support.

An interesting aspect of online identity involves the altruism involved in contributing to online projects. A classic example refers to the phenomenon of Internet hackers. Hackers often claim a strong sense of identity that revolves around the values of freedom, altruism (e.g. sharing secret codes among peers), dedication (e.g. dedicating most of your free time to hacking) and being 'anti-establishment'. To be a recognized member of the hacker community, this identity needs to be actively cultivated over a number of years, in order to develop one's reputation with other hackers. Despite popular opinion, hacking is not the prevail of privileged, Western technology workers alone. Hackers from Russia and Latin America have long been contributing. Nor is hacking always about breaking into institutional computer systems, known by the hacking community as 'cracking' (Castells, 2003). Hackers are a subgroup of individuals who contribute to open source (i.e. not tied to any one proprietary software) projects. Contributions are carefully peer reviewed, so each new line of code that is submitted is subject to the scrutiny of one's fellow hackers, even where contributors might never meet face to face.

As Castells notes, hackers 'do not depend on institutions for their intellectual existence, but they do depend on their self-defined community, built around computer networks' (2003: 47). This 'other' community is built around informal, virtual interaction, personal enjoyment and technological creativity and innovation. Traditionally, hacking is thought to have developed around twin ideologies: of freedom in technology, as with the 'free software' movement; and of freely giving (Castells, 2003). However, some authors have argued that hacking is as much about developing a reputation online, in order to enhance one's career and contribute to impressive projects, as it is about altruistic and invisible offers of help (Feller and Fitzgerald, 2002: 57). Similarly, recent research into why people contribute to the online consumer 'help' repositories, such as the reviews attached to particular products on Amazon, find that both self-oriented and other-orientated motives were cited (Peddibhotla and Subramani, 2007).

7.4 Virtual Identity, Power and Control

In Chapter 5, we saw how identity is often tied up with issues of power and control. In this section, we will explore the ways in which ICTs offer new ways in which people can be seen, monitored, evaluated, controlled and measured by management.

7.4.1 The electronic panopticon

The presence of surveillance in the workplace has long been a feature of organizations. Surveillance of the workforce was first made possible by the large-scale removal of work activities from the home into a centralized work 'place' 200 years ago. However, some argue that surveillance has been on the increase given the prevalence of new forms of ICT (Leigh Star and Strauss, 1999, with more detail in Ball and Wilson, 2000).

Zuboff (1988) draws inspiration from Foucault's concept of the panopticon (see Chapter 2, Section 2.4) to examine how technology is used to subject modern workers to constant electronic surveillance. Figure 7.2 shows one example of how technology can be used to subject employees to surveillance. For example, call centre workers can have their calls secretly 'tapped into' by managers, who listen into what they are saying to customers. Workers might also have their call speeds and durations logged and monitored by a computer, and the length of their toilet breaks measured (Sewell and Wilkinson, 1992). An extreme form of electronic surveillance is described in Wrigley's study of childcare workers, in which parents set up video cameras to capture the work of nannies, whom they suspected as not caring properly for their children (1995: 96–7).

In office settings, there is an increasing use of networked PCs that can log keystrokes, and Internet browsers that can keep track of the sites people visit. Zuboff (1988) coined the term anticipatory conformity to describe the process through which people internalize these control mechanisms and self-discipline their own

Figure 7.2 Surveillance at work

behaviour. Managers no longer have actually to control the worker – they do it for themselves thanks to the 'electronic panopticon'. For example, a call centre worker might religiously ensure they do not stray from the 'script' when talking to customers in case a manager could be listening to the call. They cannot 'be themselves' at work, they have to 'perform' as the person that management want them to be.

Poster (1996) uses the term superpanopticon to describe the impact of electronic databases on a person's identity. A 'superpanopticon', according to Poster, is one that controls the definition of a person's identity, over which the individual has little influence. Lyon (1994) argues that these 'digital selves' have considerable power to affect the 'real life' selves they represent:

> New individuals are created who bear the same names but who are digitally shorn of their human ambiguities and whose personalities are built artificially from matched data. Artificial they may be, but these computer 'selves' have a part to play in determining the life-chances of their human namesakes. Thus are subjects constituted and deviants defined within the Superpanopticon. (Lyon, 1994: 71)

An example of this involves the computerized files and records that a company holds about an employee, with records of their sickness absence, disciplinary offences and appraisal records. These files can be used to hire, fire, demote and promote that employee. Regardless of what the employee thinks they are or wants to be, this computerized identity is what holds the most power.

Ball (2005) presents a useful overview of the kinds of workplace surveillance techniques that have been used to gather and sort the 'data target'. She examines identity card schemes and the gathering of biometric data, and argues that this kind of monitoring encourages a perspective that, somehow, the bodily traits and traces captured by such technologies tell a 'truth' about an individual, reflecting Lyon's observations above. Such biometric surveillance systems then define 'the authentic person' according to the correct matching of data. People subjected to 'identity theft' can face a difficult time proving that they really are who they say they are.

In terms of a person's identity, such surveillance can trap them into a fixed categorization of identity, by which they will continue to be labelled. For Ball, much work needs to be done in examining the complex ways in which people can engage in bodily resistances to such techniques of surveillance. An interesting in-depth study of the effect of surveillance on a sense of identity relates to Barbara Ehrenreich's experiences in her book *Nickel and Dimed* (2001). Here she finds herself the target of a recruitment process drug test when she applies for a job at the retail corporation Walmart. She describes in detail how her sense of self is transposed onto the results of the test: how her representation and categorization in this data sheet comes to inform how she is perceived by the organization hiring her, Walmart, and herself. Tunnell's (2004) book *Pissing on Demand* begins by examining drug testing in the workplace and goes on to locate these processes in the wider erosion of civil liberties worldwide.

Typically, authors in organization studies (such as Zuboff, 1988, and Poster, 1996, above) have used Foucault's panopticon metaphor to show how this process generates internalized surveillance (Foucault, 1977). Control is 'internalized' because employees are always aware of the panopticon 'eye' watching over them, leading them continually to check their own compliance with the rules. However, Ball and Wilson (2000) critique this panopticon metaphor. They draw on in-depth data of employees subject to 'computer-based performance monitoring' practices at two UK financial services firms. The authors agree that surveillance technologies enable management to render workers 'visible, classified, marked, constituted as workers and drilled as such' (ibid.: 562). However, they argue that questions of power, control and resistance are played out in different ways, at different times and in different organizational settings. In other words, the use of surveillance technology cannot be generalized to a single, dystopic scenario. Furthermore, to assume that electronic technology 'necessarily' leads to surveillance is an example of determinist thinking discussed above. Electronic technology might well be used to control employees in some situations, but this arises from the economic relationships that underpin it (e.g. capitalist forms of work organization) rather than resulting from an essential, inherent feature of the technology itself. Hence, the technology does not determine its use: it could be used in more liberating and emancipatory ways in a different situation. Employees could use the company intranet to organize resistance to corporate control measures, as we saw above with Roy Mayall (Case Point 7.2), or develop support networks for bullied colleagues, for instance.

Reporting on a study of new ICT systems that were implemented as part of a business process re-engineering (BPR) effort, Knights and McCabe (1998) agree with the argument made by Ball and Wilson (2000). They challenge the view that ICT-mediated surveillance traps workers into a continuous state of observation and categorization by their managers. While the technology in the Knights and McCabe study did indeed have the capability of monitoring how many BPR-designed tasks are performed, and how long it takes to perform each of these, this did not necessarily mean that management had 'total control' over the workforce. New technologies bring with them new spaces of resistance, which can be used to subvert surveillance. In the context of workplace identity, it seems that ICT has the power to observe, monitor and categorize employees, but that similarly complex and interrelated resistances emerge.

7.4.2 Maintaining a coherent organizational identity

Power is not a one-way street. Technologies are not just used to control workers: workers themselves can use technologies to exert their own influence, and perhaps even generate the momentum for social transformation. Technologies are opening up new ways for organizational identities to be publicly exposed, deconstructed and criticized.

For many organizations, their public face is vital for maintaining their image, brand and reputation. In Chapter 6, we see how particular organizations work hard at what Goffman calls 'impression management' (see Chapter 2, Section 2.5). In recent years, we have seen the Internet offer a plethora of critiques of large organizations, eroding the public identity that such firms have been so careful to build. The example of Roy Mayall's blog described above (see Case Point 7.2) shows the space for virtual resistance and dissent by employees, although, as we also noted, the public nature of this blog makes it accessible, and potentially useful, to management.

Organizations as well as individuals, including managers, are using the Internet to challenge, criticize and rebut organizational identity claims. Sites such as Indymedia and the Centre for Media and Democracy keep a careful eye on corporations' activities (for more information, see http://www.criticalmanagement.org). Since 2000, for example, the Internet has been used by activist group the Yes Men to erode the identity of the World Trade Organization (WTO) and other organizations that the group deem unethical and problematic (Kenny, 2009a). In 1999, two members of the group set up their own website, which looked very similar to the WTO's. They obtained the domain name gatt.org to further the similarity to wto.org. The text of the new website was quite different, however, presenting a sharp attack on the practices of the WTO, including putting trade ahead of basic human rights such as access to drinking water, health care and so on.

Interestingly, the activists began to receive emails from people who had mistaken their prank site for the original. Eventually, one of those emails contained an invitation for a WTO representative to speak at an international conference of textile manufacturers in Finland. Pretending they were from the WTO, the Yes Men accepted. A series of pranks followed, one of which involved the Yes Men unveiling a new, gold-covered, 'manager outfit' that featured a three-foot long phallus equipped with a television monitor at the tip. The idea, the Yes Men explained to the conference audience, is to enable the effective management of an offshore workforce, through the comfortable outfit. The outfit also contained a device for administering electric shocks to a disobedient workforce. The point of the prank was, of course, to highlight the inequities in the global textile market, in front of an international audience of executives from this industry. In this way, the Yes Men's pranks are always political, including a TV appearance where one member pretending to be from Union Carbide apologized on BBC TV for the Bhopal disaster, promising reparations on behalf of 'his' company.

Since they began, the Yes Men and similar groups have gone 'viral', their reputations spreading across a variety of media and reaching audiences of millions. The Yes Men have used the Internet and related technologies to great effect: to manufacture their parodies, to attract new members by inviting people to engage in the kinds of 'identity corrections' they carry out, and to spread the word about their activities (Kenny, 2009a). This example shows how organizational identities can be put into jeopardy by the easy access, low cost and free availability of the Internet. This is enhanced by the growing number of cheap and easy-to-use technologies for recording sound and video.

7.5 Teleworking and Identity

In the 1980s, there was much focus on the changes in the ways organizations were being run, and how ICTs facilitated this. Changes included teleworking, BPR, flexible firms and virtual teams. Here, we focus on the example of teleworking. Teleworking is a very general term that is used to refer to many different sorts of changes in work using ICTs, including working from home and working while 'mobile' or 'on the road'. Some people also include things like virtual teams and call centres in their definition, because they also involve using ICT rather than face-to-face communications with colleagues or customers.

Teleworking is increasingly important to study because of its prominence in debates on work. For example, as part of their UK On-line project (formerly the Information Society Initiative), the UK government encouraged more organizations to telework, emphasizing the benefits for the employee as well as the organization, and the overall competitiveness of the UK economy (Department of Trade and Industry, 2000). Telework has been heralded as the solution to a wide range of individual, organizational and societal problems, such as the problem of work-life balance (by enabling people to reduce wasted commuting time by working from home), the problem of recruitment and retention (by recruiting talent from further afield and enabling mothers to continue working after having children), the problem of rising real estate costs (by reducing the amount of office space required) and even the problem of global warming (by reducing the carbon emissions from commuters). A social constructionist perspective would be sceptical of such grand claims about the 'impact' of ICTs, pointing instead to the fact that what teleworking does depends on who sets it up, and for what purposes.

There has been considerable interest and excitement about the potential of telework from governments and organizations around the world. In 1994, the European Union set the ambitious target of 10 million teleworkers throughout the region by the year 2000 (Qvortrup, 1998). Interestingly, the seismic 'boom' in teleworking that was expected has not so far happened – by 2005, the average proportion of workers teleworking across the EU had increased to only 7 per cent from the level of 5 per cent in 2000 (Weiz and Wolf, 2010). Teleworking continues to be an important part of workplace structures, however. It is better to think of teleworking not as a unique and different style of working, but as part of a more general trend towards using ICT in the workplace. For example, many employees would not be classified as 'teleworkers', but might regularly use ICTs such as mobile phones, email, the Internet, an internal company intranet and/or virtual collaboration software (such as Lotus Notes, for example) to communicate with colleagues and customers. In this section, we examine these new forms of working to consider in more depth some of the questions arising around the area of virtual identity.

7.5.1 Teleworking, isolation and identification

At a time when ICTs were first being used to enable employees to work remotely, Olson and Primps (1984) interviewed employees across 20 teleworking organizations and found that people who engaged in teleworking often perceived that it might hamper their promotion prospects. Research to date is inconclusive about whether or not this is actually the case, but, nonetheless, Olson and Primp's respondents seemed to feel that it was, and reported a willingness to 'trade off' career prospects for a greater sense of freedom. This fear can relate to prospects internally in the organization, or externally, in the wider career market. In identity terms, it seems that teleworkers faced the dilemma of choosing between their attachment to their career and their attachment to their home life, such as family or community activities.

Several studies have suggested that teleworking can have negative effects on internal promotion (Bertin and Denbigh, 2000; Fireman, 1998; Johnson, 1998). Mirchandani (1998) draws on qualitative research to show this. As one interviewee reported:

> if you are actively seeking a promotion or you're looking for a new direction, the home is not the place to be ... (at work) they are seeing you every day and you're socializing and you're talking and you're on their mind when it comes to promotions.
> (Mirchandani, 1998: 67)

It is important to bear in mind that nowadays these concerns may be less relevant, because teleworking is far more widespread and accepted, in some industries at least, and managers are more used to managing a 'virtual' workforce.

From a social constructionist perspective, whether teleworking helps or hinders career prospects is not an outcome of the properties of the technology per se. Rather, it depends on a range of social, economic and political factors, such as who is teleworking (e.g. is it only senior managers who are allowed?), how they are teleworking (e.g. are they communicating with colleagues frequently or infrequently, in structured or unstructured ways?), and why they are teleworking (e.g. is it to reduce office-space costs or to give employees better work-life balance?).

Nonetheless, the perception that teleworking hampers career prospects is of interest in the context of workplace identity. Employees have certainly reported feeling like they are not seen as 'one of us' in the same way as office-based employees. In other words, teleworking is thought to influence how employees identify with the organization. This outcome is not determined by the use of technology, though. In some cases, employees could feel a strong sense of belonging and attachment to their organization and their colleagues in work even though they work 'at a distance'. For example, Noronha and D'Cruz's (2008) study of female home-based medical transcriptionists based in Bangalore, India, found that lack of physical proximity to colleagues did not stop them feeling like a coherent group and acting like a collective, for example when facing disputes with their employer.

7.5.2 Teleworking and impression management

As permanent employment becomes rarer nowadays, insecurity is said to plague modern workers. A 'human capital' approach to career (Nicholson, 1996), is said to offer a way of combating increasing job insecurity. This increasingly common approach (Boltanski and Chiapello, 2006) sees people perceiving themselves as managers of a project-style career (Grey, 1994). This management partly involves keeping up with contacts in one's network, and presenting a 'front' that shows the person as competent and professional.

Literature on impression management (IM) discusses the ways this occurs: how people attempt to construct their social identity and monitor their own behaviour to ensure that they are perceived as they feel they ought to be. This relates to our discussion of Goffman's presentation of self, discussed in Chapter 2. Grey (1994) shows how accounting trainees begin this process from early on in their school lives: taking on particular out-of-school activities, like sports and perhaps volunteering, partly because they know that these will 'look good' on the CV. IM continues into working careers, with the accountants that Grey studies ensuring that they choose presentable spouses and carry out the 'right' after-work activities, like golf.

In the case of teleworkers, performance appraisals are an important site for 'virtual' impression management. As Grint (1995a) notes, performance appraisals are increasingly popular as means by which prospective employees can be assessed by firms. For Riordan et al. (1994), the display of appropriate behaviours is one of the most important ways in which people gain the approval necessary to 'get ahead' in an organization. According to Galpin and Sims (1999), this is often achieved through story-telling and narrative creation. They argue that for teleworkers, this kind of construction of social identity, or impression work, is particularly pertinent. Because they are physically absent, teleworkers often depend on the kinds of 'objective' performance appraisals discussed above, rather than more informal ways of presenting self. It is important for teleworkers to be sending out particular signals to their bosses: to engage in IM. Their 'virtual' status means that they must work hard at presenting favourable impressions, to ensure their careers are not disadvantaged.

7.5.3 Teleworking, identity and organizational control

Interestingly, in light of issues of organizational control highlighted in Chapter 5, a key theme in telework research is a presumed lack of attachment, identification and commitment to the organization (Depickere, 1999; Forseback, 1995). As Stanworth and Stanworth have found, this can be a problem for organizations, where isolation leads to a 'failure' on behalf of the employee to 'internalize attitudes, values and behaviour, which are often absorbed through informal messages at work' (1991: 28). If we take a critical approach to organizational culture efforts, it could be argued that teleworking and similar forms of virtual presence in working lives might in certain cases lessen such forms of control. This may have implications for managerial identity. For example, how can managers establish their sense of being 'in control' when they cannot physically see their workers? Presence and visibility are the traditional methods of organizational control; both are absent when workers telework.

However, in some organizations, telework could heighten and intensify control over employees. For example, if employees are given the responsibility and autonomy of being able to work from home or 'on the road' using ICTs, without the usual 'watchful eye' of their boss, this could heighten employees' sense of duty, obligation and commitment to the organization. Sending emails late at night or at weekends could be a deliberate IM (see discussion of Goffman in Chapter 2, Section 2.5) tactic to create the impression of a dedicated employee, for example.

Taskin and Edwards' (2007) study of teleworkers in a Belgian public sector agency found exactly that. Workers engaged in 'self-discipline' (see discussion of Foucault in Chapter 2, Section 2.4) by constantly striving to show others how hard they were working, and how available and committed they were. For example, staff tended to send more electronic messages than their office-based counterparts, and answer emails more quickly, in order to appear more 'visible'. Being 'trusted' to work from home meant that workers felt they had to repay that trust. Taskin and Edwards view this as a form of identity regulation, where trust 'acts as a socio-ideological form of control, as a norm internalised by employees to the point of regulating their identity' (2007: 203). Alternatively, in organizations with low levels of trust in their workforce, new forms of 'electronic surveillance' (see Section 7.5 above) could be used instead, such as records of the time that an employee logged into their computer, or logs of the web pages they have viewed.

Call centres are a form of 'telework' in the sense that the employee is communicating remotely with the customer, sometimes located thousands of miles away. A customer of a bank, for instance, calling from the United States may be unaware that their call is being routed to somewhere in Asia. The call centre worker may be based in a large office or might be based at home, but their main method of communicating is ICT.

D'Cruz and Noronha's (2006) study of Indian call centre workers found very similar patterns of identification and control as Taskin and Edwards (2007) mentioned above. They also found that management used forms of 'socio-ideational' control, where they attempted to control the 'values, ideas, beliefs, emotions, and identification of employees' (D'Cruz and Noronha, 2006:343). In their case, the company used the idea of 'professionalism' to define what the organization deemed to be appropriate attitudes and behaviour, such as always being polite to customers and never losing their temper when customers are rude or insulting. Employees developed an intense sense of identification with these socio-ideational norms, leading them to internalize the expectations of the company, becoming 'company men' and 'company women'. For example, one employee accidentally broke one of the company rules, by forgetting to leave his mobile phone in his locker. When his friend and co-worker saw the phone, he insisted that he should hand it in and pay the fine for his transgression, telling him: 'Friendship outside, be professional inside' (D'Cruz and Noronha, 2006: 347). Socio-ideational control works by getting employees to override any other identities and identifications, such as 'I am your friend', with their identification for the company.

Mirchandani (2004) studied call centre workers in New Delhi, India, who provided services for customers in North America. She found that the workers were being asked to perform a completely different identity when they were on the phone to customers. The workers were taught how to change their accents to sound more 'American', they were given false names that would sound more 'Western' and encouraged to watch US TV shows to pick up the latest news and gossip as well as the accent, perhaps to help them develop 'trust' and 'rapport' with the customers. The workers had to 'shed' their normal identity when they got to work each day, to put on a different 'mask' and pretend to be someone they were not. Mirchandani (2004) links this process of 'hiding' the identity of the workers to what she calls 'location masking' – the process of trying to hide where the workers are located to better 'match' the nationality of the customer. Location masking can be seen as an extreme form of organizational control over identity: employees are literally made to change their identity for the benefit of the organization. Figure 7.3 shows an example of a 'fake' virtual identity. Forms of 'electronic surveillance', such as managers secretly listening into calls (as we

Figure 7.3 Call centres and fake identities

discussed above in Section 7.5), are typically used to ensure workers are presenting the 'correct' identity to customers.

7.5.4 Diversity in teleworking identities and experiences

What causes the effects we have described on teleworkers and their identities? A technological determinist perspective (see Section 7.2 above) would argue that the technology used in teleworking arrangements (e.g. Internet, email, telephone) causes certain predictable effects on the workforce. In contrast, a social constructionist perspective would argue that the effects of teleworking depend on the social, economic and political context in which the technology is used. This context includes the type of division of labour and organization of work. The experience that workers have of teleworking depends on the broader organizational and economic context that shapes how their work is organized. The study by Galpin and Sims (1999) (see Case Point 7.4) shows how the same kinds of technology (such as Internet-based communication) led to very different identities for 'operatives' who had tightly controlled and low-skilled tasks, compared with 'knowledge workers' who had more autonomy and highly skilled jobs.

> #### Case Point 7.4 Teleworking Operatives and Knowledge Workers
>
> Galpin and Sims (1999) used a narrative approach (see Chapter 2, Section 2.6) to study the identities of two different types of teleworkers – home-based workers who predominantly used technology to communicate. The first group are labelled 'operatives', who tend to have a carefully controlled work process and highly formalized interactions, with little opportunities for unstructured story-telling. For example, home-based call centre operatives typically have a strict numbers of calls they must complete every day and a 'script' they are expected to follow with customers. The second group are labelled 'knowledge workers', who tend to have more control and autonomy over their work process and more opportunities for telling stories about themselves and their experiences to colleagues, managers and clients.
>
> *(Continued)*

(Continued)

Galpin and Sims (1999) argue that the lack of opportunity to hear (and participate in) narratives in and about their organization meant that 'operatives' were unable to construct a meaningful identity at work. For example, they were cut off from the usual office stories and gossip through which people establish a sense of 'bond' or identification with their work group or organization. Operatives often report feeling more like extensions of the machines they work with, such as computer terminals and telephone headsets, than people with thoughts, feelings and ideas. They also fail to feel a sense of attachment to the organizations they work for. The situation for 'knowledge workers' was very different. They had many opportunities to tell and share stories with clients and colleagues. The 'virtual project teams' they were part of also gave them an opportunity to play out their identity as a 'facilitator', 'communicator' or 'problem-solver', for example.

7.6 Conclusion

Virtual identity is not a new phenomenon. For hundreds of years, people have been sending letters: that is, presenting their identity without being physically co-present. Certain jobs have always been done from home (e.g. child minding) or 'on the road' (e.g. taxi drivers), despite the recent 'hype' about telework. However, new information and communication technologies have made virtual communication a more pervasive feature of modern working life. What is new is the way in which these virtual interactions form part and parcel of not only what we do at work, but also who we are.

In this chapter, we presented an overview of the many ways in which our working lives are increasingly mediated by ICTs, and explored the impact of this on the worker's sense of identity. While much hype has surrounded the 'information revolution' in recent years, implying a seismic shift in societal relations as a result, the picture that emerges is complex. On the one hand, it appears that ICTs open up new and exciting ways for us to engage in identity work; ideas of 'postmodern identity play' on the Internet invite us to think about ways in which new identities can be formulated and acted out for others whom we might never meet. The brave new world of ICT-enabled teleworking promises to open up the world of work, such that we are not restricted to types of employment that require us to be physically present. Online communities such as those relating to our professions, or problems we might be experiencing, or our passions and hobbies, enable us to develop aspects of our identity that we might find difficult to share or explore in an offline world.

However, adopting a social constructionist approach, in place of a determinist one, means that we must appreciate how our involvement in, and interpretation of, specific political, social and cultural contexts shape how we are affected by technologies. Our relationship to technology is shifting and ambivalent. Just as ICTs enable people to be 'trusted' to work away from the office, they may simultaneously enable systems of surveillance that are experienced as oppressive and intrusive. For example, the opportunity afforded by ICTs for 'playing' with our identity has been criticized for its exploitation of call centre workers who are pressured to adopt a 'fake' identity. For these reasons, it is important to be cautious about sweeping generalizations about the positive (or negative) 'impact' of ICTs, and instead to explore how and why certain technologies are used in particular ways, and for what ends.

Suggested Reading

Benwell, B. and Stockoe, L. (2006) *Discourse and Identity*. Edinburgh: Edinburgh University Press. Ch. 7.

MacKenzie, D. and Wajcman, J. (eds) (1999) *Introductory Essay in the Social Shaping of Technology* (2nd edn). Buckingham: Open University Press. Part Two.

Turkle, S. (1995) *Life on the Screen: Identity in the Age of the Internet*. New York: Simon & Schuster.

Whitty, M.T. and Joinson, A.N. (2009) *Truth, Lies and Trust on the Internet*. New York: Routledge/Taylor & Francis.

Woolgar, S. (ed.) (2002) *Virtual Society? Technology, Cyberbole, Reality*. Oxford: Oxford University Press.

Sample Exam/Assignment Questions

- Compare and contrast the technological determinist and social constructionist perspectives on the relationship between virtuality and work-based identity.
- Critically evaluate the idea that virtual interaction leads to new forms of postmodern 'identity play'. To what extent is 'identity play' possible or desirable in contemporary organizations?
- Discuss and debate the identity issues that might arise from being a teleworker.

The Future of Identity   8

[A]s we move from modernity into the great unknown that lies ahead, old prisons and old chimeras are losing their grip. Old forms of entrapment and suffering do not appear so threatening any more, but ambivalence, confusion and anxiety become associated with new, different forms of entrapment for which the glass cage offers a fair evocation. New forms of consolation also appear – new breads, new circuses and new opiates, bringing with them hopes, anxieties and confusions of their own. (Gabriel, 2005: 25)

8.1 Introduction

In this concluding chapter, we explore what the future might hold for identity and organizations. We focus on different aspects of how modern management practices are implicated in shaping the identities of the modern workforce. The chapter is divided into five parts.

First, we consider the trend, particularly in the 'core' workforce of large organizations, towards strengthening the attachment of workers to the firm. We refer to this as creating more 'totalizing' workplaces where everything the worker is and does is through the company. Second, we explore the opposing trend, particularly among those who are deemed 'peripheral' to the core activities of the firm, towards a weakening of attachments and identification, where workers are increasingly employed in 'flexible' ways, such as temporary contracts and subcontracting.

In the third section, we discuss recent trends towards new forms of public management, particularly a trend towards making public bureaucracies more 'responsive' and 'innovative'. Fourth, we describe some of the changes and challenges that are likely to arise as organizations become more 'global' in their scale and also more 'virtual' as communications and interactions are increasingly mediated by new technology. Fifth, and finally, we discuss how diversity is being understood and acted upon, at a time when organizations are employing an increasingly diverse workforce and facing a more diverse customer base.

8.2 Strong Attachments and Totalizing Workplaces?

As we discussed in Chapter 5, many organizations rely heavily on employees developing a stronger and more positive sense of identification with the organization as a means of engendering trust, 'buy-in' and commitment to the organization. It is believed that employees are more likely to 'go the extra mile' (known as 'discretionary effort') if they have a keen sense of attachment to the firm and, hence, share the norms and values advocated by their employer. However, opinion is somewhat mixed about what will happen to organizational identification in the future. In this section, we consider the argument that there will be increasing levels of attachment, particularly in the case of workers in high-pressure, high-status jobs who more readily gain a sense of purpose and pleasure from meeting the challenges that are accompanied by such pressures. Then, in the next section, we discuss the arguments that anticipate decreasing levels of attachment for other staff, particularly those who work at the 'periphery' of work organizations, who are employed on a casual or part-time basis. Our view is that these arguments are consistent insofar as they reflect and reinforce the existence, and further development, of a divided workforce. For an elite, the future holds out the prospect of intensifying work pressures compensated by comparatively high earnings and job security. For the mass of workers, whose skills are more readily acquired and are therefore more easily replaced, the prospect is for increased 'casualization' of work, especially in the form of, for example, agency work involving short-term, temporary contracts.

Some commentators have suggested that 'individuals' desire for some kind of work-based identification is likely to increase' (Ashforth et al., 2008: 326) as other affiliations (e.g. to community, family and so on) become more fractured, tenuous and less reliable as a consequence of social and geographical mobility. For example, if a person has very few strong emotional ties to their family, community and/or religion, it is expected that they are more likely to view their job as an important part of 'who I am'. Conversely, if there are few opportunities to develop ties, or identifications, with the workplace, it follows either that people will become more 'anomic' (rootless) and find their lives increasingly meaningless, or that they will find purpose and meaning elsewhere, and therefore leave their current employment (e.g. 'downshift') or endeavour to build a life outside of work in community, family, politics and so on.

Strong attachments are thought to be fostered by certain changes in (1) the nature and meaning of work and (2) the nature of the workplace. We will look at these two aspects in turn.

8.2.1 The nature and meaning of work

Work is increasingly becoming identity defining, at least for certain, mainly 'elite' types of workers. For those in high-status jobs in particular (such as lawyers, accountants, senior managers, etc.), work is often the most important aspect of 'who I am'. It could be the first thing that a person mentions when someone asks the question 'who are you?' In some industries and occupations in particular, work is typically given the highest priority in organizing the person's life. Meriläinen et al. (2004: 552) found an unquestioning commitment to the ideal of 'long hours, essential mobility and selfless devotion to the organization' among the management consultants that they studied. Instead of 'working in order to live', and deriving their sense of identity primarily from family, community, leisure, and so on, such employees 'live to work'. Even when they are not physically at work, they are thinking about it and all other activity becomes secondary. For the firm, this type of obsessive and addictive dedication to (and sacrifice for) the firm is often seen as a sign of commitment to be rewarded with promotion (ibid.: 553).

 Thinkpoint

Would you agree (or disagree) that the following are on the increase?

- Suicide among workers who lose their jobs, unable to live with the idea of not being 'somebody'.

- Workers (men as well as women) who delay starting a family in order to establish their careers.

- The number of workers who uproot their whole families in order to move where their company requires them, not because there is little alternative (e.g. relocate or be made redundant) but because the move is key to career.

- Workers who voluntarily take jobs which require them to spend long periods of time away from their families, resulting in relationship breakdown.

- Workers who let hobbies, passions, community activities and friendships suffer as a result of 'putting work first'.

- Do you agree that these forms of attachments to work are on the increase? If so, what social, economic and political consequences might result from this?

Given that for many people work is increasingly viewed as highly important, not simply as a means of earning a living wage but as an identity-defining aspect of a person's life, it is perhaps no surprise that some observers have questioned the sanity and morality of this trend. Popular culture is full of books giving advice to people on how to achieve a better 'balance' between their work and home life. Women in particular are being targeted for advice on how to balance or 'juggle' work-life and home-life, given that they continue to be identified as (and also identify with the role of) 'homemaker' and 'carer'. 'Being a worker' and 'being a wife/mother' are often viewed as a tension that women have to trade off. For example, Hewlett (2002) advises women either to have children in their twenties or thirties and sacrifice having a career, or to sacrifice having a family altogether to focus on having a career.

This kind of pop-culture prescription gets to the heart of what workers identify with most (e.g. being a parent/partner or being a worker) as well as what subject positions are made available to, or pressed upon, people in certain societies (e.g. what being a 'good worker' or a 'good father' means). The latter means that certain identity discourses have a normalizing effect (see discussion of Foucault in Chapter 2, Section 2.4), as they act to shape 'who and what is "normal", standard and acceptable' (Meriläinen et al., 2004: 544). Meriläinen et al. (2004) found that the discourse in the UK of 'work-life balance' meant that workers talked about themselves as having actively to 'choose' not to work long hours because the 'normal', default option was 'presenteeism' (i.e. the idea that long hours in the office is a sign of commitment). Those who diverted from the 'norm' of long working hours were seen as 'resisting' and even as subverting the dominant ideal of what work should be like. In Finland, by way of contrast, the discourse of the 'balanced individual' meant that workers (both men and women) could talk about themselves as having a duty to both their work and their home-life. That shared and agreed sense of duty made it not only 'normal' but responsible to leave work early to collect children from school, for instance. What this study by Meriläinen et al. (2004) shows us is that the types of discourses about work available in different contexts are crucial for shaping our sense of 'who (or what) I am' and 'who (or what) I should be'.

8.2.2 The nature of the workplace: total institutions?

Workplaces are also changing. Work is encroaching on more and more aspects of worker's 'private' spaces as a result of technological devices like Blackberries (see Section 8.5 below). And the workplace itself is changing. Large, prestigious, 'progressive', high-tech, multinational firms compete to attract and retain (ideally 24/7) elite staff by offering much more than simply a place to work. Such firms are increasingly equipped with facilities such as a gym, bars, restaurants, crèche, library, and socializing spaces. Day trips, activities and events are often organized for workers to get together in evenings and weekends. Counsellors or 'life coaches' may be made available to support workers through difficult life events. Some offices even come with hotel-style rooms and apartments, so that employees never physically have to leave. Workers are encouraged to see their work not merely as a source of income (well paid as it is), but also as an enviable 'lifestyle' – encompassing their whole life and whole sense of self. Of course, these firms are the exception but they are symptomatic of how, at the extreme, the workplace is colonizing domestic and communal spaces. They are also seen by aspirant firms seeking to recruit elite employees as a model to emulate. In such firms, the employee is invited to adopt the life of an exotic caged animal, psychologically as well as physically. There is no 'need' to have any other life because everything is, apparently, provided. It is the contemporary equivalent of the model factory and village, such as Saltaire or Bournville, built by industrial philanthropists where, in addition to the workplace, there were houses, shops, a school, recreation facilities and churches for workers and their families (see Chapter 5, Section 5.4.2). But, there again, maybe that 'caged animal' is pleased to have everything provided, and never gives a thought to what lies beyond the world of the cage? As Gabriel has observed:

> In place of the controls that were associated with the modern bureaucracy … today's organizations resort to far subtler, yet deeper, controls, controls that are pervasive and invasive, that do not merely constrain a person but define a person. These include cultural and ideological controls … affirming the business enterprise as an arena for heroic or spiritual accomplishments, structural controls (continuous measurements and benchmarking, flatter organizational hierarchies), technological controls (electronic surveillance of unimaginable sophistication) and spatial controls (open-plan offices, controlled access). (2005: 17, emphasis added)

Take, for example, the following list of some of the additional 'perks' and benefits that Google offers its employees:

Food

Hungry? Check out our free lunch and dinner – our gourmet chefs create a wide variety of healthy and delicious meals every day. Got the munchies? Google also offers snacks to help satisfy you in between meals.

On-site doctor

At Google headquarters in Mountain View, California you have the convenience of seeing a doctor on-site. Physical therapy and chiropractic services are also available.

Shuttle service

Google is pleased to provide its Mountain View employees with free shuttles to several San Francisco, East Bay and South Bay locations.

Financial planning classes

Google provides objective and conflict-free financial education classes. The courses are comprehensive and cover a variety of financial topics.

Other on-site services

At Google headquarters in Mountain View, you'll find on-site oil change and car wash services, dry cleaning, massage therapy, gym, hair stylist, fitness classes and bike repair.

Other great benefits

Halloween & holiday party, health fair, credit union, roller hockey, outdoor volleyball court, discounts for products and local attractions.

Source: http://www.google.com/intl/en/jobs/lifeatgoogle/benefits/

Companies that offer a whole 'lifestyle' rather than just a job can, or course, be interpreted (or constructed) in different ways. They may be viewed as 'progressive' and 'caring' because they pay close attention to the needs of their employees. A more critical interpretation is that such 'care' is highly instrumental. Such firms contrive to create totalizing workplaces where, in principle, they can exercise control over the whole person – when they are 'at rest' and 'at play' as well as when they are 'at work'. Indeed, ideally, such distinctions become meaningless as work is expected to be playful and opportunities to play are intended to enhance the capacity to work. The strength of the physical, relational and emotional connection between the workers and the company thereby acts as a form of control in the guise of 'best practice' and care. The presumption is that workers are more likely to be loyal and committed if a strong attachment to the firm can be developed or engineered.

Those who advocate the creation and development of such 'progressive' workplaces rightly point out that no one is forced to work in them. The benefits that they provide are undoubtedly valued by many of their employees, and these benefits are key to recruiting and retaining the best qualified/motivated/malleable staff. Doubtless, you would be less likely to leave a firm if it meant saying goodbye to many, perhaps all, of your friends, the social activities in which you have participated and your sources of support. And while you remain employed, you are probably less likely to question or resist the culture and power relations of the firm, especially if you sense that you are being 'watched' or at least 'managed' 24/7. At an extreme level, when you go to the gym after work, your boss could be there, taking a close interest in the level of effort you are putting in or the videos you are choosing to watch.

8.2.3 The nature of the workplace: can work be fun?

Another trend that has been noticed in recent years involves companies starting to encourage employees to have 'fun' at work. Bolton and Houlihan (2009) argue that increasing numbers of companies, such as Google, Ben & Jerry's (ice cream) and Innocent (drinks and 'smoothies'), design 'packaged fun' for their employees in order to try to 'tap into' the potential of play and laughter for increasing employee motivation, creativity, commitment and retention. Put simply, staff who find their work (or at least elements of it) 'fun' are thought to be more likely to work hard and stay loyal to the company (see Fleming, 2005).

Think about the following types of activities:

- Corporate activity days like paintballing or watersports.
- Company pantomime performances where senior managers don silly costumes and make fun of themselves.
- Parties at Christmas, or any other religious festival, where comedy awards for 'best-dressed employee' are given out.

These are all examples of the kind of 'packaged fun' that some companies believe will make their workforce more satisfied and motivated in their jobs. According to Bolton and Houlihan (2009: 564), packaged fun is designed to foster 'an "us" identity and unitarist identification with the organisation', just like corporate culture management attempted to do before (see Chapter 5, Section 5.3).

 Thinkpoint

Do you think that 'having fun' at work amounts to extra work? Or a form of reprieve or respite from the demands of work?

Think about an organization that you have worked for, or that you are familiar with, in which employees are encouraged or required to 'have fun'. To what extent is this demand seen as a form of pleasure or stress?

The idea behind 'fun' activities is that employees are encouraged to 'be themselves' and express their unique differences, their 'authentic self' at work. Some people view this as a liberal and free-thinking philosophy, where employees are valued as individuals and diversity is encouraged. Fleming and Sturdy (2009), however, view the idea of just 'being yourself' as a way of subtly controlling employees, what they call 'neo-normative control' (ibid.: 570). In the Australian call centre they studied (see also Case Point 3.3 in Chapter 3), employees were encouraged to express their personalities in their style of dress, and were allowed to dye their hair any colour they liked, and have piercings or tattoos. 'Fancy dress' and 'pyjama' days were organized, the office walls were covered in fun cartoon strips, and staff were allowed to play mini-golf at work. Company away days often involved satirical plays and musical performances, along with lots of drinking, sexual banter and flirting.

Fleming and Sturdy (2009) argue that encouraging fun and self-expression enables the company to draw more of the person into its remit of control, including the very personal aspects of ourselves such as our character, temperament and sense of humour. Management encouraged employees to use their uniqueness to benefit the company, not because of any moral concern for the psychological well-being of the employee. Any problems, such as a telesales worker failing to sell enough to meet their targets, can also be placed squarely on the shoulders of the individual, which in turn encourages individualization (placing responsibility onto individuals) and self-discipline (expecting employees to discipline themselves, rather than being disciplined by a manager). Employees could be told that they failed to meet their targets either because they are the wrong type of person for the job (and therefore they should leave), or because they have failed to 'be themselves', for instance by 'winning over' customers with their wit, enthusiasm and personality (and therefore they should be more self-disciplined). Unsurprisingly, some employees felt alienated by the culture of fun and freedom of expression at the call centre studied by Fleming and Sturdy. They did not want to drink alcohol and flirt, at least not with their work colleagues; or they felt pressured to wear the latest designer fashions; or they just thought that the ethos of the company was too childish. Employees were only encouraged to 'be yourself' if their 'self' fitted with the type of person the company wanted: fun, sexy, stylish and charismatic.

8.3 Weak Attachments and the 'Flexible' Firm

Other commentators have pointed out that identification with the organization could in future be diminishing, for some groups at least, with the seemingly irreversible growth of casual labour and subcontracting. These trends have 'made identity maintenance something of an ongoing worry' (Hatch and Schultz, 2004; see also Fiol, 2001) for managers and HRM specialists. If employees, or contract workers feel no identification with their workplace, why would they bother to do a good job, provide a reliable service or 'go the extra mile'? Nonetheless, the idea of the 'flexible firm', where people are employed on a just-in-time basis to work only the hours where they are absolutely needed, is as popular as ever. To provide this 'flexibility', and thereby reduce their staffing costs to a minimum, firms use part-time workers, subcontractors, temporary contracts and agency staff as a means of adapting to volatile market conditions, including 'peaks and troughs' in demand. Figure 8.1 shows the experience of being on the 'periphery', working as a 'temp'. The 'core–periphery' model of the firm remains influential, albeit with some new types of flexibility added to the model originally proposed by Atkinson (1984) – such as time–space flexibility associated with virtual teams and satellite offices in other countries. Atkinson's thinking was that having a large, flexible 'peripheral' workforce would enable the organization to downsize or grow very quickly, without the rigidity and expense of hiring and firing full-time, permanent staff – or alternatively having people left 'idle' while demand is low. However, as we have indicated, the rise in this 'peripheral' labour force also has implications for employee identification amongst those employees that are 'peripheralized' by the architects and advocates of the model.

Figure 8.1 Being on the periphery

Let's consider the following examples:

- People who work only a few hours for an organization.
- People who work for the organization for very short periods.
- People who work for many different organizations.
- People who work for an organization through an agency or subcontractor.

People in these 'peripheral' categories are, in general, less likely to have a strong sense of attachment to the organization unless strenuous and often costly efforts are made to nurture and boost this identification. This can be a major issue for managers when it affects performance, as a consequence of high turnover, lack of continuity and a 'poor attitude' to timekeeping, customer service, etc. Ogbonna and Wilkinson (1990) found that managers struggled to implement culture change in the supermarket chains that they studied as many workers were part-time or employed on a casual basis. They had little personal or career interest in paying any attention to, let alone adopting, the values and behaviour demanded by culture change programmes. They were indifferent to the new attitudes and norms that managers attempted to instil in them. At best, they minimally complied at a surface level, a process Ogbonna and Wilkinson (1990: 14) describe as 'resigned behavioural compliance' – a response that is perhaps more credibly attributed to workers' fear of losing their jobs than to even the most minimal identification with the organization and its prescribed values.

What are the implications of the 'flexible periphery' for managing identity? Competitive pressures addressed through cost cutting are often the instigator of recurrent 'flexibilization' initiatives. But unintended consequences arise when these 'flexible', peripheralized workers are unresponsive to managerial efforts to secure even a minimal degree of identification with the organization. In the UK National Health Service, the rise of compulsory competitive tendering increased the subcontracting of cleaning. Hiring external contractors was often cheaper than employing cleaners directly as employees. According to the trade union UNISON (2005), who conducted interviews in the UK with agency cleaners, cleaners working for agencies are less likely to see themselves as a valued part of the organization and less likely to work as an integrated member of the hospital team. This has some serious unintended consequences including potentially contributing to the deaths of patients from the spread of infections.

What, you might ask, has identity and identification got to do with so-called 'superbugs' like MRSA? Many factors undoubtedly influence the rise of secondary infection rates in hospitals, including material factors such as cost cutting by reducing the time available to clean each ward. However, what might be termed identity factors, including the degree of identification with the task of cleaning as well as the organization being cleaned, may also be important. Agency cleaners are hired by private firms to make money from selling cleaning services. Unless these workers have a particular appetite for, or obsession with, cleaning, they are unlikely to feel any identification with the (quality of service provided by the) firm. As contract cleaners, they have little or no control over where they work, whether it is an office block, an airport or a hospital. As a consequence, they are unlikely to develop a strong affiliation or identification with any of the organizations where they clean. That may not be such an issue if the organization is a commercial firm located in an office block. But, if agency cleaners do not see themselves as part of the NHS as a public service organization, they are less likely to concerned about, or identify with, the particular goals of the organization or the relevance of cleaning in respect of their realization. As a result, agency cleaners may be less well informed about, as well as less inclined to appreciate, the importance of standards of cleaning for patient well-being. One UNISON representative described the implications in this way:

> I think a big factor is that the people working as permanent staff become part of the system, and see themselves as part of the care team. … But when you have people coming in on pretty much an ad-hoc basis … there are some who have no commitment, they are just there to pick up the money and go home. Standards will fall. (UNISON, 2005: 12, emphasis added)

The example illustrates the broader point that, in other words, not feeling identified with the organization and like 'part of a team' has major knock-on implications – including life-threatening implications in the case of infections caused by a poorly cleaned hospital.

8.4 New Public Management

The example of contract cleaners working in the NHS is illustrative of widespread changes in the public sector happening in many countries around the world. In the name of cost reduction and improved service quality, much direct labour (i.e. where workers are employees of the public sector organization) has been outsourced to private sector agencies. For example, articles in a special issue of the *International Journal of Public Sector Management* (Volume 19, Issue 6, 2006) are dedicated to discussing the impact of these changes on the identity of public servants across a range of European societies. The very identity of the public sector and those who work within it has been challenged by a variety of 'post-bureaucratic' initiatives – such as internal markets, the creation of arm's-length agencies, market testing, public–private partnerships, and the private financing of public amenities such as schools and prisons.

Markets (where service provision is tendered out to the private sector) and quasi-markets (where internal departments are made to act as if they were in competition), are championed as the favoured – more flexible and dynamic – means of allocating scarce resources. Increased competition is assumed to remove bureaucratic 'fat', 'waste' and 'inefficiency' from all areas and levels of service provision. These developments form part of a re-visioning of the public sector that has been termed new public management (NPM). NPM promotes the values and media of 'enterprise' and the 'free spirit' of competition. In some cases, the identities of 'end users' have also been changed. Students in higher education, patients in hospitals, victims of crime dealt with by police are all re-envisioned as 'customers'.

Changing the identity of workers lies at the heart of many NPM initiatives (see also Chapter 4, Section 4.5.3). Public sector workers are deemed to be too inflexible, too slow to respond and not responsive enough to their 'customers' because of their 'bureaucratic mentality' and 'slavish' adherence to rules and procedures. A widespread 'jobsworth' mentality (see box below) – where a sense of power as well as identity are derived from adhering to rules regardless of the consequences – is understood to stifle initiative and inhibit the risk-taking necessary to provide a dynamic, innovative service responsive to changing needs.

Council Orders Family Having Picnic to Remove £12.99 Windbreak – Branding it 'Semi-permanent Structure'

Jobsworth council officers ordered a family picnicking on a public park to remove a windbreak – because it was a 'semi-permanent structure'.

Jon Hacker was enjoying a day out with wife Claire and daughters Sophie, 11, and Emily, eight, when he put up the plastic sheet to protect them from the elements.

But he was stunned when council officers sped across the grass in a 4×4 and told him he was 'breaking the law' and ordered him to take it down.

Source:http://www.dailymail.co.uk/news/article-1298290/Council-orders-family-having-picnic-remove-12-99-windbreak--branding-semi-permanent-structure.html

---

At the heart of changing this 'mentality' is changing the identity of public sector employees. For example, in many countries, doctors are now expected to be fund holders of their medical practice. They act as managers of budgets with which they procure services for their patients. Providers of these services also compete with each other to reduce the unit cost of medical services. Similar changes have also been applied to head teachers of schools. Instead of relying upon a remote bureaucracy to allocate resources, doctors and head teachers are required (and rewarded or punished accordingly) to juggle a hybrid identity – as an 'entrepreneur' (acting like an owner of a small business) as well as a 'professional expert'. Governing organizational life in an enterprising manner involves, as du Gay (1996b: 158) has observed, '"making up" new ways of people to be; it refers to the importance of individuals acquiring and exhibiting specific "enterprising" capacities and dispositions' (see also Chapter 5, Section 5.3.2).

If or when doctors or head teachers assume the identity of business managers, increased emphasis is put on business values and priorities over professional or public service ideals. For example, a head teacher may be encouraged to prioritize attracting the most able students in order to raise the ranking of the school in a league table, instead of teaching those students who need help the most. As Fountain (2001: 65) points out, when public sector workers are encouraged to 'listen' to the customer, less attention is paid to customers who are less able to exercise 'voice' and express their preferences clearly. Fountain argues that more attention needs to be paid to the disparities of power and social inequalities within the category 'customer'. What is also lost is the 'public service' ethos that encouraged employees to identify strongly with their sense of duty to the public, delivering services based on 'need'.

When seeking to cut through 'red tape' by advocating a less regulated, more entre-preneurial identity for public sector employees, it can easily be forgotten that much of the 'tape' is there to ensure equity and fairness and, hence, to garner confidence and trust in systems of public governance (Willmott, 2011a). Of course, bureaucratic organization can be abused by 'jobsworths' who use 'red tape' to secure and defend their position and delight in enforcing petty regulations. But the possibility of devel-oping a narcissistic identification with a bureaucratic role, in which the role comes to serve the person rather than vice versa, should not be regarded as an inherent feature, or as a necessary effect, of bureaucratic organization. The identity of the 'jobsworth' is, arguably, the antithesis of the public servant, not its exemplar. 'Jobsworthiness' is actually a perversion of the principles of bureaucratic organization, which demand a strict separation of personal preferences, attitudes and interests from the fulfilment of the role. While it might not be easy to ensure this separation in practice, it does highlight the need for recognizing the moral importance of the principle of separat-ing personal preferences from executing the bureaucratic role.

For some commentators like du Gay, bureaucracy is not the 'problem', the new 'enterprise' initiatives are. As one manager who had been transferred from working for an NHS hospital to work for a private sector provider of 'hotel services' to the hospital observed of how she monitored cleaning standards:

> When I was doing the monitoring job I was still thinking – like the Hospital – you don't do things like that ... I was failing things that I knew were dirty and on the other hand I was being told not to and being told to pass it. That was not me. That was not 'me' at all. (Hebson et al., 2003: 491)

Clearly, there was an issue of identity for this manager who identified very strongly with getting things clean as a top priority, and now found herself acting (accepting a substandard level of cleanliness) in ways that conflicted with her sense of identity ('not "me" at all'). For workers employed by a private company who subcontract to public organizations, like schools and hospitals, maintaining a sense of identity as a provider of a public service is more difficult. For some, NPM means losing or com-promising an identity vested in a public service ethos.

8.5 Identity and the Global, Virtual Firm

In recent years, the concept of globalization has received much attention. Traditionally, the term has described the increasing connection between societies that were once geographically and culturally disconnected (Giddens, 1990). Globalization is thought to lead to a growing homogenization of products, services, finance, knowledge, education and labour. For example, cities all around the world are starting to look very similar, dominated by the same multinational corporations such as McDonald's and the Hilton Hotel Group. These changes are happening alongside unprecedented advantages in science and technology, causing faster and easier movements of some things like services, information and money. Whether these changes are necessarily positive, though, is a source of much debate. Some critics argue that with the restrictions in place on the movement of people, but with free flows of finance being allowed, globalizing processes have led to increased inequality (Stiglitz, 2004: 73). Some commentators are critical of the 'demolition' of local identities and cultures, as global companies such as Coca-Cola and McDonald's colonize local communities. Whether these changes are necessarily new is another source of debate, with some authors pointing to highly globalized aspects of the world's economy, such as the UK's, before the First World War (Hirst and Thompson, 1999).

What we do know is that globalization is likely to have an impact on topics relating to workplace identity. Many developed countries have seen fundamental shifts in their economies, as manufacturing and service sector activities have been 'offshored' to countries with lower wages. These changes have resulted in large-scale redundancies, increased job insecurity and other challenges to people's material well-being and sense of identity, as was described in Chapter 4 (see Section 4.7). The global mobility of labour has also led some workers to identify themselves in terms of 'us' and 'them', the in-group and the out-group (see discussion of social identity theory in Chapter 2, Section 2.2): for example, by viewing 'cheap' immigrant labour from developing countries as a 'threat' to 'their' jobs.

Multinational corporations face challenges in dealing with different national cultures and identities across the many countries they operate in. The idea of 'managing identity' by defining a set of shared norms and values (see discussion of corporate culture in Chapter 5, Section 5.3) becomes more complicated with a global workforce comprising people from many different countries. To achieve a common, shared organizational culture, a person's existing sense of identity, derived from their upbringing in a particular national culture, may be eroded. The identities and values of the global firm can sometimes clash with the indigenous population, as a recent study contrasting Western business texts with discourses of self in parts of China shows (Xu, 2008). The relevance to identity is that, across the world, people – consumers as well as employees – are being encouraged to see themselves through a predominantly (though not exclusively) Western lens. From a social identity theory perspective (see Chapter 2, Section 2.2), multinational firms might experience problems with a lack of common identity within the firm, as employees develop their own sense of in-group (e.g. 'us from China') and out-group (e.g. 'them from the United States') that hampers collaboration and knowledge sharing.

8.5.1 New technology

As we discussed in Chapter 7, some commentators believe that new information and communication technology heralds a new era of 'postmodern identity play'. They emphasize the pleasure people experience when they are able to develop new and different versions of themselves online. ICTs are thought to offer the chance to escape from restrictive, 'real-world' categories, such as gender or class (see e.g. Turkle, 1995). They also highlight the emancipatory potential of being able to 'express' oneself in new ways, and connect with others who share similar values and ideals online. For some commentators, however, online identity is not as emancipatory as we might like to think. For Pellitier (2005), for example, when we are online a new 'law' with which we identify comes to replace the 'old' rules that govern our real-world identity. She illustrates this point in her overview of online training programmes. Pellitier notes that there has been a growth in excitement about the potential for digital games to help people learn. These games are thought to allow players the freedom to control their self-presentation online, and to construct their own learning experience. In this way, learning becomes 'fun'. Paradoxically, Pelletier notes, the pleasure inherent in such games comes from submitting to a new form of authority: a consumer-oriented, speed-driven brand of capitalism.

Another reason why Zizek (1999) and others critique the idea of 'free identity play' is that online role play can require stronger forms of identification than are needed in the offline world. Zizek here is discussing identity in cyberspace, the 'digitalized universe of simulation' (ibid.: 11): environments such as virtual communities, Second Life and other such online worlds. In order to ensure an online identity that is recognizable to others, the online player often has to commit themselves to a certain 'identity' position which may involve submitting to discourses that are oppressive in the 'real world', for example ethnicity, patriarchy and so on. In order for an identity to make sense in the online world, characteristics have to be exaggerated. So, for example, male characters might appear and act in an exaggerated, stereotypically masculine way. So, Zizek argues, rather than the free and open role playing promised by technology, we experience a restricted form of self when constructing and playing out our online identities. Identity play is, perversely, more limited online than offline. In organizations, therefore, identity markers (e.g. manager versus employee) could become more pronounced, or reproduced in new ways (e.g. with different 'avatars').

8.6 The Future of Diversity

In the organization of the future, particular issues raised in Chapter 3 look likely to become more important. One issue is the ways in which certain identity categories are (or are not) becoming recognized as 'disadvantaged' and in need of 'protection'. As we write this book, a new Equality Act (2010) has been passed in the UK parliament that gives 'protected' status to certain social groups. It is too early for us to say how such legislation will impact upon workers' sense of identity and identification. Nonetheless, it is relevant to note that in addition to the inclusion of categories that have been 'protected' for many years, such as gender, disability and race, this legislation introduces some new categories such as age, sexual orientation and religious belief. As we have seen from the past legislation, such as that outlawing discrimination or permitting same-sex marriage, it can have profound implications for how people come to form and exhibit their identity: Who am I? What group do I belong to? What kinds of rights do I have?

We can view these new 'protected' identities as forms of subject positions (see Glossary) opened up by the discourse of equality. For example, workers in countries where no such legislation exists are likely to have rather different, perhaps more covert and compromised, understandings of 'who I am'. For example, a gay man in the UK might see himself as someone who is 'equal' to heterosexual people, and seek to enforce his 'rights'. In contrast, a gay man in, say, Iran would likely conceive of himself quite differently, given the institutionalized prejudice against homosexuality in that country. The future of diversity and identity is therefore bound up with the interrelationship between a range of social, economic and political factors: how social movements are formed through a sense of collective identity and struggle to establish rights and remove forms of inequality.

The future of diverse identities is likely to shift profoundly as government legislation both reflects and informs how people with 'Othered' identities conceive of themselves. Perhaps new social movements (e.g. street protests and marches) will emerge around 'age', 'environmentalism' or 'religious belief' akin to the women's rights or black rights movements in the early twentieth century. It is also important to see how identities that are not enshrined in legislation in many countries (e.g. according to, say, hair colour, weight, marital status or accent) might lead to different senses of 'self' for people in those categories. A person with ginger hair, or someone who is particularly tall or short, say, could be subject to insulting and offensive jokes at work but be less able to take up the subject position (see Glossary) – with associated feelings of a sense of struggle and solidarity – as a 'member of a disadvantaged social group', in comparison with, say, a person subjected to racist or sexist insults.

With regard to the future of workplace identity, a striking issue involves the changes that are not happening in some of the areas discussed in Chapter 3. A recent study shows that the number of women occupying managerial positions is either growing at a slow rate or, in some countries like Ireland and Canada, has been declining (ILO, 2004). One of the most significant trends in employment, in recent years, has been the expansion of the care economy – work that includes preparing and serving food, caring for children and the elderly, cleaning and so on that has traditionally been carried out in the domestic sphere, usually by women. These activities have increasingly moved into the paid economy where they continue to be carried out largely by women. In this process, something of a 'care penalty' has emerged which effectively penalizes people who take on this form of work. According to England (2005), such work tends to pay less – between 5 and 15 per cent – than equivalent occupations. In societies that place a premium upon material prosperity, it is likely that the material devaluation of caring work in society will be detrimental for the quality of care provided, and will also contribute to a reluctance to take it on. For these and related reasons, issues pertaining to gender identity outlined in Chapter 3 continue to impact starkly upon women's working lives.

With regard to ethnicity and race, studies have shown that discrimination continues to persist, with little improvement since the 1970s in the UK, for example (EOC, 2004). This manifests in ethnic minority men and women becoming concentrated in low-paid sectors of the economy – such as the hospitality industry and low-skilled nursing jobs. Changing the position of disadvantaged groups, such as women and ethnic minorities, involves more than just introducing new legislation to tackle discrimination. Even in countries where discrimination over pay has been against the law for decades, only marginal progress has been made in removing it. That, we suggest, is because change requires not only the removal of overcoming assumptions and stereotypes associated with such identities, but the institutionalized protection of advantage. The problem is not only sexist or racist individuals, but the dominant discourses (see Glossary) through which people make sense of what other people are 'like', and what types of work they are most 'suited' to. Social change is needed to challenge these entrenched ideas. When we look back at the social transformations that have been made over the last century – back to the turn of the twentieth century when women and ethnic minorities were not allowed to vote or apply for certain jobs – there are reasons to be optimistic. 'Identity change' can happen, but such social transformations require determined and extended political struggles.

8.7 Conclusion

This chapter has extended an invitation to think about aspects of the future of identity especially in the context of the workplace. The question of how workplaces affect our sense of self and our identifications remains an ongoing challenge for academics and practitioners. We have presented some tentative ideas about how this might take shape but the discussion is continuously evolving. In the field of scholarship, contributions regularly appear in journals such as *Organization*, *Organization Studies*, *Organization Science*, *Human Relations* and *Ephemera*, which we encourage you to consult in order to keep abreast with developments.

Overall, our concern has been to present, open up and illustrate different perspectives on identity and organizations. This has promoted a wide-ranging exploration of issues relating to age, gender, ethnicity, professional roles, external organizations, new forms of ICTs and so on. Our intention has been to demonstrate the significance of workplace identity, and to reflect critically upon how it involves us in flows of power, both subtly and overtly, and so affects our life-chances and well-being. We look forward to seeing how the myriad of identity-forming practices and struggles occurring in modern organizations evolve in coming years, and we urge you to take up the challenges of exploring the relevance of this text to your everyday working experiences. In doing so, you will undoubtedly discover omissions and limitations in our discussion that we invite you to expose and correct.

Suggested Reading

du Gay, P. (2007) *Organizing Identity: Persons and Organizations 'After Theory'*. London: Sage.

Pullen, A., Beech, N. and Sims, D. (eds) (2007) *Exploring Identity: Concepts and Methods*. Basingstoke: Palgrave Macmillan.

Webb, J. (2004) 'Organizations, self-identities and the new economy', *Sociology*, 38 (4): 719–38.

Wetherell, M. and Mohanty, C.T. (eds) (2010) *The Sage Handbook of Identities*. London: Sage.

Glossary of Terms

Discourse   This term means different things in different research perspectives and traditions. For some, discourse refers to actual practices of language use – talk and text (things that are said or written). For others, particularly those inspired by poststructuralist thought (see below), the term discourse refers to a set of ideas that are dominant in a particular period of time that shapes how we see ourselves and the world around us. In this book, we (mainly) refer to this latter conception (ethnomethodology and conversational analysis is one exception, which focuses more on former conception: the actual practices of talk-in-interaction). A good overview of the different meanings of 'discourse' is provided by Alvesson and Karreman (2000).

Dis-identification   The process through which a person detaches their sense of self from an organization, for example through distancing, cynicism, humour or resistance.

Foucauldian   The body of work which has taken inspiration from the work of French philosopher Michel Foucault. We explain the Foucauldian perspective on identity in Chapter 2, Section 2.4.

Ideology   A set of ideas that serves to maintain or further the power of one particular group.

Identification   The process through which a person attaches themselves to an organization, feels a sense of belonging with the organization and defines themselves according to the ideas, beliefs and values of the organization (e.g. 'I love being an Apple employee').

Identity   The answer to the question 'who am I'? Can refer to an individual's self-identity ('who I am') or a collective identity ('who we are').

Identity work   The more or less conscious effort and activities that are undertaken to build, maintain, protect or defend our sense of 'who I am'.

Personality   The idea deriving from the field of psychology that we have relatively stable and distinct attitudes, orientations, values and behavioural patterns that make us different from one another.

Poststructuralism   A body of work that rejected the claims of 'structuralism' to objectivity and instead emphasizes the power involved in the search for 'truth'. Associated primarily with certain continental European philosophers and theorists such as Michel Foucault, Jacques Derrida and Gilles Deleuze. Often associated with the idea of 'deconstructing' established truths and expert knowledge and binary oppositions (e.g. male and female, subjectivity and objectivity, agency and structure). For identity in particular, poststructural thought holds that the 'self' is not a bounded, discrete and autonomous entity, but instead is 'de-centred': positioned in and through discourse (see definition above) and is itself a medium and outcome of power relations.

Psyche   The notion that there is an organ or function that directs, whether consciously or unconsciously, thought and emotion by governing behaviour – for example, by adjusting responses to the social and physical environment.

Stereotype   An oversimplified and biased opinion or image that we hold about all members of another social group.

Subjectivity   An open capacity to develop a state of awareness and self-understanding that is not reducible to biology or the effects of social conditioning.

Subject position   The 'location' people are invited ('hailed' to or 'called upon') to inhabit in a particular discourse (see definition above). Compare, for example, the predominantly Western notion of 'individual human rights' with the predominantly non-Western notion of 'duty' and 'honour' to society and family. The idea is that, when a person takes up a particular subject position, they see themselves and the world around them from the vantage point of that position – for instance, as having 'rights' or 'duties'. In some cases, different discourses can open up alternative, and perhaps even contrasting, subject positions that people can occupy.

Notes on citation terminology

Ibid.   An abbreviation of the Latin phrase *ibidem* – 'the same place', meaning the source is from the previous citation.

Et al.   An abbreviation of the Latin phrase *et alia*, which means 'and others', used for referencing work that has three or more authors.

References

Acker, J. (1990) 'Hierarchies, jobs, bodies: a theory of gendered organizations', *Gender and Society*, 4 (2): 139–58.

Ackers, P. and Preston, D. (1997) 'Born again? The ethics and efficacy of the conversion experience in contemporary management development', *Journal of Management Studies*, 34 (5): 677–701.

Ackroyd, S. and Crowdy, P. (1990) 'Can culture be managed? Working with "raw" material, the case of English slaughtermen', *Personnel Review*, 19 (5): 3–13.

Ainsworth, S. and Hardy, C. (2007) 'The construction of the older worker: privilege, paradox and policy', *Discourse & Communication*, 1 (3): 295–313.

Ainsworth, S.A. and Cutcher, L. (2008) 'Staging value and older women workers: when "something more" is too much', *International Journal of Work Organisation and Emotion*, 2 (4): 344–57.

Albert, S. and Whetten, D.A. (1985) 'Organizational identity', in L.L. Cummings and B.M. Staw (eds), *Research in Organizational Behavior*, Vol. 7. Greenwich, CT: JAI Press. pp. 263–95. Reprinted in Hatch, M.J. and Schultz, M. (2004) *Organizational Identity: A Reader*. Oxford: Oxford University Press. pp. 89–118.

Alvesson, M. (1990) 'Organization: from substance to image?', *Organization Studies*, 11: 373–94.

Alvesson, M. and Empson, L. (2008) 'The construction of organizational identity: comparative case studies of consulting firms', *Scandinavian Journal of Management*, 24: 1–16.

Alvesson, M. and Karreman, D. (2000) 'Varieties of discourse: on the study of organizations through discourse analysis', *Human Relations*, 53: 1125–49.

Alvesson, M. and Willmott, H. (2002) 'Identity regulation as organizational control: producing the appropriate individual', *Journal of Management Studies*, 39 (5): 619–44.

Anderson-Gough, F., Grey, C. and Robson, K. (1998) *Making Up Accountants: The organizational and professional socialization of trainee chartered accountants*. London: Ashgate.

Andriopoulos, C. and Gotsi, M. (2001) '"Living" the corporate identity: case studies from the creative industry', *Corporate Reputation Review*, 4 (2): 144–54.

Anzaldúa, G. (1987) *Borderlands/La Frontera: The New Mestiza*. San Francisco: Spinsters/Aunt Lute.

Armstrong, P. (2011) 'From bourgeois sociology to managerial apologetics: a tale of existential struggle', in P. Armstrong and G. Lightfoot (eds), in 'The Leading Journal in the Field': Destabilizing Authority in the Social Sciences of Management. Available at www.mayflybooks.org.

Ashforth, B. and Kreiner, G.E. (1999) '"How can you do it?": Dirty work and the challenge of constructing positive identity', *Academy of Management Review*, 24: 413–34.

Ashforth, B.E. and Mael, F. (1989) 'Social identity theory and the organization', *Academy of Management Review*, 14: 20–39.

Ashforth, B.E., Harrison, S.H. and Corley, K.G. (2008) 'Identification in organizations: an examination of four fundamental questions', *Journal of Management*, 34: 325–74.

Atkinson, J. (1984) 'Manpower strategies for flexible organisations', *Personnel Management*, 16 (8): 28–31.

Ball, K. (2005) 'Organization, surveillance and the body: towards a politics of resistance', *Organization*, 12 (1): 89–108.

Ball, K. and Wilson, D. (2000) 'Power, control and computer based performance monitoring: a subjectivist approach to repertoires and resistance', *Organization Studies*, 21 (3): 539–65.

Barker, J.R. (1993) 'Tightening the iron cage: concertive control in self-managing teams', *Administrative Science Quarterly*, 38 (3): 408–34.

Barley, S.R. (1983) 'The codes of the dead: the semiotics of funeral work', *Urban Life*, 12: 3–31.

Batnitzky, A., McDowell, L. and Dyer, S. (2009) 'Flexible and strategic masculinities: the working lives and gendered identities of male migrants in London', *Journal of Ethnic and Migration Studies*, 35 (8): 1275–93.

Bell, E. and Nkomo, S. (2001) *Our Separate Ways: Black and White Women and the Struggle for Professional Identity*. Boston, MA: Harvard Business School Press.

Benwell, B. and Stockoe, L. (2006) *Discourse and Identity*. Edinburgh: Edinburgh University Press.

Bertin, I. and Denbigh, A. (2000) *The Teleworking Handbook* (3rd edn). Kenilworth: Telecottage Association.

Bishop, V., Cassell, C. and Hoel, H. (2009) 'Preserving masculinity in service work: an exploration of the underreporting of customer anti-social behaviour', *Human Relations*, 62 (1): 5–25.

Boje, D.M. (1991) 'The storytelling organization: a study of storytelling performance in an office supply firm', *Administrative Science Quarterly*, 36: 106–26.

Boje, D.M. (1995) 'Stories of the storytelling organization: a postmodern analysis of Disney as "Tamara-land"', *Academy of Management Journal*, 38 (4): 997–1035.

Boje, D.M. (2003) 'Using narrative and telling stories', in D. Holman and R. Thorpe (eds), *Management and Language*. London: Sage. pp. 41–53.

Boltanski, L. and Chiapello, E. (2006) *The New Spirit of Capitalism*. London: Verso.

Bolton, S. and Houlihan, M. (2009) 'Are we having fun yet? A consideration of workplace fun and engagement', *Employee Relations*, 31 (6): 556–68.

Bouchikhi, H. and Kimberley, J.R. (2003) 'Escaping the identity trap', *Sloan Management Review*, Spring: 20–6.

Bratton, J., Callinan, M., Forshaw, C. and Sawchuk, P. (2010) *Work and Organizational Behaviour: Understanding the Workplace* (2nd edn). Basingstoke: Palgrave Macmillan.

Brewis, J. (2004) 'Refusing to be "Me"', in R. Thomas et al. (eds), *Identity Politics at Work: Resisting Gender, Gendering Resistance*. London: Routledge.

Brewis, J. and Linstead, S. (2000) *Sex, Work and Sex Work: Eroticizing Organization*. London: Routledge.

Brockmeier, J. and Carbaugh, D. (2001) 'Introduction', in J. Brockmeier and D. Carbaugh (eds), *Narrative and Identity*. Amsterdam: Benjamins. pp. 1–22.

Brown, A.D. (1997) 'Narcissism, identity, and legitimacy', *Academy of Management Review*, 22: 643–86.

Brown, A.D. (2001) 'Organization studies and identity: towards a research agenda', *Human Relations*, 54 (1): 113–21.

Brown, A.D. and Humphreys, M. (2006) 'Organizational identity and place: a discursive exploration of hegemony and resistance', *Journal of Management Studies*, 43 (2): 231–57.

Brown, A.D. and Starkey, K. (2000) 'Organizational identity and organizational learning: a psychodynamic perspective', *Academy of Management Review*, 25 (1): 102–20.

Brown, T.J., Dacin, P.A., Pratt, M.G. and Whetten, D.A. (2006) 'Identity, intended image, construed image, and reputation: an interdisciplinary framework and suggested terminology', *Journal of the Academy of Marketing Science*, 34 (2): 99–106.

Brubaker, R. and Cooper, F. (2000) 'Beyond "Identity"', *Theory and Society*, 29 (1): 1–47.

Bryant, S. (2000) 'At home on the electronic frontier: work, gender and the information highway', *New Technology, Work and Employment*, 15 (1): 19–33.

Buchanan, D. and Huczynski, A. (2004) *Organizational Behaviour* (5th edn). Harlow: Pearson.

Burawoy, M. (1979) *Manufacturing Consent*. Chicago: University of Chicago Press.

Burchell, B., Fagan, C., O'Brien, C. and Smith, M. (2007) 'Gender and Working Conditions in the European Union, Report for the European Foundation for the Improvement of Living and Working Condition'. Available at http://www.eurofound.europa.eu/pubdocs/2007/108/en/1/ef07108en.pdf (accessed 15 March 2010).

Butler, J. (1990) *Gender Trouble: Feminism and the Subversion of Identity*. London: Routledge.

Butler, J. (1993) *Bodies That Matter: On the Discursive Limits of 'Sex'*. London: Routledge.

Butler, J. et al. (2000) *Contingency, Hegemony, Universality: Contemporary Dialogues on the Left (Phronesis)*. London: Verso.

Cara Ellison (2010) 'The Enron Blog by Cara Ellison'. Available at http://caraellison.wordpress.com/ (accessed 7 April 2011).

Carozza, N. (2007) 'Constant warning', *Fraud Magazine*, January/February. Available at http://www.fraud-magazine.com/article.aspx?id=583 (accessed 20 November 2010).

Carroll, B. and Levy, L. (2008) 'Defaulting to management: leadership defined by what it is not', *Organization*, 15 (1): 75–96.

Casey, C. (1995) *Work, Self and Society*. London: Routledge.

Castells, M. (1996) *The Rise of the Network Society*, Vol. 1. Oxford: Blackwell (2010 edn).

Castells, M. (2003) *The Internet Galaxy: Reflections on the Internet, Business, and Society*. Oxford: Oxford University Press.

Chattopadhyay, P., Tluchowska, M. and George, E. (2004) 'Identifying the ingroup: a closer look at the influence of demographic dissimilarity on employee social identity', *Academy of Management Review*, 29: 180–202.

Clair, J., Beatty, J. and Maclean, T. (2005) 'Out of sight but not out of mind: managing invisible social identities in the workplace', *Academy of Management Review*, 30 (1): 78–95.

Clarke, C.A., Brown, A.D. and Hope Hailey, V. (2009) 'Working identities? Antagonistic discursive resources and managerial identity', *Human Relations*, 62 (3): 323–52.

Cockburn, C. (1983) *Brothers: Male Dominance and Technological Change*. London: Pluto Press.

Collinson, D. (1992) *Managing the Shopfloor: Subjectivity, Masculinity and Workplace Culture*. Berlin: de Gruyter.

Collinson, D. (2003) 'Identities and insecurities: selves at work', *Organization*, 10 (3): 527–47.

Computerworld (2009) '54% of companies ban Facebook, Twitter at work'. Available at http://www.computerworld.com/s/article/9139020/Study_54_of_companies_ban_Facebook_Twitter_at_work (accessed 29 April 2011).

Contu, A. and Willmott, H. (2006) 'Studying practice: situating talking about machines', *Organization Studies*, 27 (12): 1769–82.

Cooley, C.H. (1902) *Human Nature and the Social Order*. New York: Scribner's.

Corley, K. and Gioia, D. (2004) 'Identity ambiguity and change in the wake of a corporate spin-off', *Administrative Science Quarterly*, 49: 173–208.

Cornelissen, J.P. (2002) 'On the "organizational identity" metaphor', *British Journal of Management*, 13: 259–68.

Costas, J. and Fleming, P. (2009) 'Beyond dis-identification: a discursive approach to self-alienation in contemporary organizations', *Human Relations*, 62 (3): 353–78.

Creed, W.E.D.; Scully, M. and Austin, J.R. (2002) 'Clothes make the person? The tailoring of legitimating accounts and the social construction of identity', *Organization Science*, 13 (5): 475–96.

Cushman, P. (1991) 'Ideology obscured: political uses of the self in Daniel Stern's infant', *American Psychologist*, 46 (3): 206–19.

Czarniawska, B. (1997) *Narrating the Organization: Dramas of Institutional Identity* (2nd edn). Chicago: University of Chicago University Press.

Czarniawska, B. (1998) *Narrative Approach to Organization Studies*. London: Sage.

Czarniawska-Joerges, B. (2004) *Narratives in Social Science Research*. Thousand Oaks, CA: Sage.

Daft, R.L. and Lengel, R.H. (1986) 'Organizational information requirements, media richness and structural design', *Management Science*, 32 (5): 554–71.

Dalton, M. (1959) *Men Who Manage: Fusions of Feeling and Theory in Administration*. New York: Wiley.

D'Cruz, P. and Noronha, E. (2006) 'Being professional: organizational control in Indian call centers', *Social Science Computer Review*, 24 (3): 342–61.

De Bruin, A. and Firkin, P. (2001) 'An exploration of ageing and self-employment', in C. Massey et al. (eds), *Creating Innovative Growth Companies: Proceedings of the 4th Conference of the Small Enterprise Association of Australia and New Zealand,* September 2001, Wellington, New Zealand. New Zealand Centre for SME Research, Massey University.

Deal, T.E. and Kennedy, A.A. (1982) *Corporate Cultures: The Rites and Rituals of Corporate Life*. Reading, MA: Addison-Wesley.

Department of Trade and Industry (2000) *Working Anywhere: Exploring Telework for Individuals and Organisations*. London: Department of Trade and Industry.

Depickere, A. (1999) 'Managing virtual working: between commitment and control?', in P. Jackson (ed.), *Virtual Working: Social and Organisational Dynamics*. London: Routledge. pp 99–120.

Down, S. and Reveley, J. (2009) 'Between narration and interaction: situating first-line supervisor identity work', *Human Relations*, 62 (3): 379–401.

Driver, M. (2005) 'From empty speech to full speech? Reconceptualizing spirituality in organizations based on a psychoanalytically-grounded understanding of the self', *Human Relations*, 58 (9): 1091–1110.

Driver, M. (2009) 'Encountering the Arugula leaf: the failure of the imaginary and its implications for research on identity in organizations', *Organization*, 16: 487–504.

du Gay, P. (1996a) *Consumption and Identity at Work*. London: Sage.

du Gay, P. (1996b) 'Organizing identity: entrepreneurial governance and public management', in S. Hall and P. du Gay (eds), *Questions of Cultural Identity*. London: Sage. pp 151–69.

du Gay, P. (2000) 'Enterprise and its futures: a response to Fornier and Grey', *Organization*, 7 (1): 165–83.

Dukerich, J.M., Kramer, R. and Parks, J.M. (1998) 'The dark side of organizational identification', in D.A. Whetten and P.C. Godfrey (eds), *Identity in Organizations: Building Theory Through Conversations*. London: Sage.

Dutton, J. and Dukerich, J. (1991) 'Keeping an eye on the mirror: image and identity in organizational adaptation', *Academy of Management Review*, 34: 517–54.

Dutton, J., Dukerich, J. and Harquail, C.V. (1994) 'Organizational images and member identification', *Administrative Science Quarterly*, 39: 239–63.

Dyer, J. and Keller-Cohen, D. (2000) 'The discursive construction of professional self through narratives of personal experience', *Discourse Studies*, 2 (3): 283–304.

Ehrenreich, B. (2001) *Nickel and Dimed*. Granta Books: London.

Ehrenreich, B. (2006) *Bait and Switch: The Futile Pursuit of the Corporate Dream*. London: Granta.

Elsbach, K.D. (2003) 'Relating physical environment to self-categorizations: identity threat and affirmation in a non-territorial office space', *Administrative Science Quarterly*, 48 (4): 622–54.

Elsbach, K.D. (2004) 'Interpreting workplace identities: the role of office decor', *Journal of Organizational Behavior*, 25 (1): 99–128.

Elsbach, K.D. and Bhattacharya, C.B. (2001) 'Defining who you are by what you're not: organizational disidentification and the National Rifle Association', *Organization Science*, 12: 393–413.

Elsbach, K. and Kramer, R. (1996) 'Members' responses to organizational identity threats: encountering and countering the Business Week rankings', *Administrative Science Quarterly*, 41: 442–76.

Elstak, M.N. and Van Riel, C.B.M. (2004) 'Closing ranks: how a collective threat shifts salience from organizational to corporate identity', *Best Papers, Proceedings of the 64th Annual Meeting of the Academy of Management, New Orleans*.

Empson, L. (2001) 'Fear of exploitation and fear of contamination: impediments to knowledge transfer in mergers between professional services firms', *Human Relations*, 54 (7): 839–62.

England, P. (2005) 'Emerging theories of care work', *Annual Review of Sociology*, 31: 381–99.

EOC (2004) *Ethnic Minority Women and Men* (eds S. Botcherby and K. Hurrell). Manchester: EOC.

Equality Act (2010) Available at http://www.legislation.gov.uk/ukpga/2010/15/contents (accessed 7 April 2011).

Essers, C. and Benschop, Y. (2007) 'Enterprising identities: female entrepreneurs of Moroccan and Turkish origin in the Netherlands', *Organization Studies*, 28 (1): 49–69.

Ezzamel, M. and Willmott, H. (1998) 'Accounting for teamwork: a critical study of group-based systems of organisational control', *Administrative Science Quarterly*, 43 (2): 358–97.

Ezzamel, M., Willmott, H.C. and Worthington, F. (2004) 'Accounting and management-labour relations: change initiatives and worker resistance', *Accounting Organizations and Society*, 29: 269–302.

Ezzy, D. (1997) 'Subjectivity and the labour process: conceptualising "good work"', *Sociology*, 31 (3): 427–44.

Fairclough, N. (1992) *Discourse and Social Change*. Cambridge: Polity Press.

Feller, J. and Fitzgerald, B. (2002) *Understanding Open Source Software Development*. Edinburgh: Pearson.

Ferguson, K.E. (1984) *The Feminist Case Against Bureaucracy*. Philadelphia, PA: Temple University Press.

Fine, G. (1996) 'Justifying work: occupational rhetorics as resources in restaurant kitchens', *Administrative Science Quarterly*, 41 (1): 90–116.

Fineman, S. (2011) *Organizing Age*. Oxford: Oxford University Press.

Fiol, C.M. (2001) 'Revisiting an identity-based view of sustainable competitive advantage', *Journal of Management*, 27: 691–9.

Fiol, C.M. (2002) 'Capitalizing on paradox: the role of language in transforming organizational identities', *Organization Science*, 13 (6): 653–66.

Fiol, C.M., Pratt, M.G. and O'Connor, E.J. (2009) 'Managing intractable identity conflicts', *Academy of Management Review*, 34: 32–55.

Fireman, S. (1998) 'Evolution of the telecommuting withdrawal model: a US perspective', in P. Jackson and J.M. van der Wielen (eds), *Teleworking: International Perspectives*. London: Routledge. pp. 281–92.

Fleming, P. (2005) 'Workers' playtime: boundaries and cynicism in a "culture of fun" program', *Journal of Applied Behavioural Science*, 41 (3): 285–303.

Fleming, P. (2007) 'Sexuality, power and resistance in the workplace', *Organization Studies*, 28: 239–56.

Fleming, P. and Sturdy, A.J. (2009) 'Just be yourself – towards neo-normative control in organisations', *Employee Relations*, 31(6): 569–83.

Fombrun, C. (1996) *Reputation: Realizing Value from the Corporate Image*. Boston, MA: Harvard University Press.

Ford, J. (2006) 'Discourses of leadership: gender, identity and contradiction in a UK public sector organization', *Leadership*, 2 (1): 77–99.

Ford, J., Harding, N. and Learmonth, M. (2008) *Leadership as Identity: Constructions and Deconstructions*. Basingstoke: Palgrave Macmillan.

Forseback, L. (1995) '20 Seconds to work: home-based telework, Swedish perspectives from a European perspective, state of the art 1995', *Teldok Report 101E*. Stockholm: Teldok.

Foster, D. and Fosh, P. (2010) 'Negotiating "difference": representing disabled employees in the british workplace', *British Journal of Industrial Relations*, 48(3): 560–82.

Foucault, M. (1977) *Discipline and Punish: The Birth of the Prison*. London: Allen Lane.

Foucault, M. (1988) 'Technologies of the self', in L.H. Martin et al. (eds), *Technologies of the Self*. Amherst: University of Massachusetts.

Fountain, J. (2001) 'Paradoxes of public sector customer service', *Governance*, 14 (1): 55–73.

Fournier, V. (1999) 'The appeal to "professionalism" as a disciplinary mechanism', *Sociological Review*, 47 (2): 280–307.

Fournier, V. and Grey, C. (1999) 'Too much, too little and too often: a critique of du Gay's analysis of enterprise', *Organization*, 6 (1): 107–28.

Fuss, D. (1991) *Inside/out: Lesbian Theories, Gay Theories*. London: Routledge.

Gabriel, Y. (1999) *Organizations in Depth: The Psychoanalysis of Organizations*. London: Sage.

Gabriel, Y. (2000) *Storytelling in Organizations: Facts, Fictions and Fantasies*. Oxford: Oxford University Press.

Gabriel, Y. (2005) 'Glass cages and glass palaces: images of organization in image-conscious times', *Organization*, 12 (8): 9–27.

Gabriel, Y., Grey, D. and Goregaokar, H. (2009) 'Temporary derailment or the end of the line? Unemployed managers at 50', Working Paper Series SoMWP–0903, School of Management, Royal Holloway University of London.

Galpin, S. and Sims, D. (1999) 'Narratives and identity in flexible working and teleworking organizations', in P. Jackson (ed.), *Virtual Working: Social and Organizational Dynamics*. London: Routledge. pp. 76–94.

Gardner, W.L. and Avolio, B.J. (1998) 'Charismatic leadership, a dramaturgical perspective', *Academy of Management Review*, 23 (1): 32–58.

Garfinkel, H. (1967) *Studies in Ethnomethodology*. Englewood Cliffs, NJ: Prentice Hall.

Garrett-Peters, R. (2009) 'If I don't have to work anymore, who am I? Job loss and collaborative self-concept repair', *Journal of Contemporary Ethnography*, 38 (5): 547–83.

Garrety, K., Badham, R., Morrigan, V., Rifkin, W. and Zanko, M. (2003) 'The use of personality typing in organizational change: discourse, emotions and the reflexive subject', *Human Relations*, 56 (2): 211–35.

Gibson-Graham, J.K. (1996) 'Queer(y)ing capitalist organisation', *Organization*, 3 (4): 541–5.

Giddens, A. (1990) *The Consequences of Modernity*. Cambridge: Polity Press.

Gilmore, S. and Warren, S. (2007) 'Emotion online: experiences of teaching in a virtual learning environment', *Human Relations*, 60: 581–608.

Gioia, D.A. and Thomas, J. (1996) 'Identity, image and issue interpretation: sensemaking during strategic change in academia', *Administrative Science Quarterly*, 41: 370–403.

Gioia, D.A., Schultz, M. and Corley, K.G. (2000) 'Organizational identity, image, and adaptative instability', *Academy of Management Review*, 25 (1): 63–81.

Gioia, D.A., Schultz, M. and Corley, K.G. (2002) 'On celebrating the organizational identity metaphor: a rejoinder to Cornelissen', *British Journal of Management*, 13: 269–75.

Glynn, M. (2000) 'When cymbals become symbols: conflict over organizational identity within a symphony orchestra', *Organization Science*, 8 (6): 593–611.

Glynn, M.A., Barr, P.S. and Dacin, M.T. (2000) 'Pluralism and the problem of variety', *Academy of Management Review*, 25 (4): 726–33.

Goffman, E. (1961) *Asylums: Essays on the Social Situation of Mental Patients and Other Inmates*. New York: Doubleday Anchor.

Golden-Biddle, K. and Rao, H. (1997) 'Breaches in the boardroom: organizational identity and conflicts of commitment in a nonprofit organization', *Organization Science*, 8 (6): 593–611. Reprinted in Hatch, M. J. and Schultz, M. (2004) *Organizational Identity: A Reader*. Oxford: Oxford University Press. pp. 313–348.

Goldthorpe, J., Lockwood, D., Bechhofer, F. and Platt, J. (1968) *The Affluent Worker: Industrial Attitudes and Behaviour*. Cambridge: Cambridge University Press.

Goleman, D. (1998) *Working with Emotional Intelligence*. New York: Bantam Books.

Gossett, L. and Kilker, J. (2006) 'My job sucks: examining counter-institutional websites as locations for organizational member voice, dissent, and resistance', *Management Communication Quarterly*, 20 (1): 63–9.

Gotsi, M., Andriopoulos, C., Lewis, M. and Ingram, A. (2010) 'Creative workers: managing tensions of multiple identities', *Human Relations*, 63 (6): 781–805.

Gouldner, A.W. (1954) *Patterns of Industrial Bureaucracy*. New York: Free Press.

Grandy, G. (2008) 'Managing spoiled identities: dirty workers' struggles for a favourable sense of self', *Qualitative Research in Organizations and Management*, 3 (3): 176–98.

Grey, C. (1994) 'Career as a project of the self and labour process discipline', *Sociology*, 28 (2): 479–97.

Grey, C. (1997) 'Management as technical practice: professionalization or responsibilization?',

Systemic Practice and Action Research, 10: 703–26.

Grey, C. (1999) 'We are all managers now; we always were. On the emergence and demise of management', *Journal of Management Studies*, 36: 561–86.

Grint, K. (1995a) *Management: A Sociological Introduction*. Cambridge: Polity Press.

Grint, K. (1995b) *The Sociology of Work* (3rd edn). Chichester: Wiley.

Grint, K. (2005) *Management: A Sociological Introduction*. Oxford: Polity Press.

Groß, C. and Kieser, A. (2006) Consultants on the way to professionalization?, in R. Greenwood and R. Suddaby (eds), *Research in the Sociology of Organizations*. Bingley: Emerald. pp. 69–100.

Grugulis, I., Dundon, T. and Wilkinson, A. (2000) 'Cultural control and the "culture manager": employment practices in a consultancy', *Work, Employment & Society*, 14 (1): 97–116.

Gullette, M.M. (1997) *Declining to Decline: Cultural Combat and the Politics of the Midlife*. Charlottesville, VA: University Press of Virginia.

Hakim, C. (1995) 'Five feminist myths about women's employment', *British Journal of Sociology*, 46 (3): 429–55.

Hales, C. (2002) '"Bureaucracy-lite" and continuities in managerial work', *British Journal of Management*, 13 (2): 51–66.

Hall, M. (2008) 'Contextualizing leadership: Jamaican managers' sense-making accounts of leading in a post-colonial context', paper presented at the National Communication Association, San Diego, CA.

Hallowell, E.M. (1999) 'The human moment at work', *Harvard Business Review*, 71(1): 58–64.

Hammersley, M. (2003) 'Conversation analysis and discourse analysis: methods or paradigms?', *Discourse and Society*, 14 (6): 751–81.

Harding, N. (2003) *The Social Construction of Management: Texts and Identities*. London: Routledge.

Hatch, M.J. and Schultz, M. (1997) 'Relations between organizational culture, identity and image', *European Journal of Marketing*, 31 (5): 356–65.

Hatch, M.J. and Schultz, M. (2004) *Organizational Identity: A Reader*. Oxford: Oxford University Press.

Hatch, M.J. and Schultz, M. (2008) *Taking Brand Initiative: How Corporations Can Align Strategy, Culture and Identity through Corporate Branding*. San Francisco: Wiley/Jossey Bass.

Hebson, G., Grimshaw, D. and Marchington, M. (2003) 'PPPs and the changing public sector ethos: case-study evidence from the health and local authority sectors', *Work, Employment and Society*, 17 (3): 481–501.

Heckscher, C. (1994) 'Defining the post-bureaucratic type', in C. Heckscher and A. Donnellon (eds) *The Post-Bureaucratic Organization*. Thousand Oaks: Sage. pp. 14–62.

Hewlett, S.A. (2002) *Creating a Life: Professional Women and the Quest for Children*. New York: Talk Miramax Books.

Hill, L.A. (2003) *Becoming a Manager: How New Managers Master the Challenges of Leadership*. Boston, MA: Harvard Business School Press.

Hirst, P. and Thompson, G. (1999) *Globalization in Question* (2nd edn). Cambridge: Polity Press.

Hochschild, A. (1983) *The Managed Heart: Commercialization of Human Feeling*. London: University of California Press.

Hodgson, D. (2005) 'Putting on a professional performance: performativity, subversion and project management', *Organization*, 12 (1): 51–68.

Hoedemaekers, C. (2010) '"Not even semblance": exploring the interruption of identification with Lacan', *Organization*, 17: 379–93.

Holmes, J. (2005) 'Story-telling at work: a complex discursive resource for integrating personal, professional and social identities', *Discourse Studies*, 7 (6): 671–700.

Humphreys, M. and Brown, A.D. (2002) 'Narratives of organizational identity and identification: a case study of hegemony and resistance', *Organization Studies*, 23 (3): 421–47.

Hutchby, I. and Wooffitt, R. (1998) *Conversation Analysis: Principles, Practices, and Applications*. Cambridge: Polity Press.

Ibarra, H. (1993) 'Personal networks of women and minorities in management: a conceptual framework', *Academy of Management Review*, 18 (1): 56–87.

ILO (2004) 'Global Employment Trends, January'. Available at http://www.ilo.org/empelm/what/pubs/lang--en/docName--WCMS_114353/index.htm (accessed 11 June 2010).

International Journal of Public Sector Management (2006) Special Issue on *Public Management Reform and its Impact on Public Servant's Identity*, 19 (6).

Izraeli, D. and Adler, N (1994) 'Competitive frontiers: women managers in a global economy', in N. Adler and D. Izraeli (eds), *Competitive Frontiers: Women Managers in a Global Economy*. Oxford: Blackwell.

Jack, G. and Lorbiecki, A. (2007) 'National identity, globalization and the discursive construction of organizational identity', *British Journal of Management*, 18 (1): S79–94.

Jacka, T. (1997) *Women's Work in Rural China: Change and Continuity in an Era of Reform*. New York: Cambridge University Press.

Jacobs, G., Christe-Zeyse, J., Keegan, A. and Pólos, L. (2008) 'Reactions to organizational identity threats in times of change: illustrations from the German police', *Corporate Reputation Review*, 11 (3): 245–61.

Jenkins, R. (1996) *Social Identity*. London: Routledge.

Johnson, S.A. (1998) 'Teleworking service management: issues for an integrated framework', in P. Jackson and J.M. van der Wielen (eds), *Teleworking: International Perspectives*. London: Routledge. pp. 185–206.

Jones, C. and Spicer, A. (2005) 'The sublime object of entrepreneurship', *Organization*, 12 (2): 223–46.

Kanter, R.M. (1977) *Men and Women of the Corporation*. New York: Basic Books.

Kärreman, D. and Alvesson, M. (2004) 'Cages in tandem: management control, social identity, and identification in a knowledge-intensive firm', *Organization*, 11 (1): 149–75.

Kärreman, D. and Rylander, A. (2008) 'Managing meaning through branding – the case of a consulting firm', *Organization Studies*, 29 (1): 103–25.

Kenny, K. (2009a) 'The performative surprise: parody, documentary and critique', *Culture and Organization*, 15 (2): 221–35.

Kenny, K. (2009b) 'Heeding the stains: Lacan and organizational change', *Journal of Organizational Change Management*, 22 (2): 214–28.

Kenny, K. and Bell, E. (2011) 'Representing the sucessful Managerial Body' in E. Jeanes, D. Knights and M.P. Yancey (eds) *Handbook of Gender, Work and Organization*. Oxford: Blackwell/Wiley.

Kitay, J. and Wright, C. (2007) 'From prophets to profits: the occupational rhetoric of management consultants', *Human Relations*, 60 (11): 1613–40.

Knights, D. (2002) 'Writing organizational analysis into Foucault', *Organization*, 9 (4): 575–93.

Knights, D. and Kerfoot, D. (2004) 'Between representations and subjectivity: Gender binaries and the politics of organizational transformation', *Gender, Work and Organization*, 11(4): 430–454.

Knights, D. and McCabe, D. (1998) 'What happens when the phone goes wild? Staff, stress and spaces for escape in a BPR regime', *Journal of Management Studies*, 35 (2): 163–94.

Knights, D. and Willmott, H. (1989) 'Power and subjectivity at work', *Sociology*, 23 (4): 535–58.

Knights, D. and Willmott, H.C. (1999) *Management Lives: Power and Identity in Contemporary Organizations*. London: Sage.

Kondo, D. (1990) *Crafting Selves: Power, Gender and Discourses of Identity in a Japanese Workplace*. Chicago: University of Chicago Press.

Kosmala, K. and Herrbach, O. (2006) 'The ambivalence of professional identity: on cynicism and jouissance in audit firms', *Human Relations*, 59 (10): 1393–1428.

Kunda, G. (1992) *Engineering Culture: Control and Commitment in a High-Tech Corporation*. Chicago: University of Chicago Press.

Laclau, E. and Mouffe, C. (1985) *Hegemony and Socialist Strategy: Toward a Radical Democratic Politics*. London: Verso (2nd edn, 2001).

Legge, K. (1994) 'Managing culture: fact or fiction?', in K. Sisson (ed.), *Personnel Management*. Oxford: Blackwell. pp. 397–433.

Leigh Star, S. and Strauss, A. (1999) 'Layers of silence, arenas of voice: the ecology of visible and invisible work', *Computer Supported Cooperative Work*, 8 (1–2): 9–30.

Leonard, P. (2010) 'Organizing whiteness: gender, nationality and subjectivity in post-colonial Hong Kong', *Gender, Work and Organization*, 17 (3): 340–58.

Lieberman, M. and Goldstein, B. (2005) 'Self-help on-line: an outcome evaluation of breast cancer bulletin boards', *Journal of Health Psychology*, 10 (6): 855–62.

Llewellyn, N. (2008) 'Organization in actual episodes of work: Harvey Sacks and organization studies', Organization Studies, 29 (5): 763–91.

Llewellyn, N. and Burrow, R. (2007) 'Negotiating identities of consumption: insights from conversation analysis', in A. Pullen et al. (eds), *Exploring Identity: Concepts and Methods*. Basingstoke: Palgrave Macmillan. pp. 302–15.

Llewellyn, N. and Hindmarsh, J. (2010) 'Work and organization in real time: an introduction', in N. Llewellyn and J. Hindmarsh (eds), *Organization, Interaction and Practice*. Cambridge: Cambridge University Press.

Lockwood, D. and Glass, R. (1958) *The Black Coated Worker: A Study in Class Consciousness*. London: Allen & Unwin.

Lucas, K. and Buzzanell, P.M. (2004) 'Blue-collar work, career, and success: occupational narratives of sisu', *Journal of Applied Communication Research*, 32: 273–92.

Lucas, N. and Koerwer, S. (2004) 'Featured interview Sherron Watkins, former Vice President for Corporate Development of Enron', *Journal of Leadership & Organizational Studies*, 22 June. Available at http://goliath.ecnext.com/coms2/gi_0199-3637056/Featured-interview-Sherron-Watkins-former.html (accessed 20 November 2010).

Luxton, M. (1997) 'The UN, women, and household labour: measuring and valuing unpaid work', *Women's Studies International Forum*, 20 (3): 431–9.

Lyon, D. (1994) *The Electronic Eye: The Rise of Surveillance Society*. Minneapolis: University of Minnesota Press.

Macdonald, K.M. (1995) *The Sociology of the Professions*. London: Sage.

MacKenzie, D. and Wajcman, J. (1999) *The Social Shaping of Technology* (2nd edn). Buckingham: Open University Press.

MacKinnon, C.A. (1979) *Sexual Harassment of Working Women*. New Haven, CT: Yale University Press.

Maloney-Krichmar, D. and Preece, J. (2005) 'A multilevel analysis of sociability, usability, and community dynamics in an online health community', *ACM Transactions on Computer-Human Interaction*, 12 (2): 201–32.

Mangham, I. (1986) *Power and Performance in Organizations: An Exploration of Executive Process*. Oxford: Blackwell.

Markus, L.M. (1996) 'Finding a happy medium: explaining the negative effects of electronic communication on social life at work', in R. Kling (ed.), *Computerization and Controversy: Value Conflicts and Social Choices* (2nd edn). San Diego, CA: Academic Press.

Matthewman, L.J., Rose, A. and Hetherington, A. (eds) (2009) *Work Psychology: An Introduction to Human Behaviour in the Workplace*. Oxford: Oxford University Press.

Mayall, R. (2010a) '"The Unsorting Office". Going Postal: Occasional thoughts from an overworked postie, October 14th 2010'.

Available at http://roymayall.wordpress.com/ (accessed 23 November 2010).

Mayall, R. (2010b) '"No united front at the Royal Mail". Going Postal: Occasional thoughts from an overworked postie, October 27th 2010'. Available at http://roymayall.wordpress.com/ (accessed 23 November 2010).

McGuire, T. (2010) 'From emotions to spirituality: "spiritual labor" as the commodification, codification, and regulation of organizational members' spirituality', *Management Communication Quarterly*, 24 (1): 74–103.

McKinsey (2007) *Women Matter: Gender Diversity, a Corporate Performance Driver.* McKinsey & Company, Inc.

McNay, L. (2003) 'Agency, anticipation and indeterminacy in feminist theory', *Feminist Theory*, 4 (2): 139–48.

Meriläinen, S., Tienari, J., Thomas, R. and Davies, A. (2004) 'Management consultant talk: a cross-cultural comparison of normalizing discourse and resistance', *Organization*, 11 (4): 539–64.

Mintzberg, H. (2011) *Managing.* Harlow: Financial Times/Pearson.

Mirchandani, K. (1998) 'No longer a struggle? Teleworkers' reconstruction of the work/non-work boundary', in P. Jackson and J.M. van der Wielen (eds), *Teleworking: International Perspectives.* London: Routledge. pp. 118–35.

Mirchandani, K. (2004) 'Practices of global capital: gaps, cracks and ironies in transnational call centres in India', *Global Networks: A Journal of Transnational Affairs*, 4 (4): 355–74.

Mueller, F. and Carter, C. (2007) '"We are all managers now": managerialism and professional engineering in U.K. electricity utilities', *Accounting, Organizations and Society*, 32 (1–2): 181–95.

Mueller, F., Sillince, J., Harvey, C. and Howorth, C. (2004) '"A rounded picture is what we need": rhetorical strategies, arguments and the negotiation of change in a U.K. Hospital Trust', *Organization Studies*, 25 (1): 85–103.

Mueller, F., Valsecchi, R., Smith, C., Elston, M.A. and Gabe, J. (2008) '"We are nurses, we are supposed to care for people": professional values among nurses in NHS Direct call centres', *New Technology, Work & Employment*, 23 (1–2): 2–17.

Muir, R. and Wetherell, M. (2010) *Identity, Politics and Public Policy.* London: IPPR.

Musson, G. and Cohen, L. (1999) 'Understanding the language process: a neglected skill in the management curriculum', *Management Learning*, 30: 27–42.

Nag, R., Corley, K. G., Gioia, D. A. (2007) 'The intersection of organizational identity, knowledge and practice: Attempting strategic change via knowledge grafting', *Academy of Management Journal*, 50(4): 821–847.

Nelsen, B.J. and Barley, S.R. (1997) 'For love or money: commodification and the construction of an occupational mandate', *Administrative Science Quarterly*, 42: 619–53.

Newton, T. (1998) 'Theorizing subjectivity in organizations: the failure of Foucauldian studies?', *Organization Studies*, 19 (3): 415–48.

Nicholson, N. (1996) 'Career systems in crisis: change and opportunity in the information age', *Academy of Management Executive*, 10 (4): 40–52.

Nixon, D. (2009) '"I can't put a smiley face on": working-class masculinity, emotional labour and service work in the "new economy"', *Gender, Work and Organization*, 16 (3): 300–22.

Noon, M. (2007) 'The fatal flaws of diversity and the business case for ethnic minorities', *Work, Employment and Society*, 21 (4): 773–784.

Noronha, E. and D'Cruz, P. (2008) 'The dynamics of teleworking: case studies of women medical transcriptionists from Bangalore, India', *Gender, Technology and Development*, 12 (2): 157–83.

O'Connor, E.J. and Annison, M.H. (2002) 'Building trust and collaboration between physicians and administrators', *The Physician Executive*, 28: 48–52.

O'Doherty, D. and Willmott, H. (2000) 'The question of subjectivity and the labor process', *International Studies of Management & Organization*, 30 (4): 112–32.

Ogbonna, E. and Harris, L.C. (2006) 'The dynamics of employee relationships in a diverse workforce: an ethnic minority perspective', *Human Relations*, 53 (3): 379–407.

Ogbonna, E. and Wilkinson, B. (1990) 'Corporate strategy and corporate culture: the view from the checkout', *Personnel Review*, 19 (4): 9–15.

Olson, M.H. and Primps, S.B. (1984) 'Working at home with computers: work and non-work issues', *Journal of Social Issues*, 40 (3): 97–112.

Parker, I. (1997) 'Discourse analysis and psycho-analysis', *British Journal of Social Psychology*, 36: 479–95.

Parker, M. (2001) 'Fucking management: queer, theory and reflexivity', *Ephemera*, 1 (1): 36–53. Available at www.ephemeraweb.org (accessed 8 June 2010).

Parker, M. (2004) 'Becoming manager - or, the werewolf looks anxiously in the mirror, checking for unusual facial hair', *Management Learning*, 35 (1): 45–59.

Parker, M. (2007) 'Identification: organizations and structuralisms', in A. Pullen et al. (eds), *Exploring Identity: Concepts and Methods*. Basingstoke: Palgrave Macmillan. pp. 61–82.

Peddibhotla, N. and Subramani, M. (2007) 'Contributing to public document reposi-tories: a critical mass theory perspective', *Organizational Studies*, 28 (3): 327–46.

Pelletier, C. (2005) 'Reconfiguring interactivity, agency and pleasure in the education and com-puter games debate – using Žižek's concept of interpassivity to analyse educational play', *E-Learning and Digital Media*, 2 (4): 317–26.

Pelletier, C. (2009a) 'Education, equality and emancipation: Rancière's critique of Bourdieu and the question of performativity', *Discourse: studies in the cultural politics of education*, 30 (2): 137–50.

Pelletier, C. (2009b) 'Ranciere and the poetics of the social sciences', *International Journal of Research and Method in Education*, 32 (3): 267–84.

Peters, T.J. and Waterman, R.H. (1982) *In Search of Excellence: Lessons from America's Best-Run Companies*. New York: Harper & Row.

Pettinger, L. (2005) 'Gendered work meets gendered goods: selling and service in clothing retail', *Gender, Work and Organization*, 12 (5): 460–78.

Phillips, L. and Jørgensen, M. (2002) *Discourse Analysis as Theory and Method*. London: Sage.

Poggio, B. (2000) 'Between bytes and bricks', *Economic and Industrial Democracy*, 21 (3): 381–402.

Porter, T. (2001) 'Theorizing organizational identity', *Best Papers, Proceedings of the 2001 Academy of Management Meeting*, Washington, DC.

Poster, M. (1996) 'Databases as discourse; or, electronic interpellations', in D. Lyon and E. Zureik (eds), *Computers, Surveillance, and Privacy*. Minneapolis: University of Minnesota Press. pp. 175–92.

Posthuma, R. and Campion, M. (2009) 'Age stereotypes in the workplace: common stereotypes, moderators, and future research directions', *Journal of Management*, 35 (1): 158–88.

Potter, J. and Hepburn, A. (2008) 'Discursive constructionism', in J. A. Holstein and J.F. Gubrium (eds), *Handbook of Constructionist Research*. New York: Guilford Press. pp. 275–93.

Potter, J., Stringer, P. and Wetherell, M. (1984) *Social Texts and Context: Literature and Social Psychology*. London: Routledge.

Prasad, A. (2009) 'Contesting hegemony through genealogy: Foucault and cross cultural manage-ment research', *International Journal of Cross Cultural Management*, 9 (3): 359–69.

Pratt, M.G. and Foreman, P.O. (2000) 'Classifying managerial responses to multiple organiza-tional identities', *Academy of Management Review*, 25 (1): 18–42.

Pratt, M.G. and Rafaeli, A. (1997) 'Organizational dress as a symbol of multilayered social identi-ties', *Academy of Management Journal*, 40 (4): 862–98.

Pringle, R. (1989) *Secretaries Talk: Sexuality, Power and Work*. London: Verso.

Pritchard, C. (1990) 'Suicide, unemployment and gender variations in the western world 1964–1986', *Social Psychiatry and Psychiatric Epidemiology*, 25 (2): 73–80.

Pullen, A. and Simpson, R. (2009) 'Managing difference in feminized work: men, otherness and social practice', *Human Relations*, 62 (4): 561–87.

Putnam, R. (2000) *Bowling Alone: The Collapse and Revival of American Community*. New York: Simon & Schuster.

Qvortrup, L. (1998) 'From teleworking to net-working: definitions and trends', in P. Jackson and J.M. van der Wielen (eds), *Teleworking: International Perspectives*. London: Routledge. pp. 21–39.

Ranciere, J. (1989) *The Nights of Labor: The Worker's Dream in Nineteenth Century France*. Philadelphia, PA: Temple University Press.

Ranciere, J. (1991) *The Ignorant Schoolmaster: Five Lessons in Intellectual Emancipation*, transl. K. Ross. Stanford, CA: Stanford University Press.

Ravasi, D. and van Rekom, J. (2003) 'Key issues in organizational identity and identification theory', *Corporate Reputation Review*, 6 (2), 118–32.

Ren, Y., Kraut, R.E. and Kiesler, S. (2007) 'Applying common identity and bond theory to design of online communities', *Organization Studies*, 28 (3): 377–408.

Riordan, C. A. Gross, T. and Maloney, C. C. (1994) 'Self-monitoring, gender, and the personal consequences of impression management', *American Behavioural Scientist*, 37(5): 715–25.

Roberts, J. (2005) 'The power of the "imaginary" in disciplinary processes', *Organization*, 12 (5): 619–42.

Robertson, M. and Swan, J. (2003) '"Control – what control?": culture and ambiguity within a knowledge intensive firm', *Journal of Management Studies*, 40 (4): 831–58.

Rose, M. (1988) *Industrial Behaviour: Theoretical Development Since Taylor.* Harmondsworth: Penguin.

Rose, N. (1990) *Governing the Soul: The shaping of the private self.* London: Free Association Press.

Rosener, J. (1990) 'Ways women lead', *Harvard Business Review*, November–December: 119–25.

Ross, D.A.R. (2007) 'Backstage with the knowledge boys and girls: Goffman and distributed agency in an organic online community', *Organization Studies*, 28 (3): 307–25.

Rudy, I.A. (1996) 'A critical review of research on electronic mail', *European Journal of Information Systems*, 4: 198–213.

Rumens, N. and Kerfoot, D. (2009) 'Gay men at work: (re)constructing the self as professional', *Human Relations*, 62 (5): 763–86.

Samra-Fredericks, D. (2003) 'Strategizing as lived experience and strategists' everyday efforts to shape strategic direction', *Journal of Management Studies*, 40(1): 141–174.

Samra-Fredericks, D. (2004) 'Managerial elites making rhetorical/linguistic "moves" for a moving (emotional) display', *Human Relations*, 57 (9): 1103–43.

Sanders, T. (2005) '"It's just acting": sex workers' strategies for capitalizing on sexuality', *Gender Work and Organization*, 12 (4): 319–42.

Schwartz, H.S. (1987a) 'On the psychodynamics of organizational disaster: the case of the space shuttle Challenger', *Columbia Journal of World Business*, 22 (1): 59–67.

Schwartz, H.S. (1987b) 'Anti-social actions of committed organizational participants: an existential psychoanalytic perspective', *Organization Studies*, 8 (4): 327–40.

Schwartz, H.S. (1990) *Narcissistic Process and Corporate Decay: The Theory of the Organization Ideal.* New York: New York University Press.

Sedgwick, E.K. (1990) *Epistemology of the Closet.* Berkeley: University of California Press.

Sennett, R. and Cobb, J. (1972) *The Hidden Injuries of Class.* New York: Vintage Books.

Sewell, G. and Wilkinson, B. (1992) 'Someone to watch over me: surveillance, discipline and the just-in-time labour process', *Sociology*, 26 (2): 271–89.

Sheppard, D.L. (1989) 'Organizations. power and sexuality: the image and self-image of women managers', in J. Hearn et al. (eds), *The Sexuality of Organization.* London: Sage. pp. 139–157.

Simpson, R. (1998) 'Presenteeism, power and organizational change: long hours as a career barrier and the impact on the working lives of women managers', *British Journal of Management*, 9 (s1): 37–50.

Sims-Schouten, W., Riley, S.C.E. and Willig, C. (2007) 'Critical realism in discourse analysis', *Theory & Psychology*, 17 (1): 127–50.

Skeggs, B. (1997) *Formations of Class and Gender: Becoming Respectable.* London: Sage.

Soenen, G. and Moingeon, B. (2002) 'The five facets of collective identities: integrating corporate and organizational identity', in G. Soenen and B. Mongeon (eds), *Corporate and Organizational Identities.* London: Routledge.

Sosteric, M. (1996) 'Subjectivity and the labor process: a case study in the restaurant industry', *Work, Employment and Society*, 10 (2): 297–318.

Speer, S.A. (1999) 'Feminism and conversation analysis: an oxymoron?', *Feminism and Psychology*, 9 (4): 471–8.

Spivak, G. (1988) 'Can the subaltern speak?', in C. Nelson and L. Grossberg (eds), *Marxism and the Interpretation of Culture.* Basingstoke: Macmillan. pp. 271–313.

Sproull, L., Dutton, W. and Kiesler, S. (2007) 'Introduction to the special issue: online communities,' *Organization Studies*, 28 (3): 277–81.

Stanworth, C. and Stanworth, J. (1991) *Telework: The Human Resource Management Implications*. London: Institute of Personnel Management.

Stein, M. (2007) 'Oedipus Rex at Enron', *Human Relations*, 60 (9): 1387–1410.

Stiglitz, J. (2004) 'An end to global trade?', *New Perspectives Quarterly*, 21: 58–9.

Stockoe, E. and Edwards, D. (2006) 'Story formulations in talk-in-interaction', *Narrative Inquiry*, 16 (1): 56–65.

Sumara, D.J. and Luce-Kapler, R. (1996) '(Un) becoming a teacher: negotiating identities while learning to teach', *Canadian Journal of Education*, 21 (1): 65–83.

Sveningsson, S. and Larsson, M. (2006) 'Fantasies of leadership: identity work', *Leadership*, 2: 203–24.

Sykes, A. (1965) 'Economic interest and the Hawthorne researches: a comment', *Human Relations*, 18 (3): 253–63.

Symons, G.L. (1992) 'The glass ceiling is constructed over the gendered office', *Women in Management Review*, 7: 18–22.

Tannen, D. (1994) *Gender and Discourse*. Oxford: Oxford University Press.

Taskin, L. and Edwards, P. (2007) 'The possibilities and limit of telework in a bureaucratic environment: lessons from the public sector', *New Technology, Work and Employment*, 22 (3): 195–207.

Taylor, F.W. (1911) *The Principles of Scientific Management*. New York: Harper & Brothers. Essay available at http://melbecon.unimelb.edu.au/het/taylor/sciman.htm.

Taylor, S. (2006) 'Narrative as construction and discursive resource', *Narrative Inquiry*, 16 (1): 94–102.

THE (Times Higher Education newspaper supplement) (2011) 'Average salary of full-time academic staff, 2009–2010', 24 March: 44.

Thomas, R. and Davies, A. (2005a) 'Theorizing the micro-politics of resistance: new public management and managerial identities in the UK public services', *Organization Studies*, 26 (5): 683–706.

Thomas, R. and Davies, A. (2005b) 'What have the feminists done for us? Feminist theory and organizational resistance', *Organization*, 12 (5): 711–40.

Thompson, P. (1990) 'Crawling from wreckage: the labour process and the politics of produc-tion', in D. Knights and H. Willmott (eds), *Labour Process Theory*. London: Macmillan. pp. 95–124.

Thompson, P. and Ackroyd, S. (1995) 'All quiet on the workplace front? A critique of recent trends in British industrial sociology', *Sociology*, 29 (4): 615–33.

Thompson, P. and McHugh, D. (2009) *Work Organizations: A Critical Approach* (4th edn). Basingstoke: Palgrave Macmillan.

Tracy, S.J. and Scott, C. (2006) 'Sexuality, masculinity, and taint management among firefighters and correctional officers', *Management Communication Quarterly*, 20 (1): 6–38.

Tretheway, A. (1999) 'Disciplined bodies: women's embodied identities at work', *Organization Studies*, 20 (3): 423–45.

Tretheway, A. (2001) 'Reproducing and resisting the master narrative of decline: midlife professional women's experiences of aging', *Management Communication Quarterly*, 15 (2): 183–226.

Tunnell, K. (2004) *Pissing on Demand: Workplace Drug Testing and the Rise of the Detox Industry*. New York: NYU Press.

Turkle, S. (1995) *Life on the Screen: Identity in the Age of the Internet*. New York: Simon & Schuster.

UNISON (2005) 'Cleaners' voices: interviews with hospital cleaning staff', UNISON report.

Van Gelder, L. (1996) 'The strange case of the electronic lover', in R. Kling (ed.), *Computerization and Controversy: Value Conflicts and Social Choices* (2nd edn). New York: Academic Press. pp. 533–46.

Van Maanen, J. (1990) 'The smile factory: work at Disneyland', in P.J. Frost et al. (eds), *Reframing Organizational Culture*. London: Sage. pp. 58–76.

Van Rekom, J., Corley, K. and Ravasi, D. (2008) 'Extending and advancing theories of organizational identity', *Corporate Reputation Review*, 11 (3): 183–8.

Vásquez, C. (2007) 'Moral stance in the workplace narratives of novices', *Discourse Studies*, 9 (5): 653–75.

Vurdubakis, T. (2007) 'Technological determinism', in D. Knights and H. Willmott (eds), *Introducing Organizational Behaviour and Management*. London: Thompson. pp. 405–38.

Wajcman, J. (1998) *Managing Like a Man: Women and Men in Corporate Management*. Cambridge: Polity Press.

Walkerdine, V. (2009) 'Steel, identity, community: regenerating identities in a South Wales town', in M. Wetherell (ed.), *Identities in the 21st century*. Basingstoke: Palgrave Macmillan. pp. 59–75.

Warhurst, C. and Nickson, D. (2001) *Looking Good, Sounding Right: Style Counselling in the New Economy*. London: The Industrial Society.

Watson, T.J. (1994) *In Search of Management: Culture, Chaos and Control in Managerial Work*. London: Thompson Business Press.

Watson, T.J. (2000) 'Ethnographic Fiction Science: Making Sense of Managerial Work and Organisational Research processes with caroline and Terny', *Organization*, 7(3): 31–3.

Watson, T.J. (2005) *Sociology, Work and Industry* (3rd edn). London: Routledge.

Watson, T.J. (2008) 'Managing Identity: identity work, personal predicaments and structural circumstances', *Organization*, 15 (1): 121–43.

Watson, T.J. (2009) 'Narrative life story and the management of identity: a case study in auto-biographical identity work', *Human Relations*, 62 (3): 1–28.

Watson, T.J. and Bargiela-Chiappini, F. (1998) 'Managerial sensemaking and occupational identities in Britain and Italy', *Journal of Management Studies*, 35 (3): 285–301.

Weber, M. (1992) *The Protestant Ethic and the Spirit of Capitalism*. London: Routledge.

Weierter, S.J.M. (2001) 'The organization of charisma: promoting, creating, and idealizing self', *Organization Studies*, 22 (1): 91–115.

Weiz, C. and Wolf, F. (2010) 'Telework in the European Union', Eurofound Report TN0910050S. Available at http://www.eurofound.europa.eu/eiro/studies/tn0910050s/tn0910050s_7.htm (accessed 23 November 2010).

Wentworth, D.K. and Chell, R.M. (2005) 'Gender identity at home: comparing the role of househusband to housewife', in J.W. Lee (ed.), *Psychology of Gender Identity*. Hauppauge, NY: Nova Biomedical Books. pp. 113–26.

Westwood, R.I. and Leung, A. (1994) 'The female expatriate manager experience: coping with gender and culture', *International Studies of Management and Organisation*, 24 (3): 64–85.

Wetherell, M. (1998) 'Positioning and interpretative repertoires: conversation analysis and post-structuralism in dialogue', *Discourse and Society*, 9 (3): 413–16.

Wetherell, M. and Potter, J. (1992) *Mapping the Language of Racism: Discourse and the Legitimation of Exploitation*. Hemel Hempstead: Harvester Wheatsheaf.

Wetherell, M., Stiven, H. and Potter, J. (1987) 'Unequal egalitarianism: a preliminary study of discourses concerning gender and employment opportunities', *British Journal of Social Psychology*, 26: 59–71.

Whetten, D.A. (1998) 'Preface: why organizational identity and why conversations?', in D.A. Whetten and P.C. Godfrey (eds), *Identity in Organizations: Building Theory through Conversations*. Thousand Oaks, CA: Sage. pp. vii–xi.

Whetten, D.A. (2006) 'Albert and Whetten revisited: strengthening the concept of organizational identity', *Journal of Management Inquiry*, 15 (3): 219–34.

Whittle, A., Mueller, F. and Mangan, A. (2009) 'Storytelling and "character": victims, villains and heroes in a case of technological change', *Organization*, 16 (3): 425–42.

Whitty, M. (2002) 'Liar liar! An examination of how open, supportive and honest people are in chat rooms', *Computers in Human Behaviour*, 18: 343–52.

Whitty, M. (2003) 'Cyber-flirting: playing at love on the Internet', *Theory & Psychology*, 13 (3): 339–57.

Whitty, M.T. and Carr, A.N. (2003) 'Cyberspace as potential space: considering the web as playground to cyber-flirt', *Human Relations*, 56 (7): 869–91.

Widdicombe, S. and Wooffitt, R. (1995) *The Language of Youth Subculture*. Brighton: Harvester.

Willis, P. (1977) *Learning to Labour*. Farnborough: Saxon House.

Willmott, H. (1993) 'Strength is ignorance; slavery is freedom: managing culture in modern organizations', *Journal of Management Studies*, 30 (4): 515–46.

Willmott, H. (1997) 'Rethinking management and managerial work – capitalism, control, and subjectivity', *Human Relations*, 50 (11): 1329–59.

Willmott, H.C. (2011a) 'Back to the future: what does studying bureaucracy tell us?', in S. Clegg et al. (eds), *Managing Modernity: Beyond Bureaucracy?* Oxford: Oxford University Press.

Willmott, H.C. (2011b) '"Institutional work" for what? Problems and prospects of institutional theory', *Journal of Management Inquiry*, 20(1): 67–72.

Women and Work Commission (2006) *Shaping a Fairer Future*. London: Department of Trade and Industry.

Woods, J.D. and Lucas, J.H. (1993) *The Corporate Closet: The Professional Lives of Gay Men in America*. New York: The Free Press.

Woolgar, S. (2003) *Virtual Society? Technology, Cyberbole, Reality*. Oxford: Oxford University Press.

Wrigley, J. (1995) *Other People's Children*. New York: Basic Books.

Xu, Q. (2008) 'A question concerning subject in the spirit of Chinese capitalism', *Critical Perspectives on International Business*, 4 (2/3): 242–76.

Zizek, S. (1999) 'Is it possible to traverse the fantasy in cyberspace?', in E. Wright and E. Wright (eds), *The Zizek Reader*. Oxford: Blackwell. pp. 102–24.

Zlolniski, C. (2006) *Janitors, Street Vendors, and Activists: The Lives of Mexican Immigrants in Silicon Valley*. Berkeley: University of California Press.

Zuboff, S. (1988) *In the Age of the Smart Machine*. New York: Basic Books.

Index

Tables and Figures are indicated by page numbers in bold.